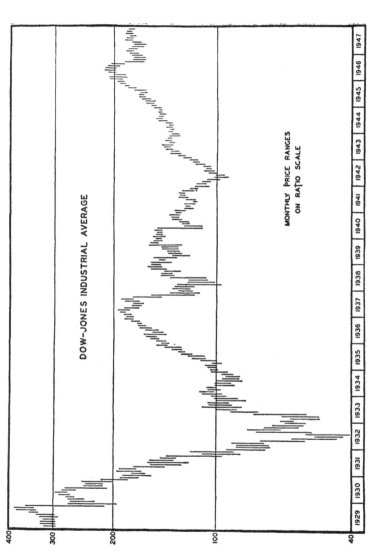

DOW-JONES INDUSTRIAL AVERAGE

MONTHLY PRICE RANGES
ON RATIO SCALE

FRONTISPIECE

New Methods *for* Profit
in the Stock Market

with a
critical analysis
of established systems

by

GARFIELD A. DREW

Winner of Barron's Open Forum on the Best Securities for
Recovery or Inflation; *Director of Accounts*—UNITED INVEST-
MENT COUNSEL, INC.

Martino Publishing
Mansfield Centre, CT
2011

Martino Publishing
P.O. Box 373,
Mansfield Centre, CT 06250 USA

www.martinopublishing.com

ISBN   978-1-61427-126-0

Cover design by T. Matarazzo

Printed in the United States of America On 100% Acid-Free Paper

New Methods *for* Profit
in the Stock Market

with a
critical analysis
of established systems

by

GARFIELD A. DREW

Winner of Barron's Open Forum on the Best Securities for
Recovery or Inflation; *Director of Accounts* — UNITED INVEST-
MENT COUNSEL, INC.

THE METCALF PRESS · BOSTON, MASSACHUSETTS

FOREWORD

THIS revised and expanded edition of "New Methods for Profit in the Stock Market" makes two major contributions to the art of solving the market problem.

Like the 1941 book, it presents a classified analysis of easily understood and tested specific methods for timing stock market operations—some of them entirely new. The scope has been broadened to include the major developments in the field during the past few years.

Secondly, in the until now only hastily sketched theory of popular psychology in relation to stock prices, Mr. Drew expands his original discussion and states clearly a principle of which successful traders have long been conscious. This principle is tied to the statistical indexes of odd lot trading developed by Mr. Drew and given briefly in the 1941 text. The valuable correlation between these statistics and theory is here fully explained for the first time.

As was so aptly said about the original edition, it is seldom that one finds a book on the stock market that is really unique in its approach. This is not just another collection of generalities and confusing details. Unlike the usual intricate expositions of technical study, it has a simplicity of approach which makes it usable by the inexperienced investor as well as the advanced market student. The limitations as well as the advantages of each specific technique are carefully pointed out, and the reader can easily decide just what may be best suited to his own particular desires and needs.

In a practical way, Mr. Drew has tied together the loose ends in a field of market procedure that is often maligned because it is commonly misunderstood. I commend this thoughtful book to those who seek a better understanding of logical approaches to the problem of stock market timing.

CLARK M. CAVENEE
Member, NEW YORK STOCK EXCHANGE

CONTENTS

ILLUSTRATIONS

INTRODUCTION

THE general background for this 1948 edition of "New Methods for Profit in the Stock Market" is so radically different from that of the original book in late 1941, that some perspective on the whole problem is necessary.

A long bear market was then drawing to a close — a prediction made in the first edition of this book — but naturally unprovable at the time. Despite definition according to strict Dow Theory on some of the interim moves, perspective from the vantage point of 1948 suggests that — in terms of the Dow-Jones Industrial Average — the period from March, 1937, to April, 1942, constituted one major downtrend, or bear market (see Frontispiece or Figure 7). It was, however, marked by the most violent intermediate swings in both directions, particularly between the middle of 1938 and 1940 when the prospects of war and later the actualities of war, were the dominant short-term influences. Investment "values" seemed to mean nothing and investors thus had their attention focused on "timing" to a greater than average degree.

New Interest in Timing

Moreover, the whole picture of the '30s was still fresh in mind. The depression of 1932, the New Deal, the market collapse of 1937, and the onset of a great war; all had made investors realize that they could not divorce the speculative element from investment holdings. They were taught that fundamental changes in the world economy or a political setup could reduce what had appeared to be

1

high grade investment media to the status of rank specu-
lations overnight.

The extreme difficulty of foreseeing such changes accurately, naturally emphasized the possible protection to be
found in taking advantage of the more extensive market
swings. Obviously, the individual who can meet these with
reasonable accuracy has an automatic safeguard against the
unforeseeable longer term contingencies. Hence the search
for dependable methods that may provide such protection.
Most market methods are concerned with "timing," because
there are situations which are advantageous to the buying
of almost all stocks, while at other times the conditions are
entirely unfavorable. Moreover, although the degree of advance or decline may vary widely, almost every stock will
synchronize with the general trend of "The Market" during
any important move.

Between 1942 and 1946, there was somewhat less interest in this aspect of the matter than when the first edition
of this book was published in late 1941. As opposed to the
violent ups and downs of the 1937-1941 period, there was
the background of the steadily ascending 1942-1946 bull
market, during the course of which the most important consideration was *what* stocks were held. Except for those who
at various points saw, or believed they saw, an end of the
uptrend, "timing" tended to lose its importance to most investors. The break in late 1946, however, — which, according to Dow Theory, at least, — heralded the change from a
bull market to a bear market, reawakened them to a considerable extent.

Growth of New Methods

In any event, "timing" has lost none of its fundamental
importance. The market will always fluctuate, sometimes

gently but sometimes violently. If timing seemed less important in 1942-1946 than in 1937-1941, who shall say to what extent it may appear vital between 1947 and 1952? Obviously, not everyone can be right on "timing," or there would be no one from whom to buy or to whom to sell at the correct times. In order for one group to be right, another group must be wrong.

Whatever the degree of emphasis may be at any given time, there is no doubt that the interest in taking advantage of the major or intermediate stock market trends has grown steadily during the last twenty-five or thirty years. If nothing else, the existence of so many specialized financial services covering the subject, would be testimony to the fact.

Public Familiarity

There have been times when it has seemed that "forecasting the market" had become a national game. Every brokerage office is haunted by someone with an infallible method, and the large financial services have a steady flow of callers wanting to sell their own systems or forecasts which they can always demonstrate would have avoided any mistake made by the service.

The rapid growth of these ideas for taking the speculation out of speculating has been mostly within the last fifteen years. Despite some lessening, perhaps, in the number of people actively interested in the market since the three and four million share trading days of 1929, it is probably safe to say that ten times as many individuals know that there is such a thing as the Dow Theory.

Yet the Dow Theory does not stand alone, nor is it new, Dow having died some forty-five years ago. Although Robert Rhea first really began to publicize the Theory in 1932 with his series of *Dow Theory Comment* letters, it was several years before it was very widely discussed. The peak of its popularity was apparently reached in early 1938, largely because of its inevitably correct recognition of a bear market in September, 1937 — some 65 points above the ultimate low. In the subsequent period of erratic market movements, however, it fell more or less into public disfavor because, as a "forecasting" device — which it is not — it proved neither very clear nor profitable. Not having had any spectacular "successes" as in 1937 for some years, the present popularity of the idea is relatively low. Yet the Theory — for which the author holds no particular brief — has not outlived whatever usefulness it possesses. It is merely that too much has been expected of it in periods to which it was ill adapted.

Such lack of comprehension with respect to market methods is quite common, even among those otherwise well versed in investment matters. This book is intended to clarify the general haze of misunderstanding, and to cover various approaches with a concise treatment of their underlying principles, techniques, and reasonable expectations, so that any individual may make an intelligent appraisal of their worth to his own particular needs. Some of these methods will be found suited to one purpose and some to another. In some cases, they can be easily applied by any individual. In others, they represent the work of some published financial service which would be difficult or even impossible to duplicate without more time and facilities than the average individual possesses.

Additions to Book

In any event, the methods included are those which seem worth while in the realm of mechanical or semi-mechanical "forecasting," as well as some special approaches that are worthy of discussion. The omission of any specific method is not necessarily to be construed as condemnation, since it may merely mean that the approach is either closely allied to one that is discussed, or is in a field outside the scope of this analysis.

Some of the "methods" included in the original 1941 edition of this book do not appear here for various specific reasons. For example, the "Divergence Curve" used by "Trendographs" of Rochester, N. Y. is no longer published. On the other hand, certain important additions have been made, some of which were only covered briefly in the original text, while others are entirely new. Thus, Cycle Forecasting and Formula Plans — which were barely touched on in the earlier edition — are discussed at much greater length. Interest in cycle studies received a tremendous impetus in 1947 by Henry Holt & Co.'s publication of Dewey and Dakin's book "Cycles (the Science of Prediction.)." Similarly, the study and development of Formula Plans — scarcely heard of in 1941 — has proceeded rapidly during the intervening years.

Scope of New Edition

One of the primary purposes of this book is to segregate the classes of approach; to show why some must be used only by themselves; why some others may be combined, and to suggest what sort of program would be logical. The following arrangement was therefore followed:

Section I is largely background material, although covering the relation of fundamental statistics to the market.

Section II takes up one specific class of methods — those setting up criteria for defining the trend.

Section III discusses the other broad and well-known group seeking to determine points of reversal in price trends.

Section IV covers the now more familiar formula plans —
a highly specialized approach aimed more at modest long-
term investment results than at immediate profits.

Section V deals with almost the only form of pure forecasting, i.e. the use of assumed cyclical rhythms. This
section may be skipped by the hard-headed and practical.
It is given for whatever it is worth, and the author affirms
neither his belief nor his disbelief.

Section VI really comes back to Section III as a matter
of broad classification. However, the subject is just enough
different to deserve separate treatment, to say nothing of
length, and the fact that it concludes with a new approach
developed by the author on the basis of data which have
only become available within recent years. This appeared
in relatively brief form in the 1941 edition, and the passage
of time has only enhanced its validity. The allied theory
and discussion of the "why" of intermediate market movements in the first part of Section VI is, it is believed, pre-
sented here in complete form for the first time.

Section VII ties together all that has gone before, and
suggests more concretely just how the individual may find
the solution to his own investment problem.

The concluding "Prediction" in Section VIII is dictated
somewhat by the fact that the 1941 edition had a similar
forecast (reprinted in full in the Supplement). The author
can only hope that whatever prescience was displayed seven
years ago will be equalled in the future.

No System is Perfect

It is often said that no mechanical system can be devised
which will accurately forecast the market or show profits
all the time. That is quite true. The mechanistic "trend
systems", for example, frequently seem to "go haywire",

but, when they do, it simply means that entirely in accordance with normal expectations, they are encountering the type of seesaw market in which their nature makes it impossible for them to operate profitably. As soon as the character of the market changes and important moves recur, they will just as surely be "right."

Nothing will show profits *all* the time, and it may be inquired of those who scoff at "systems" whether they know of any "forecasting" or "management" sources that can lay claim to better *results* over any adequate period of time than several of the best modern methods described in this book. Notice that this does not refer to accuracy in forecasting the probabilities, but to dollars and cents results in specific buying and selling.

Field Misunderstood

In a speech on investment management, an official of a well-known investment trust devoted to common stocks once remarked, "Amusing are the mechanical schemes for diagnosing the market and arriving at automatic forecasts. These range all the way from the Dow Theory . . . to intricate systems of stock market clairvoyance." The performance of this trust at the time had been mediocre, the value of its portfolio merely fluctuating very closely in accordance with the Dow-Jones Industrial Average, whereas good investment management of stocks should — at the very least — do better than the Average over any reasonable period of time.

Since the results which would indisputably have been attained by many of the methods to be described were far ahead of any Average performance, it is difficult to see why they should have been regarded as "amusing". It is perfectly true, however, that many wild and illogical theories have been propounded. The secret was once imparted to the author in the strictest of confidence that the real key to the market is that "They" (the Big Operators) always move stocks in multiples of 3½ points. But, the fact that a lunatic fringe exists is no reason for wholesale condemnation of the mechanical or semi-mechanical methods, particularly since there are very few who can show that their interpretation of events, "investment analyses", or whatever orthodox approach is used, have yielded anywhere near as good results. The proof of the pudding is in the eating.

GARFIELD A. DREW.

Boston, Mass., September, 1948.

THE EVOLUTION OF FORECASTING

EARLY METHODS

THE evolution of market forecasting has followed what can be seen as a quite natural course. Before World War I, comparatively few people (outside of New York and Boston) were interested in the stock market or even securities in general. Study of the price movement was largely limited to individuals, although there are a few writings from the early part of the century such as Nelson's *ABC of Stock Speculation* (1903), which discussed in part what is now known as the Dow Theory. However, market forecasting was largely limited to "tape-reading", or to the use of "figure charts".

Tape-Reading and Figure Charts

Tape-reading, particularly in individual stocks, was a more practical affair then than it is now. Not only was the total volume of trading comparatively small, but there were infinitely fewer issues listed on the Exchange. The more prominent of these were often identified with some individual, as in the case of James M. Waterbury and National Cordage, or H. O. Havemeyer and American Sugar. Since such individuals often conducted manipulative operations in the stocks in which they were interested, there were certain characteristics in their technique of buying or selling that were likely to betray to close observers of the price movement what was coming.

Use of figure charts — in a forecasting sense — was also widespread some forty years ago. A figure chart is merely a method of depicting the price movement by showing all fluctuations of one point or some other unit instead of the usual price range. For example, a stock might have a high of 71 and a low of 70 for any one day, but during that day, it might have gone up and down several times between these two figures, in which case the number of "one point moves" (between 70 and 71) would be shown on the chart. Such charts are very useful in general study for showing details of the action at a time of trend reversal, but it was — or is — sometimes believed that they can be used to measure the extent of a future move. One writer outlined this theory in detail in 1904, and it has merely been repeated rather than improved since. (For a detailed explanation, see Gartley's *Profits in the Stock Market* or de Villier's *The Point and Figure Method.*)

BUSINESS BAROMETERS

After World War I, market forecasting took an entirely different tack. The key to the future was felt to lie in the statistics which were becoming available in volume on such factors as pig-iron production, business failures, bank clearings, etc. Comparatively little of this material had been widely disseminated before, and it was only natural that it should be seized upon as providing the answer. Here were the cold facts relating to business conditions. Why should they not coldly show what was likely to happen in the future?

One of the best-known specific "forecasters" was Colonel Ayres' "Blast Furnace Index" which moved someone to write in 1927, "The accuracy with which Colonel Ayres' 60% blast furnace barometer has predicted the wide swings of the stock market has for some time focused attention on the value of the production figures." The idea here was that when the average rate of blast furnaces in operation crossed 60% on the way up, the market was high enough to be sold, and when it crossed 60% on the way down, the price level was low enough to be bought. This was merely applying a specific yardstick to the obviously correct general procedure of selling stocks when business is good and prices high, and buying them when business is bad and stock prices consequently low. Yes, this method had "predicted" the market, but the comment quoted above was written in 1927. Subsequently, it appeared far less accurate, simply because it had been dealing with what had been regarded as a normal relationship, whereas the next few years were extremely abnormal.

Another similar theory at that time held that when pig-iron production showed a 20% decline from a high point, stocks were a buy, and vice versa. This was knocked askew not only by the abnormal conditions that destroyed the force of the "Blast Furnace Index", but also by the fact that more scrap than pig iron began to go into steel ingots in the late '20s.

Changes in money rates were likewise once regarded as a reliable indicator of major turning points in the market, but one does not have to be an economist to realize that, with the degree of power exercised by the Treasury since 1933, indications in this sphere — which were based on the free play of supply and demand — may be quite invalidated by artificial controls.

Changing Relationships

The inherent danger of all economic barometers is that when used as rigid formulas, they may be applicable in one period, but not in another. One ambitious attempt is recalled to link the monthly movements of stock prices to the monthly figures on nineteen factors like bond yields, coke prices, etc. One hundred and twenty-five such factors had been checked for ten years, and the nineteen were those which had seemed to move consistently in a certain direction before the market did — some of them by one month, and others by longer periods. The "barometer" was thus based purely on what *had* happened. There was really little logical connection and, as might be expected, the next ten years were a different story.

As a matter of fact, it is possible to take almost any series of changing figures and, by suiting various statistical adjustments to the known facts, arrive at something approximating what would have been a "forecast" of the stock market or, indeed, of any other series of fluctuating data. Hence, the frequent later disappointment of the research enthusiasts who, by trial and error, so often find the apparent key to the trends *of the past.*

An Example of Absurdity

A perfect "reductio ad absurdum" argument is the non-serious "Gridiron Method of Forecasting Stock Prices". All one needs are a few football scores. If, in any year, the loser of the Harvard-Yale game fails to score, that is a buy signal for the succeeding year unless there is no difference between the points scored by California in the Stanford game and those scored by Army in the Navy game. The selling is easy. Just sell the year after California beats Stanford. To know exactly when to buy or sell if a signal has been given, add the scores of all six teams, divide by 9 (disregarding fractions) and add 2. If the result is less than 3, call it 3 and if more than 10, call it 10. The answer is the month of the year in which to act, obviously always between March and October.

From 1920 to 1940, the "system" would actually have been very profitable. In fact, it would have netted something like 600 points profit (with only two small losses) in the Dow-Jones Industrial Average on just twelve changes in market position. It rode the big bear market down, for instance, from June, 1929, to March, 1932, and sold out in August, 1937, prior to the sharp collapse of that year. It is regrettable, therefore, to state that because of the unfortunate victory of California over Stanford in 1941, adherents of the "Gridiron Method" abandoned their holdings at a loss in July, 1942, just as a big bull market got under way, not to re-purchase until October, 1946, at much higher levels.

Seriously, however, it is true that a tremendous amount of time has been wasted in attempting to correlate the stock market with certain economic data that actually have no more direct relationship to it in a forecasting sense than do the football scores.

Always the Last Experience

Unfortunately, credence in any "barometer" is likely to become most widespread just when — with the benefit of hindsight — the discovery is made that it would have worked accurately in the past, which is actually all the more reason why it is less likely to work as efficiently in the future. Nevertheless, the human mind is always inclined to go back to the last experience in the market and judge the future by that. Post-mortems may be held after each largely unforeseen collapse in order to determine what the warning signals were. Attention is then focused upon them for a time in order to avoid the next crisis, but when it comes, it is usually found afterward that the primary signs of danger had shifted to another field.

Thus, the 1920-21 depression stemmed from commodity price inflation, and the 1929-32 deflation from inflated brokers' loans. Because of remembering 1921, it was held in 1929 that the situation was not dangerous because commodity prices had not risen, the evidences of inflation elsewhere being ignored. Similarly, in 1937, it was argued that the stock market could not be vulnerable while brokers' loans were so low, and the risks of swollen inventories in the face of declining demand for goods were overlooked.

Books could be — and have been — written on the subject of economic barometers for forecasting the cycles of business and the stock market, but it is unnecessary to elaborate upon them further. Until 1931, such indices remained popular, but since virtually without exception they had indicated that stocks were cheap and should be bought in 1930, a more skeptical attitude grew up. Their failure at that time was not surprising. Just as the 1929 boom grew to abnormal proportions, so the 1932 depression went to unprecedented extremes, whereas these barometers were based on the supposedly "normal" limits of the business cycle. *But "normal" at any given time merely means an average of the past. It does not allow for changed conditions, whereas the current or future "normal" may be something quite different.*

TOWNSEND-SKINNER'S FINANCIAL ACCOUNTING

Although such oversimplified "barometers" as the "Blast Furnace Index" have been dismissed, it should not be inferred that all avenues of fundamental approach are to be neglected. Obviously, for example, there should be some validity in an analysis of the banking figures released by the Federal Reserve Board. As the late Richard Dana Skinner put it, the banking figures show the "actions and moods of men through what they do with their money". Hence, an important change in the money picture often foreshadows a change in business and, therefore, the trend of stock prices.

However, since short-term — although extensive — market movements may have psychological rather than economic backgrounds, it will be seen that such an approach is primarily concerned with the detection of the broad turning points in business trends and therefore those of the stock market, rather than relatively short price swings.

Theory of Interpretation

The theory of the meaning of bank figures as analyzed by the firm of Townsend-Skinner resolves itself into an interpretive or accounting control method of basic forecasting, although Skinner always maintained that no more forecast is involved than with a doctor who correctly diagnoses a case of whooping cough from preliminary symptoms before there are any "whoops".

In this interpretation of the banking figures, all the people and businesses in the U. S. are visualized as one huge corporation, part of whose balance sheet and operating statement may — in substance — be read by reversing the Federal Reserve Board's weekly composite reports of the condition of the member banks in the system and related factors. That is, certain bank assets (reversed) represent part of the Corporation's quick liabilities, or the public's short-term debts. Likewise, bank deposit liabilities are the public's quick cash assets. The bank debits, or checks drawn against deposit accounts, which show to what extent or how actively the public is using its money, are analogous to the Corporation's total sales volume.

An Example from 1937

It will be remembered that in 1937 there occurred a sharp slump in business and also the stock market. The coming trouble was clearly foreshadowed in the facts revealed by such an analysis of the banking figures. Beginning in June, 1936, the "sales volume" of the Corporation flattened out for several months; i.e., bank debits ceased to gain. At the same time, "quick liabilities" of the Corporation (represented by commercial loans for inventory, plant expansion, etc.) grew larger. Demand was drying up, commitments were increasing, and any businessman knows that such a situation spells trouble for any individual company. In the first half of 1937, this picture became more acute with "sales" declining 15% while loans (or "quick liabilities") rose some 10%. Since assets (total bank deposits) also failed to rise as fast as liabilities (total loans), the working capital position of the Corporation was likewise deteriorating. It was evident that there were breakers ahead for business, and it was not long afterward that the stock market began to reflect what was clearly coming, even though its real crash was delayed about six months when business followed on its heels.

By June of 1938, however, a considerable improvement was manifest. The U. S. Corporation's working capital position had been improving since late 1937 and "gross sales" had been rising for many weeks, with "quick liabilities" declining. As a result, common stock investments were adjudged warranted at that time around 120 in the Dow-Jones Industrial Average. (This and the following points of market action are facts of record.)

The Running Picture

Without attempting to go into an analysis of the banking figures' meaning at each point, stocks were then sold in January, 1939, around 150, repurchased in April near 125, and sold again in October at about 155. That was a very unusual period in every respect, and ordinarily nowhere near as much market activity would be indicated by this method of basic analysis.

It is interesting that during the six months of sidewise market movement (from October, 1939, to May, 1940) preceding the fall of France and the coincident collapse of stock prices, the Townsend-Skinner banking figure studies showed fundamental conditions to be rapidly deteriorating. Not until July of 1942 was any improvement in this respect evident, although for the record, purchase of stocks was recommended in June, 1940, and sales in September between about the 110 and 125 levels. Although still in the middle of a broad basic decline at this juncture, action was advised because in June there was an unusually severe disproportion between the bank figure facts and stock prices. That is, business was in better fundamental shape than was reflected by stock prices which had temporarily declined too far.

As mentioned above, there were no signs of basic improvement in the banking figures until July of 1942, despite the impact of war and the furious Government spending for armament. This situation then showed just the reverse of that previously described for the first half of 1936. Commercial loans, or the "quick liabilities" of the theoretical corporation, were gaining, but at the same time "sales volume" (or bank debits) gained even faster. Backed up by other indications of improvement, a more bullish position was taken at this time, but a fully committed long position in stocks was not definitely recommended until October, 1942, at around 112 in the Dow-Jones Industrial Average.

The abnormalities of war conditions produced some distortions later on in the banking figures, but not of any such character as to cause a change in market position. For instance, in the fall of 1943, the "Basic Economic Trend", as shown in the Townsend-Skinner analyses, was declining as an aftermath to the War Loan "bulge", but since even these reduced figures still showed business in much sounder condition that the level of stock prices indicated, a bullish position was maintained.

Market and Business Diverge

No change had been made five years later in the fall of 1947. The stock market drop of 1946 was not considered as a direct correlation with a similar movement in the bank-figure analyses, and since that drop was not felt in general business — which, indeed, was just entering upon one of the most prosperous years in history — the "error" of interpretation (if such it was) is not surprising.

In any event, the Townsend-Skinner theory of "balance sheet analysis" from the banking figures was never intended to be a key to successful short-term speculation. The frequent changes in market position indicated during the 1938-1940 period represented an abnormality born of the unusual character of events in those years. Its value for the long-term investor under ordinary business conditions, however, is apparent.

MARKET AS ITS OWN BAROMETER

With the failure of the ordinary business "barometers" as known in 1929-1932, it came to be more widely recognized that perhaps the stock market itself is its own best barometer on the logical ground that the price movement represents the sum of all knowledge pertaining to stocks, applied to discounting the future. Thus, the rapidity with which the popularity of the Dow Theory rose in the '30s is not at all surprising, since its basic assumption is that the movement of stock price averages represents (in Dow's original words) "everything everybody knows, hopes, believes, and anticipates."

This, of course, is exactly contrary to the use of business data as forecasts of the stock market. The simon-pure Dow Theorist or market technician says rather that the market forecasts what business will do. Like all such controversies, there is something to be said on both sides. It is rather like the old argument of which came first — the chicken or the egg. There have certainly been occasions when business conditions did forecast the stock market in the sense that the latter was running at high levels on the momentum of speculative enthusiasm, while business was flying storm signals at the same time.

Stock Prices Tend to Precede Business

It is the upturn from periods of depression which lends credence to the theory that the market forecasts business. As a rule, stock prices tend to precede a change in business conditions. In the twenty-six major reversals of the past ninety years, they have lagged in only five cases, one of these being 1942 when the impact of war obviously had changed the normal relationship. The time of anticipation by the market in the other twenty-one instances varied between two and six months. Why, for example, did stock prices nearly double during the depths of the depression in the summer of 1932 when there were certainly no signs of tangible improvement?

Actually, it is probable that the market rises initially at such a time less because informed individuals sense better things ahead, than because the professional speculative element realizes it is dealing with a "sold-out" market and hence — as always — is interested in *temporarily* exploiting the path of least resistance. The "sold-out" market occurs because of an "error of pessimism" on the part of many stock owners, who are selling because they (mistakenly) visualize even worse things than those existing to come. There seems, for instance, no other rational explanation, for such rare occurrences as the 20-point advance of six days in June, 1938, which came out of an entirely clear sky in a quiet market and without the benefit of any news whatsoever, either then or later.

CLASSIFICATION OF MARKET METHODS

Methods of dealing with the market fall into several distinct classifications. The term "dealing with" rather than "forecasting" is used here because very few methods in the implied sense actually attempt to forecast. One relatively successful formula system, for example, enters fixed orders simultaneously to buy both above (on stop) and below the current market without any concern as to which may be reached first. *Also, it is one thing to say that "The current established trend is assumed to continue (until proven otherwise)" or that "The recent trend will not go further", and quite another to say that prices will advance or decline so many points after such and such a date and within a given period of time.* By the term "method", something is meant which is to be employed to the exclusion of all other considerations and which specifically indicates buying or selling.

Actual Forecasting

There is one exception to the rule that almost all methods "deal with" the market rather than forecast its fluctuations. This is the theory of cycles which — since it assumes reasonably regular recurrent rhythms in the stock market as well as in other spheres — does actually attempt to forecast or predict the bull and bear markets of the future (see Section V).

The orthodox forecaster, however, who goes on record with *"why, when, and how much"* is hardly likely to use any method at all except as he may examine everything — fundamental facts, technical indications, the political outlook, etc. but without applying formulae to any of them. Thus, he emerges from his studies with some conclusion derived from his experience and reasoning superimposed upon an array of more or less factual information. The larger and well-known financial services are likely to be "forecasters" in this sense, their published opinion usually representing a composite of the conclusions independently arrived at by members of a central staff.

The Technical Approach

The most important broad classification of methods covers those using a technical approach as opposed to those based on "fundamentals", defining the latter as being concerned with facts relating to the market, but external to it, such as money rates, steel production, department store sales, etc. The pure technical approach disdains such data on the assumption that by the time they are generally available they have already been largely reflected by market price changes.

H. M. Gartley is a leading exponent of the technical school, and has done a tremendous amount of research on

price patterns, volume of trading, and all the various ramifications of the market price movement. However, his conclusions as published in the *Gartley Weekly Stock Market
Forecast (a Technical Analysis)* are the result of a synthe-
sized study employing all sorts of technical "tools" and
weighting their often diverse implications at any given time
in the light of judgment and experience. Hence, there is
no point here in attempting to cover the use of "triangles",
"trend lines", oscillators", etc. which are fully treated in
the Gartley publication, *Profits in the Stock Market* (1937).
An excellent more recent study covering this specialized
field is *Technical Analysis of Stock Trends* by Robert D.
Edwards and John Magee, Jr. (published by the Stock
Trend Service of Springfield, Mass.)

Major Technical Groups

Many of the technical methods which can stand by
themselves, and with which this book is primarily concerned, may be divided into two groups — (1) those which
attempt to define the trend in order to go with it and
(2) those which attempt to detect elements of latent
strength or weakness in the price structure, thus determining the turning point *before* a trend is established.

The first group of "trend methods" is covered in the
next section (II) and comprises the following:

Dow Theory and Various Offshoots
The "Ten Percent Rule" and its Modification
Mechanizations of the Dow Theory
Various Moving Average Methods, including the
   "Semaphore" and the "Technometer".

Section III explains and discusses various "Character-of-
the Market" methods such as:

The Parker Method

Lowry's "Buying Power vs. Selling Pressure"

Mills' "Buying and Selling"

Lamotte & Whitman's Measures of Supply and Demand

Quinn's "Moving Volume Curve"

Hood's "Group Action"

Use of Market-Breadth Data

(Also see the "Odd Lot Indexes" under Section VI)

There is likewise a negative relationship between the Cycle Theories and Formula Plans which are at completely opposite poles in their approach. Cyclical projections are pure forecasting, whereas formulas are based on the assumption that even reasonably accurate forecasting is impossible.

Formula Plans are discussed in Section IV, including

The Vassar and Yale Plans

Constant Ratio and Constant Dollar Systems

The Keystone "Seven Step" Plan

F. I. duPont Institutional Plan

The Burlingame Plan and the Howe Method

New England Plan

Section V is devoted to the theory of Cycles, covering the following:

Smith's "Decennial Pattern"

Marechal's Long-Term Forecasts

Elliott's "Wave Principle"

Sidereal Radiation and the Stock Market

Section VI comes back basically to a "character-of-the market" method (Section III), but since it represents a psychological study based on special data, the treatment is separate, covering the Theory of Contrary Opinion and the "Odd Lot Indexes".

In Section VII, some conclusions are drawn and the question of selecting stocks as mediums is discussed. Finally, in Section VIII a new "Prediction" is ventured, that of the 1941 edition being quoted *in toto* in the Supplement on page 284.

METHODS DEFINING THE TREND

DOW THEORY AND VARIOUS OFFSHOOTS

OF the methods concerned with defining the trend, the Dow Theory is by far the most widely known. So much has been written on it that an extended description is unnecessary, Robert Rhea's *Dow Theory* (*Barron's*) probably being the most comprehensive orthodox treatment. In fact, it could almost be said that its prominence represents a triumph of publicity rather than of merit.

Briefly, the fundamental concept is that at any given time the market is a composite resultant of three movements — the major trend, the secondary trend, and the minor (day to day) trend. There are other usually accepted ramifications such as the confirmation of the Dow-Jones Industrial Average by the Rail Average (or vice versa) in penetrating previous resistance points, the breakout from line formations as indicating the direction of the next move, and other minor points connected with study of the price movement.

Definition of Trends

The basic concept is definition of the trend. A Dow Theory investor, for example, would not hold stocks while he considered the major trend to be down, although a more active speculator might do so on a temporary basis if the secondary trend (lasting weeks or months) was up. Trends

25

are determined by the relation of the market to previous high and low points. The change from a bull market to a bear market in 1937 was a particularly clear-cut instance. In that year, the Industrial Average first fell from a peak of 195 to 165 and then recovered to 190, the major trend still being regarded as up by previous definition as it had been for four years. (See Frontispiece or Figure 7.) If it had exceeded 195 instead of stopping at 190, the major trend would have been reconfirmed as upward, but the downturn from 190 left the matter in doubt. Since 165 was the last important low point — or bottom of a secondary decline — this became the crucial level for determining the trend. Its later penetration meant that the major trend had changed from up to down, i.e., the heretofore "proven" bull market had ended five months before.

Not a Forecasting Device

Strictly speaking, it will be seen that the Dow Theory does not attempt to pick tops or bottoms, nor does it actually attempt to forecast. In fact, Dow himself never intended his theory to be used as a means to stock market profits, but rather as a barometer of what business conditions would be.

The unkindest thing that has been said about the Dow Theory in its ordinary usage is that it is "an attempt to forecast by definition" — a criticism that has some weight under certain conditions. In April of 1939, for instance, penetration of a previous low point signaled a change in major trend, but unlike 1937, the trend promptly reversed and later developments showed that according to the Theory, a bull market had begun only four days after a bear market had been confirmed.

It is evident, therefore, that orthodox Dow Theory will be satisfactory only when there are long sweeping movements. Acceptance of the major trend definition, for example, would have enabled an investor to have avoided the grief in the great bear market of 1929 to 1933, or to have made profits on the short side. Followed consistently over a period of years, it will unquestionably produce moderately profitable results, but it obviously requires more patience and "stick-to-itiveness" than the average person has. Months may go by with no clear indication at all, or there may be heartbreaking experiences like the one in 1939.

Conflict in Interpretations

Even the major trend is not always indisputable and the leading exponents of the Theory may differ among themselves as to its direction. On more than one occasion, the determination of the major trend has hinged upon whether a certain minor trend was sufficiently important to be classified as a true secondary move. The 1942-1946 bull market caught this at both ends. Between April and July, 1942, the Industrial Average rose from 92.92 to 108.91 and then declined to 104.80 in August. To those Dow Theorists who considered that decline as a secondary correction, a bull market was signaled in September when 108.91 was penetrated upside. The conservatives who felt that the July-August decline was only a minor move, however, then watched prices advance to 145.82 in July, 1943 before encountering what they could consider a valid secondary correction. As it worked out, they did not get conclusive confirmation that a bull market was in existence until June of 1944, more than two years after the uptrend in prices had actually started.

There was likewise a little conflict between various Dow Theorists when the trend—according to the Dow Theory—changed from bull to bear in the late summer of 1946.

Some called the turn on the penetration by the Industrial Average of one previous low point and some on another, the difference in practice being whether sales were effected around the 190 or the 178 level.

Another divergence of opinion arose in February, 1947, and again as in 1942, the side taken depended upon whether a certain reaction in the preceding month was classified as secondary or minor. To a few calling it a secondary, it meant that a new bull market had been confirmed as having begun four months before. To the others, a primary bear market remained in force.

From this, it may be seen that application of the Dow Theory—as it is usually expounded in various services and publications—is likely to be quite confusing on occasion. Sometimes the confusion arises from hair-splitting. In 1947, for example, the May low of the Industrial Average was nineteen cents above the low of the preceding October—a fact which had some bearing on future determination of the trend according to some exponents of the Theory. However, if Eastman Kodak had not happened to split its stock in the interim, the Average would have gone seven cents *below* the previous bottom, thus involving a nice point of interpretation. It seemed a bit naive for one commentator to remark nearly a year later that "Last May, it was the failure of the Dow-Jones Industrial Average to close at a new low that proved to be the correct clue to the market at that time."

Theory Now Complicated

Another cause of confusion is the lack of any clearly defined line among the interpreters as to where the Theory stops. Dow's original concept was a simple definition of the trend, but it has been carried beyond that point. Some are fond of saying that a good Dow Theorist does not wait for actual confirmation of a trend by definition before taking action. In other words, he anticipates that it will occur on the basis of his judgment concerning the price pattern and the character of the market's action. There is no quarrel with such procedure, but whether it is strictly Dow Theory is something else. Any good judge of the market might act at the same point, regardless of his acquaintance—or lack of it—with the Theory.

There is, however, a simple but little known set of rules which entirely eliminates the sort of indecision discussed above. ·These rules are given in the subsequent section called "Mechanizations of the Dow Theory". As also shown there, an excellent case has been made out for disregarding the confirmation of one average by the other, although the latter is held to be vital by the most prominent orthodox exponents of the Dow Theory.

Natural Limitations

The Theory has its merits, but it has its limitations as well. Many who have embraced it at times simply expected too much and did not realize the patience required. As pointed out in the Introduction, the unequivocal bear market signal of 1937 which was immediately followed by a violent crash of prices, caused a sudden rise in the popularity of the Theory. Its new adherents who accepted it as gospel, however, shortly encountered a sequence of unfortunate events. A bull market was indicated at around 149 in the Industrial Average in October, 1938, only to have a bear market signaled at the 131 level in April, 1939. This again proved unprofitable when another bull market was confirmed only three months later at 144.

It almost seems to be a law in these matters that the

better something has been in the immediate past, the worse
it is likely to be in the near future. Provided that any
method has some basic merit, it can be looked to with most
confidence just after it has passed through a poor or mediocre period. That is merely another way of saying that the
character of the market is different in some periods than in
others, and that nothing is likely to function with a constant degree of success in any and all types of markets.

The important points to remember for anyone contem-
plating the formulation of his investment policy according
to the Dow Theory are (1) that the Theory does not actually forecast and (2) that although it will assuredly be
profitable in the long run, at least, the initial degree of
success — or lack of it — will be a matter of chance.

Minor Allied Concepts

Other methods have been evolved on the same basis as
the Dow Theory. Jesse Livermore, of trading fame, lent
his name to a scheme called the "Livermore Market Key"
which used leading stocks within groups in the same way
that the Theory uses the Industrial and Rail Averages.
Thus, one would buy Montgomery Ward and Sears Roebuck when both stocks confirmed each other by penetrating
their previous highs. This would doubtless be satisfactory
in the case of big moves, but probably quite the opposite
in seesaw markets.

Before this, W. H. Roystone had evolved the "Heavy
Industry Theory (using Steels instead of Rails in the Dow
Theory principle)". The idea is perfectly sound, being
based as it is on the relationship between consumer goods
and heavy goods production. From a market viewpoint,
action is taken in anticipation of an important reversal of
trend whenever the "action of the main body of industrials

belies the action of the Steels". However, the operation of this theory would require considerable interpretation of the price action and relative price levels.

TEN PERCENT RULE

Although the "Ten Percent Rule" is a very simple mathematical calculation, it has exactly the same basis as the Dow Theory or any trend method, i.e., the assumption that any trend, once established, will continue further in the same direction.

This was originally publicized by the *London Financial News* with the story of an American, Cyrus Hatch (actually a mythical individual). Hatch was supposed to have evolved and used this rule which enabled him to increase an estate of $100,000 left to him in 1882 to $14,400,000 by his death in December, 1936. According to the study, he calculated the market value of his holdings at the end of each week and then averaged the weekly figures once a month. Whenever the latter average declined 10% from the previous highest point, he sold and did not buy again until the monthly average value of his former holdings had risen 10% from the lowest point recorded after liquidation. In all those fifty-three years, the rule called for a change in position 44 times. During one period (1923-1929) the same position was held for six years, although at another time stocks were held for only three months. The longest period out of the market (Hatch did not make short sales) was a little over two years. If the original purchases had been left unchanged until 1936, their value would then have been only $382,500.

As may be seen, the "Ten Percent Rule" is a sort of mechanization of the Dow Theory, using the degree of advance or decline to define the trend instead of pinning the latter on penetration of previous high or low points. It must be assumed that the mythical Hatch was able to choose better-than-average stocks because of the degree of gain shown. That does not invalidate the principle, however. If the rule is applied to the Dow-Jones Industrial Average between 1882 and 1936, it still shows a startling increase, even though not up to the supposed Hatch results.

A Modifying Improvement

Carleton Davenport did some further research on the rule as applied to the Dow-Jones Industrial Average, and found that by reducing it to the following formula (which makes it rather an "Eleven Percent Rule"), better results were obtained.

For a "buy signal," total all Saturday (or the last day in the week the market is open) closings of the Dow-Jones Industrial Average for a calendar month and divide by the number of Saturdays used. Add 11% of this monthly average figure (plus 50¢) to the Average itself. On any subsequent Saturday that the Industrial Average closes above this result, the market should be bought. In selling the highest *single* Saturday close is used. Deduct 11% from it (plus 50¢) and then sell whenever on any Saturday the Average closes below the resultant figure.

Applying this rule to the Dow-Jones Industrial Average on the long side only for fifty years from 1896, it is found that a $100,000 fund would have increased to approximately $1,548,600 in 1946 after the liquidation called for in that year. The calculation does not allow for the dividends which would have been received, nor for taxes on capital gains, non-existent before 1913, and subsequently variable at different times with the individual.

Like the Dow Theory, the "Ten Percent Rule" will always come out ahead of the game in the long run, but can encounter very difficult periods. It was badly whipsawed, for example, in 1947 when the market just fluctuated within a 15% price range without any real trend, and even for the whole ten-year period from 1937 to 1947, the net gain was only about fifty points. Nevertheless, this was still better than an investor would have fared by buying and holding for the same period.

MECHANIZATIONS OF DOW THEORY

Samuel Moment tested the Dow Theory over a long period by the application of definite rules so as to eliminate possible controversial indications. His major trend rules for this were simple: buy when the last secondary rally on both Averages is exceeded and sell when the last secondary decline is exceeded, either of which establishes a new major trend. To be "exceeded", a high or low point must be penetrated by 1 point if either Average is under 100, 1% if between 100 and 150, 1½% between 151 and 200, and 2% above 200. A secondary movement is one retracing one-third or more (regardless of time) of the last price swing in the direction of whatever major trend has been previously established. If any secondary movement fails to make the required degree of penetration, the point of "failure" becomes the level which must subsequently be exceeded (by the necessary percentage) to establish the new trend.

Results to 1932

The original study was made some years ago and covered the period from 1897 to September, 1932. It showed that application of the major trend rules given above would have resulted in the growth of a $100,000 fund to $2,937,-300 (without allowing for capital gains taxes), using the stocks in the Dow-Jones Industrial Average and assuming that when sales were made, a short position was also taken. Allowance was made for commissions and transfer taxes, but not for dividends or rights, so that results are understated to that extent. The procedure came out far ahead of the "Ten Percent Rule" which, using the long side only, had brought its $100,000 in the Industrial Average to only $485,000 by September, 1932. If short sales had been made on its sell signals, it would be better, but still behind the results of the Moment major trend rules.

Confirmation Discarded

Carrying out his studies further for the same period from 1897 to 1932, Moment demonstrated rather conclusively that the supposedly essential element in orthodox Dow Theory of confirmation by one Average of the other is unnecessary. Applying the same rules as above to the Industrial Average alone, he found that the fund would have grown to $3,679,800, or $742,500 more than one operated under the ordinarily accepted principles of interpretation.

Recent Record

This latter study has been carried further, and in early 1948, the fund was assured of a theoretical minimum value of $7,617,700 which would be realized in case a later breaking of the October, 1946, low point by the requisite percentage, should signal sales. Results of the major trend rules from 1937 on were unusually interesting because they called for a change of position only twice in the next ten years. That is, the selling position taken in

September, 1937, at around 165 was held for over five years until shortly after the ultimate low in 1942.

The "bull markets" of 1938 and 1939 according to orthodox Dow Theory were ignored. Similarly, the orthodox bear market signaled in September, 1946, did not call for selling under Moment's major trend rules and the 1942 purchases at 108 were still being held in early 1948.

Secondary Trend Rules

Moment also worked out a mechanized Dow Theory to be used on the secondary trends. In this, he likewise ignored the matter of "confirmation", basing all his operations upon the movements of the Industrial Average alone. He does, however, include the theory of "lines", defining a line as a series of twelve or more daily closing prices in the Average within a range of not more than 5½%, measured from the highest point of the range. If within a line there occur "reactions" of at least 3%, these are used instead of the line. Reactions are net rallies or declines amounting to at least 3% of the Average from the point of reversal and lasting for two days or more. For example a 3% rally in one day followed by no change or a decline the next day is not a reaction.

Resistance points are the highest or lowest daily closing prices of a line or a reaction, and, for action to be taken, these must be exceeded by 1 point when the Average is below 100, 1% between 100 and 150 and 2% above 150. Daily closing prices are used throughout. The rule is to buy whenever an advance exceeds the high point of the last line or previous rally and to sell whenever a decline exceeds the low point of the preceding line or downward movement. There are some further minor rules covering unusual sequences in the price movement, but the above are the essential requirements.

Naturally, this gives more frequent signals than the major trend rules, but over the period of time covered in Moment's original study (1897-1932), it was found to be far more profitable. During the same thirty-five years in which the major trend fund grew from its original $100,000 to $3,679,800, application of the secondary trend rules would have brought it up to the astounding total of $18,180,000.

Record Unsatisfactory Since 1937

By 1937, it would have increased to around $34,000,000, but then ran into several years of the very worst types of market for any fairly active method based on following the indicated secondary or intermediate trends. The result was that by 1947, the fund was back to its 1932 level, having lost all the 1932-1937 gains. The character of the market from 1937 to 1947 was entirely different from anything encountered in the thirty-five years covered by the original study, which — again — illustrates the danger of relying upon past performance as a guaranty of the future.

In so far as the character of the market was concerned, the 1937-1947 period was divided into two distinct phases. In the first, between 1937 and 1942, there were abrupt and erratic movements in both directions as investors endeavored to appraise the approach, and then the impact, of war. By the time a secondary trend would be confirmed in one direction, the move would be nearly over, and then an abrupt reversal in the other direction would signal another change of trend which often resulted in selling, or covering a short position, at a loss. The year 1938 was the nemesis for the secondary trend rules in this respect. There were fifteen completed transactions, only three of which resulted in profits, and a net loss of about 28% would have been sustained for the full year.

From 1942 to 1946, the character of the market was exactly the opposite, but almost as poorly adapted for attempting to capitalize on the secondary trends. The long upswing of that period was not interrupted until near its end by any important secondary reaction. Consequently, sales would be indicated on minor downward moves which almost never went far enough to permit repurchasing or covering at a profit, and the fund would be forced back to the long side at a loss. There was a net profit for the period, but it amounted to only about 18%.

Moment's experience tables for thirty-five years had shown 166 completed transactions, of which 92, or 55%, were profitable. About one-third of the profits were over 15% with the largest 72%. No loss, however, exceeded 15% and over two-thirds of them were less than 5%.

On the other hand, in the difficult 1937-1947 period, there were 48 losses to 21 profits. The highest profit was only 24%, but it still held good that no single loss ever exceeded 15%.

This, however, is inherent in the nature of any method which is constantly attempting to go with the immediately indicated trend. If the trend reverses, the position changes with it, so that, in effect, there is always an automatic stop-loss system at work. For precisely this reason, to go short on a selling indication as well as liquidating long holdings, is only logical.

Changed Character of Trading

With the experience of the past ten years, the secondary trend rules seem like an unsatisfactory basis for operations, despite their earlier success over a much longer period.

What they — or other similarly timed trend methods — need, are long major trends interrupted fairly frequently by orthodox reversals retracing one-third to two-thirds of the preceding move. Such patterns were once "normal", but the major moves of recent years have been much more in the nature of "one-way streets". The chances are that this change is permanent, because it is apparently the result of the restrictions placed on professional trading since the advent of the Securities and Exchange Commission.

In the past, floor traders were always prompt to exploit vigorously the line of least resistance, but it is now virtually impossible for them to accelerate any given movement. For example, professionals may not buy on what is called an "up-tick", or higher quotation. Or, if there are no outside buyers after a stock has advanced, they may only buy one-third of the amount offered at the higher price, or 300 shares, whichever is greater. They may not fill a bid with a short sale, nor can they effect any short sale unless at a price higher than the last transaction. In fact, there is even a general rule that they may not create more than "normal" trading activity on the upside. With such complete hamstringing of professional operations, it is only natural that there is less "follow-through" to secondary price movements.

Major Trend Rules Successful

For dealing with the major trends, however, Moment's rules have been consistently successful for fifty years. The best-known exponents of the Dow Theory have never approved of reducing it to such a formula, but the rules do have the virtue of eliminating the indecision or differences of opinion which so often mark the orthodox interpretations of the Theory. Moreover, the results covering all types of markets do seem to demonstrate conclusively that over a period of time, profits will be greater than under the accepted principles of Dow Theory interpretation.

Doubtful Value of Confirmation

As previously pointed out, Moment's study showed that final results were better if trends were accepted on the basis of the Industrial Average alone, ignoring the supposed necessity of "confirmation" by the Rails. Actual experience of more recent years has borne this out, and indeed, it seems perhaps only logical that it should. In the days when the Dow Theory was being formulated, the Rails were the most important group of stocks in which investment and speculative interest centered.

At the turn of the century, there were only 377 issues listed on the New York Stock Exchange, of which nearly 40% were rails. Moreover, they accounted for the bulk of trading volume, the peak in this respect being reached in 1902 when 75% of the total number of shares turned over represented transactions in railroad stocks. At the end of 1947, there were 1,379 stocks listed, but these included fewer rails than in 1900, and this group was only 7½% of the total. Thus, the rails are now a relatively minor group. In 1947, the value of listed rail stocks was less than $4 billion, whereas oils, chemicals and utilities were each about $8 billion and even groups like automobiles, food and retail merchandising were all more than the railroads.

The Dow Theory argument for the necessity of "confirmation" of a trend by both the Industrial and Railroad Averages is the fact that the railroads serve all industry and therefore, that any important trend in industry and trade is sooner or later reflected in rail traffic. True enough, but it can be argued with equal validity that automotive power or the use of oil are so closely enmeshed in the economy today that any broad changes in business will just as surely be reflected there. In other words, why can only the Rails "confirm" a trend — if, indeed, the trend of a broad industrial group needs to be "confirmed"?

There also seems to be considerable common sense in Moment's requirement that a crucial point must be penetrated by a fairly substantial amount, depending on the price level. Orthodox Dow Theory says that one cent is enough to constitute a "penetration", but this may be a slim peg at times. As mentioned earlier, a penetration of a previous low point would have occurred in May, 1947, if it had not been for the split in Eastman Kodak. Allowing for Moment's necessary percentage, however, there would not have been any question either way that a true penetration had not occurred.

Long-Term Results Now Modified

Some of the figures cited on the growth of funds in the preceding discussions seem very spectacular. Indeed, the *London Financial News* referred to Hatch's performance as "staggering, sensational, breath-taking, and colossal". However — successful as these methods have been — even the indisputable results seem more spectacular than they are for two reasons. The first is that the figures are compounded, no money ever being withdrawn from the funds. Consequently, in the later phases, there is capital running into the millions with which to work. The results of compounding are always startling over a period of time. If money could draw 5% interest and the interest be compounded annually, $100,000 could be raised to $1,476,740 in fifty years. Or to state it another way, when Moment arrived at $18,180,000 from $100,000 in thirty-five years, it represented only about a 15½% annual rate of appreciation at compound interest.

The second reason is that the largest gains came just after the middle 1920s during some abnormally sweeping price changes in the price level of stocks. Any method following the trend will be unusually successful when the trends continue as far and as long as they did between 1927 and 1932. The influence of the period, however, was less than might be supposed, as the average annual rate of gain was only 17½% from 1927 to 1933 which was better than the 12½% average of the preceding 20 years, but practically the same as the 1897-1906 period. However, by the '20s, these theoretical funds had a large amount of capital to use. It took 25 years, for example, for the mechanized orthodox Dow Theory fund of $100,000 to grow to $457,000, which is only about 6% at annual compound interest.

One more word of caution. Let us assume the fund available is $10,000 instead of $100,000. In that case, it would probably take twenty-five years of normal markets to increase this to $200,000. In the meantime, one could not withdraw any profits, but would have to use every penny (without borrowing however) in the new commitments on both the long and short side at any given time. And that would mean that other funds would have to be used for the payment of income taxes on capital gains. If tax payments were logically withdrawn from profits, the fund's rate of gain would be considerably retarded. It would also be necessary to have the moral courage to follow every signal given under the rules, and never deviate regardless of the circumstances at any time.

The results, therefore, may not be spectacular, but it is a fair assumption that over a twenty-five year period, ninety-nine out of a hundred people interested in stocks would come out better by sticking to, let us say, Moment's major trend rules than they actually do in practice.

Less well known, perhaps, than the Dow Theory among the methods for determining the trend, but certainly the basis of more "systems", is the use of moving averages for that purpose. A moving average is a statistical device for discerning the underlying trend of any series of erratically fluctuating figures. Suppose, for instance, that a three-day moving average of the closing price of U. S. Steel is desired beginning with some particular week. The first moving average figure would be an average of the closing prices on Monday, Tuesday, and Wednesday, the second an average for Tuesday, Wednesday, and Thursday, the third for Wednesday, Thursday, Friday, etc. Any number of days, of course, can be employed. The more that are used, the smoother will be the curve of the resulting series, but there will be a greater time lag before the moving average will pursue the trend of the actual figures.

A moving average simply requires more substantiation that a trend has been established than a mere price change in a certain direction. Suppose it is desired to follow the more important trends of some active stock which normally fluctuates over a wide price range.

An easy and workable method is to use a two-week moving average of the central weekly price range of the stock. That is, add the high and low for one week and divide by two for the center of the price range. Do the same for the preceding week, add both results and divide that by two for the moving average figure. If the high on any Monday is below the last figure obtained, sell, while if the low is above it, buy. If neither is true, then the last signal remains in effect. The same check is made for each succeeding day throughout the week until the next Monday when a new key figure is calculated.

As long as wide price fluctuations occur, such a simple formula will yield a net profit over a reasonable period of time, although any one signal or even series of signals can result in relatively small losses. Naturally, however, it will always be on the right side of the market during any important move, and short sales should always be made on a sell signal for the reasons explained on page 37.

for the reasons explained on page 37.

SEMAPHORE AND TECHNOMETER

A typical and more elaborate moving average applied to the whole market has been known as "The Semaphore", its construction being as follows. Six-week moving averages are first taken of the weekly highs and lows of some representative stock average. Plotted together, this gives a picture of a fluctuating band varying in width which is called Line A in Figure 1. This is drawn or projected two weeks ahead of the market. Then a three-week moving average of the weekly highs and lows is plotted but *not* projected ahead of the market. This band (Line B) naturally shows sharper fluctuations because of the shorter time element used, i.e., 3 weeks against 6 weeks.

As long as B is below A, the market is regarded as in a downtrend, but when B turns up and starts crossing A, the trend is assumed to be changing and one would buy. Just the opposite is true, of course, for choosing the time to sell. Because of the nature of this construction, signals do not occur until after prices have actually begun to move in the direction in which it is assumed they will continue. This is designed to take advantage of the secondary movements

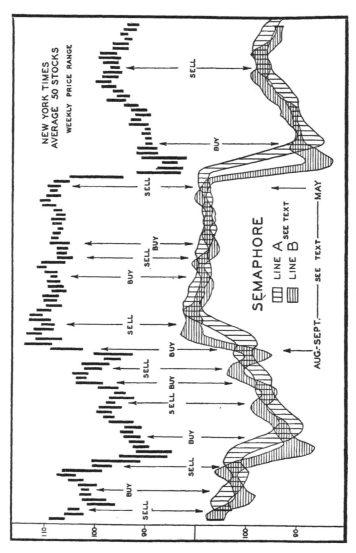

FIGURE 1

lasting weeks to months, and it does have the advantage that on any sustained move in either direction, a user will be on the right side of the market at least 75% of the time. A faster "Semaphore" might be made using, say, 3 days and 7 days, which would simply give more frequent signals with a greater number of profits and losses.

Figure 1 shows the "Semaphore" for two years computed from the weekly price ranges of the *New York Times* Stock Average with the "buy" and "sell" points of that period designated. This is the original illustration in the first edition of this book, and hence the period covered is 1939-1940. However, it serves the purpose just as well as something more recent, and illustrates both the advantages and shortcomings of the "Semaphore". As with all moving average methods, of course, there are "whipsaws"; i.e., quick reversals of position at small losses. Notice also that when a sharp reversal develops suddenly as in August-September, for example, it does not change fast enough to act at the beginning of the new trend. On the other hand, sales were indicated close to the beginning of the May, 1940, drop, because the mild sag in the market preceding that decline had already turned Line B down. A certain amount of anticipation is used with the Semaphore because, as any week draws to a close, it is obviously possible to know approximately what the picture will be after the complete weekly price range has become available.

A Faster Trend Method

Sometimes modifying factors have been introduced in the use of moving averages as in the case of the "Technometer". To quote the originator, S. M. Thompson, this is based "on the changes in direction of a four-day moving average of daily closing prices of either individual stocks or an average of a number of stocks. When the four-day moving average turns up, a buy is indicated; when it turns down, a sell is indicated. However, the signals thus given are too numerous and often of minor importance, so that another factor is introduced for confirmation of the signal, namely — volume. If increased volume accompanies the signal, it should be acted upon. In order properly to determine increased volume four criteria are used. The volume on the day of the signal must be greater than (A) the average volume for four days, (B) the volume on the fourth day previous to the signal, (C) the volume on the day before the signal, and (D) the closing price on the day of the greatest volume during the four-day period must be in a direction to confirm the signal". Saturday's volume is doubled for the purpose of these calculations.

A record may easily be kept as follows.

Date	Preliminary Signal	Closing Price	Volume of Trading	A	B	C	D	Signal Confirmed
2nd	——	66	4700	—	—	—	—	——
4th	——	. 65¼	4300	—	—	—	—	——
5th	——	63½	6200	—	—	—	—	——
6th	——	66	4600	—	—	—	—	——
7th	Buy	67¼	4700	—	0	+	—	No
8th	Buy	67	4000	—	—	—	—	No
9th	Buy	66¾	4300	—	—	+	—	No
11th	Buy	67¼	5800	+	+	+	+	Buy

A plus sign is entered in the proper column on any day that one of the requirements is filled. If not filled, a minus sign is entered. A zero means no change one way or the other. After the first zero or minus, there is no need for further calculations on that day. When all are plus, however, action is signalled. In the illustration above, it would be to buy because the price moving average turned up. If it had turned down, the signal would have been to sell. It is not necessary to calculate the moving average because its direction can be determined by comparing the price with that on the fourth preceding day. In this particular case, the close of 67¼ on the 11th is higher than the 66 on the 6th which makes the direction up. If the close on the 11th had been 65¼, the signal would have been to sell.

When there are wide price movements and volatile, active stocks are used, dollar profits of the "Technometer" seem to run in a ratio to the losses of about two to one. Figure 2 shows its specific application to Chrysler during a time selected at random except for the fact that it was taken to include both a wide move and a period of irregular price movements. In this six-month period, the net profits were roughly twice the losses, although a little over one-half of the profit came on the wide downswing in the latter part of March when the Technometer secured 62% of the total move. The irregular price movements in the last part of the period shown naturally resulted in small losses.

ADVANTAGES AND LIMITATIONS

The foregoing illustrations will suffice for this class of method. Notice that what they do is to set up some criteria for defining the trend at any given time. If these criteria indicate that the trend is up, then one buys on the assumption that the trend will continue. If the trend is down, a

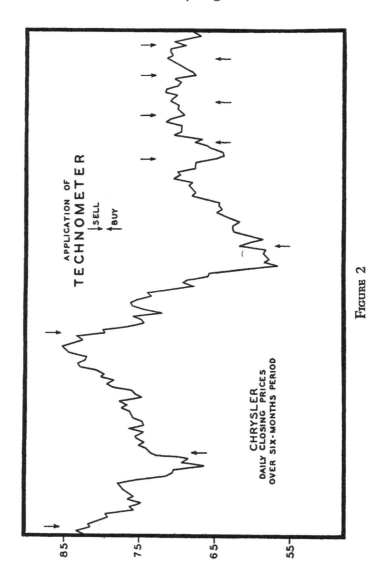

FIGURE 2

short position is taken. Therefore, such methods are an assurance of being on the right side of the market when any important move comes along. On the other hand, if the trend does not continue, but quickly reverses itself, then it usually means taking a loss. The net result is ordinarily many small losses and a few large profits. If the market stays in a narrow trading area, the series of small losses will persist for a dishearteningly long time, but there is the consolation of knowing one will be right when a substantial move does occur.

The time at which the method is adopted can also make a considerable difference. If an important move chances to occur near the beginning, the original capital will be immediately increased and a few small losses will not hurt. But, if the initial period of operations chances to be dull with only small fluctuations, perhaps 25% or 30% of the original capital will have been chipped away before there is a worth-while profit.

Notice, too, that no forecasting is involved. When a signal is given, there is absolutely no way of knowing from the method whether it will mean a large profit or a little loss, because all it says is that a trend has been established, which is no guarantee that the trend will continue. Therefore, these methods must be followed with 100% consistency on every signal given. To interpose judgment on the basis of other factors is fatal to ultimate success. Moreover, they may not be combined for a stronger "forecast", because they do not forecast. One particular method must be elected, and that one followed implicitly.

Market Background Important

It cannot be too often repeated that the character of the market for any given period determines the relative success or failure of any trend method, whether it is Dow Theory or a highly sensitive moving average. One of the latter methods, somewhat like the Semaphore, once gained 100 points with no losses on the Dow-Jones Industrial Average in one year, and then had a net loss of thirty points in the next twelve months. There was nothing "wrong" with the system. It just happened to be ideally suited to the type of intermediate moves that occurred in the first year and not to the entirely different sort of fluctuations which came along immediately afterward.

Followed consistently over a long enough period of time, however, any good trend method should show a fair to excellent profit, depending upon the opportunities offered by the market. Notice that "opportunities" does not mean rising prices. It merely means decisively *changing* prices.

METHODS ANALYZING CHARACTER
OF THE MARKET

THE other broad group of technical methods is not at all concerned with an assumed determination of the trend. In fact, such methods seek to *anticipate* the trend by determining points of reversal, or the direction in which prices will move out of an indecisive area. For example, the Dow Theorist who is confronted with a "line formation" is content to wait until it is broken one way or the other, upon which he assumes that the price movement will continue in the same direction.

On the other hand, one who uses the type of method described in this Section is interested in analyzing the character of the action during the line formation in order to decide on the probable direction in which it will be broken. The Dow Theorist awaits the verdict; the analyst of market action forecasts it. All other things being equal, such methods are obviously superior to those which must wait for the trend to be established because, if correct, they will naturally be able to secure profits on a greater proportion of any given market swing.

The analyses to be discussed are designated here as "character-of-the-market" methods, because they attempt to determine the characteristics of the buying and selling at any given time. Are stocks, for example, passing from

51

"strong hands" to "weak hands" — which would suggest a forthcoming decline — or is the buying being done preponderantly by informed interests, thus indicating a probable advance?

It is evident that nothing in this category can ever be perfect or right all the time. Modifying influences or radically changed conditions will make the "perfect" analysis of one period less perfect — or perhaps almost worthless — in another. But even though some particular study is far short of perfection does not mean that it is necessarily to be ignored. It still may be capable of a good batting average over a period of time by itself, or be a highly useful adjunct to some other method at certain junctures. Many — although not all — of the character-of-the-market methods can be used in combination, whereas the trend methods in Section II must be employed singly.

Probing Beneath the Surface

Whatever particular avenue — or avenues — of approach may be used, the character-of-the-market methods represent attempts to probe beneath the surface appearance of the price movement in order to evaluate the future probabilities. A simple chart of the price fluctuations in a market average at some given time may be likened to the photograph of an individual. It is a true picture of his physical appearance, but it tells little — if anything — about his character. If, however, one had a psychiatric report on his mental processes and responses — these to be weighed against a known background — it would be possible to predict reasonably well how that person would be likely to fare or react under some particular set of circumstances.

The parallel is illustrative — not exact. The point is that, in the stock market, there are more readily available and significant facts pertaining to the price movement than the simple surface data on average price change. There is the volume of trading, the amount of short selling, the number of new highs and lows, the most active issues for each day, the breakdown of buying and selling by New York Stock Exchange members, the transactions in odd lots by dealers and the public, etc. All have one thing in common. They are derived entirely from the records of transactions on the Stock Exchange, which represent the meeting of thousands of minds. A buyer and a seller must agree in order to make a transaction — each moved to action by varying stimuli. To the extent that the forces behind these activities may be discerned or understood, the better is it possible to see when they may have run out their influence for the time being, or what result they are likely to produce in the future.

PROFESSIONAL ACTIVITY INDEX

Purely as an illustrative example, there is a simple and logical device known as the "Professional Activity Index". This is merely the ratio of sales in the fifteen most active stocks each day to the total sales of all stocks for that day. The basic idea is that professional traders accumulate active stocks quietly, so that the ratio of the volume in the most active stocks to the total volume will be relatively small when a strong situation is developing. Conversely, the ratio will be large when stocks are being distributed around an important top.

That is perfectly correct in theory, but there are too many difficulties in practical application to make the study worth much as a method by itself. The question is always "how small is small" and "how large is large". At the time it attracted the greatest amount of interest, the reason was that for two or three years, it would have worked quite well if purchases were made whenever the ratio declined below 30% and sales were made when it rose above 45%. From then on, however, other limits were established at different periods. Thus, there are too many variable factors for consistent application, despite the essentially correct assumption on which the method is based.

Nevertheless, the "Index" is not worthless if it is used as a suggestive or corroborative indication of the market's character at any given time, rather than being reduced to a rigid formula of buy and sell signals when given limits are reached. In the latter form, it is too inconsistent.

INDEX OF CONFIDENCE

A very similar and often-used method employs the ratio of a selected group of low-priced stocks to another group of high-priced stocks. To obtain the ratio, the average price of the former is divided by the average price of the latter. Thus, the low-priced stocks are being measured in terms of the high-priced issues instead of in dollars. Normally, the ratio will rise in an advancing market, since increasing *confidence* is expressed in a willingness to buy the low-priced and more speculative stocks. However, there are times when the ratio will show a tendency to decline in a rising market. This signifies that there is less willingness to buy low-priced issues; i.e., confidence is declining. Such action is bearish, and suggests a coming reversal in trend. It is implicit in the foregoing that the action of the ratio must be observed in relation to that of the high-priced and low-priced stocks themselves.

Although it is ordinarily true that a declining ratio in a rising market is bearish, the rule does not apply rigidly to all circumstances. There is one important exception when the rising price level represents the rebound after a sharp decline or selling climax. In such a case, the ratio is likely to lag and continue down after the market has turned, because — under such circumstances — the first faint revival of confidence is expressed only in a willingness to buy the "safer" high-priced issues. The same sort of lag is also likely to be witnessed for the same reason in the case of a dull rounding bear-market bottom such as in April-May, 1942. If — in the case of an apparent selling climax — the ratio, or index, does not lag, but turns up simultaneously with the average price movement, it is likely to mean that the recovery is temporary and that the whole move is not over.

An Index of this sort has some value, but it is another excellent example of the sort of method which is better used as a corroborative adjunct of some other approach than exclusively by itself.

PARKER METHOD

This particular device — which was described in the 1941 edition of this book — also employs a specific group of stocks, but unlike the "Index of Confidence" must be used by itself rather than as confirmatory evidence. In fact, it is just as necessary to stick to it and follow every indication as in the case of the trend methods in Section II if its average profit potentialities are to be realized.

The mechanics of the Parker Method are as follows: four investment stocks in the Dow-Jones Industrial Average are used — American Telephone, Eastman Kodak, duPont, and Allied Chemical. In order to maintain continuity and give approximately equal weight to all four issues, the five-for-one split of Eastman Kodak on May 16, 1947, has been ignored. That is, its present price is always multiplied by five in the calculations. The closing prices of the four stocks (Eastman Kodak adjusted) are added together and divided by the close of the Industrial Average for the same day multiplied by 13.3. This last figure is not as mysterious as it sounds. It is simply the divisor which was used in figuring the Dow-Jones Industrial Average prior to the split of Eastman Kodak. (The current divisor is 12.2, such adjustments being necessary to maintain the continuity of the Average.)

The sum of the four issues listed above divided by the Average (multiplied by 13.3), therefore, simply shows what percentage of the Average for each day is accounted for by four investment-grade stocks out of its thirty components. This percentage result is placed on a ten-day moving average, and the moving average figure is plotted in what appears to be a smoothly fluctuating line. When this line turns down, it is taken as a signal to buy stocks, while an upturn, of course, calls for selling. As a matter of fact, one could just as well use four speculative stocks from the Average, in which case the line would simply move in the opposite direction at any time and an upturn instead of a downturn would indicate buying.

Underlying Theory

The logical theory behind the method is this. As everyone knows, speculative stocks like U. S. Steel move over a wider range than investment issues such as American Telephone. Therefore, as the market rises, the speculative stocks in the Dow-Jones Industrial Average make up an increasingly larger part of the Average while the investment stocks account for a smaller part. The opposite, of course, is true during a decline. Hence, when the market is at a bottom, the investment stocks are a relatively large part of the Average and the moving average "index line" is at a peak. Theoretically, one should buy when the line is high and sell when it is low, but to attempt to apply it that way runs into the same difficulty mentioned in the case of the "Professional Activity Index" of knowing "how high is high", or "how low is low". The reason for taking action when the line reverses is that, characteristically, it does so rather infrequently, and hence a reversal usually means that the extreme point of the phase has been reached.

The disadvantage of the Parker Method is that, like the moving average trend systems, there is no way of judging whether the move will go further or be quickly reversed. Thus, it is not a "forecasting" method, and occupies a hybrid position between the methods of Section II and those of the current Section. Mistaken indications usually result from resumption of an important trend in the moving average line after it has apparently reversed, thus indicating that the final high or low has not been reached. In such a case, one may be "whipsawed", but no loss is ever large, and this usually occurs when there are sharp and erratic week-to-week fluctuations within approximately the same price range — always a difficult sort of market with which to deal. In this respect, it has elements of similarity to the moving average systems, but it has ordinarily the distinct advantage as compared with the latter of losing considerably less in sidewise price movements. Like them, however, it can be relied upon to be always on the right side of the market when a big move gets under way. For the same reason, it cannot be expected to pick exact bottoms or tops of the climactic type unless the price pattern is extremely unusual.

There is a slight element of judgment involved in determining just how much of a reversal in the "index line" is necessary to be accepted as an indication that it has reached a definite high or low. Ordinarily, this is perfectly clear, although it may sometimes be necessary to make allowances for whether the reversal is primarily due to what is happening currently or to the dropping off of figures in the moving average. For example, the latest figures used might show no change from the preceding day, but the elimination of the eleventh day back could change the moving average figure if that eleventh day was materially greater or smaller than the latest calculation.

Record in Different Periods

It must be said, however, that the record at the time the 1941 edition of this book was published looked better than it does today. From its nature, the method would be expected to do very well — as it did — in a year like 1937 with its sweeping trends. Since 1938 and 1939 were very erratic periods, however, the relatively excellent results shown then by the Parker Method seemed to stamp it as quite outstanding in its particular class. In 1938, for example, it gave fourteen signals with a net profit of about 50 points in the Dow-Jones Industrial Average, assuming that a short position was taken on selling indications. This resulted from fairly large profits on five of the signals, the others resulting in no gains or minor losses. Similarly, in 1939, there were twelve signals, eight of which were profitable. The largest loss was about five points while the net profit was approximately 60 points.

More recent performance has, therefore, been somewhat disappointing — not that it has "gone haywire" and resulted in a net loss for any year, but simply that net profits have not been so large as might have been expected from the earlier record. For example, in 1946, there were 13 signals with completed transactions showing six gains and six losses, the net gain amounting to only 14 points — hardly more than a "break-even" performance after expenses. It might be borne in mind, however, that most investors suffered losses in 1946. The most important "sell" was rather late, not coming until August 29 when the market had already lost about 22 points of what was to be nearly a 50-point decline. In 1947, there were nine signals, with six profits and two losses, the net gain being over 37 points.

As a simple and completely mechanical method to be used entirely by itself, however, the Parker Method has attraction for those desiring something in this particular class.

BUYING POWER VS. SELLING PRESSURE (LOWRY)

One of the best-known "character-of-the-market" methods is represented by the calculations of "Buying Power vs. Selling Pressure" published by Lowry's Investment Reports (formerly Lowry and Mills). The basic concept had been used by many, but the Lowry approach and analysis were the most completely worked out presentation when first made available in 1938.

Principle Employed

Stated briefly, the Lowry principle of analyzing the relative strength of "Buying Power vs. Selling Pressure" is that the total net daily gains and/or losses for all round-lot issues traded on the New York Stock Exchange are indicative of the increase or decrease of Buying Power and/or Selling Pressure in inverse ratio to the volume of trading on which such gains and/or losses may be registered.

To take an oversimplified example — if it requires 10,000 shares traded to advance a certain stock 2 points, whereas it had formerly risen the same amount on a volume of only 5,000 shares — the rise is meeting more resistance and hence the situation is that much weaker. To apply such simple reasoning to any and all individual stocks would prove misleading without making allowance for a great many other factors. However, by using all active stocks listed and placing results on a moving average basis, individual distortions are so greatly minimized as to have no appreciable effect upon the total.

Actual Calculations

Anyone could make the Lowry basic calculations, but it is such a long process that it would be rather impractical. The procedure is to segregate the daily gains and losses (measured by closing prices) in all stocks except the "inactives", or those traded in less than 100 share units.

Dividing the total gain of stocks showing a plus sign by the volume of trading for the same issues, gives the "average gain per upside share". Similarly, the "average loss per downside share" is calculated from the total loss for stocks showing minus signs. The underlying assumption is that if stocks are moving easier on the upside than the downside, the average gain per share will be greater than the average loss per share, while the reverse will be true if the path of least resistance is downward.

In addition to these tabulations, Lowry provides two major Indexes derived from them for observing the undertone of the market. These are moving averages using a time period of approximately two months. One is based on the data concerning the gains and is called "Buying Power", while "Selling Pressure" reflects the strength of downside activity and losses.

A much shorter-term (around 2½ weeks) moving average of the upside figures is also calculated, called the "Short-Term Measurement of Buying Power". (See Figure 3.) The index figures are released each day for plotting on

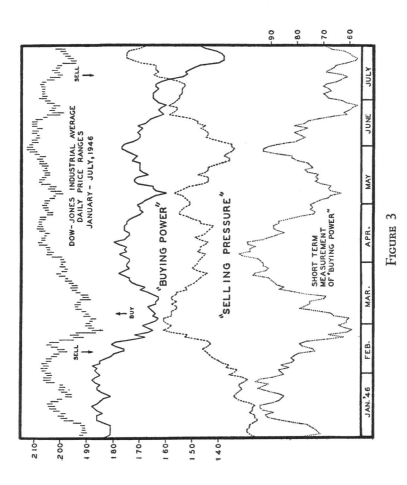

FIGURE 3

a prepared graph, certain levels on which may be used in determining the proper time of action. For example, one of the most certain indications to buy (usually occurring on a "selling climax") is a drop in the Short-Term Measurement below 60 on the Lowry chart, followed either by a rebound of six points, or the establishment of a zigzag upward trend in the index.

Interpretation

In general, a rising trend to the main "Buying Power" index has bullish connotations, while increasing "Selling Pressure" has the opposite meaning. However, there are exceptions, as, for example, if one index or the other has progressed to such an extreme point that a reversal can be logically expected. Trend lines are also employed to a certain extent in determining probable reversals.

Lowry has published a detailed discussion on how to interpret the action of the Indexes. It is pointed out that the analysis is not an absolutely rigid system as it might be made if the only factor to which any attention was paid was a crossing of the two Indexes. Such a crossing is important, and is assumed to give a definite "signal", but previous interpretation may — and often does — anticipate it.

However, Lowry has set up sufficiently definite rules or controls to apply to almost any situation that may be found on the graph of measurements which extends back to 1933. Hence, in evaluating the past record later, it is these controls and Lowry's specific application of them which are taken as the basis.

One point should be emphasized in connection with the Lowry approach. Although not a trend method, it does have one thing in common with such studies. This is that — because of its nature and the rules or "controls" — it will never be caught for very long on the wrong side of any big move. Depending on the circumstances, it may or may not act close to the beginning of an important advance or decline, but if not, the correct indication must be given before the move has progressed very far.

The Lowry 1942-1946 Record

By the same token, of course, it is also vulnerable to an occasional whipsaw and small loss — again just as in the case of a trend method and for the same reason. But when such a mistake is made, the nature of the method is such that it always gets back on the right side of the market. For example, during the course of the long 1942-1946 bull market, intermediate sales were indicated five times — once in 1943, twice in 1944, once in 1945, and once again in the first part of 1946. In 1943 and 1946, repurchases were advantageously indicated at lower levels than the sales had been made. In 1944 and 1945, however, it was necessary to re-enter the market at a somewhat higher point than when the sales had been effected. Nevertheless, from May 2, 1942, to July 16, 1946, the Lowry score stood at a total of approximately 110 points gained in the Industrial Average on purchases only (no short sales assumed). If advantage of the declines is assumed, however, the "score" would have been raised to about 115 points.

Considering that from extreme low (92.92 in April, 1942) to extreme high (212.50 in May, 1946) the scope of the whole upward price movement was 119.58 points, actually to clinch 109.44 points during approximately the same period is certainly doing even better than might be reasonably expected.

Since the record is definite and complete in the wires sent and the published Lowry analyses, the advantages and limitations can best be understood by checking through the actual performance of recent years on major (or basic) signals and the evidences of intermediate buying or selling points. Basic signals are relatively infrequent and are covered by just one buying rule and three selling rules. It does not appear wise, however, to proceed entirely on these indications, even though the greater activity inherent in the intermediate signals may not be individually desired. That is, a basic signal may fail to appear when it should, and keep the investor out of an important move. The greater — and sometimes undesirable — frequency of the intermediate indications represents the price which must be paid for the added assurance of having the right position on the more important trends. As far as the very short-term indications are concerned, it is felt that these are too frequent for practical use by the average investor.

Identifying the Bottom

Going back to the beginning of the bull market in 1942, the Lowry analysis gave the most clear-cut basic buying indication of which it is capable on May 2 — virtually at the extreme bottom in the Dow-Jones Industrial Average. All requirements were fulfilled. (1) The market had been declining. (2) The short-term measurement of Buying Power had turned up over six points from below its 60 level. (3) The main lines of Buying Power and Selling Pressure — after having been unusually far apart — had each clearly evidenced a change of trend in the desired direction.

Unreserved purchases were, therefore, indicated and advised at about the 96 level (Dow-Jones Industrial Average) in the face of apparently gloomy surface conditions — some 30 points lower than the preceding sale. From then on, nothing occurred in the picture to cause any selling until over a year later on June 22, 1943, at around 138, this move of some 42 points representing the virtually uninterrupted first leg of the bull market. The next definite evidence was to buy on an intermediate term basis at around 130 on November 30 of the same year, thus repurchasing stock sold in June at about a nine-point advantage.

Whipsaws in 1944-1945

Again selling indications appeared by April 19, 1944, when the November purchases could be liquidated at about 136 for a nominal six-point profit. As pointed out earlier, this was one of the two bull-market years when it was necessary to re-enter the market at a higher level than when the previous sales had been made. Thus, intermediate buying evidence appeared on May 19, 1944, when the market had risen nearly four points above the previous selling level. The process was repeated with the May purchases being sold at a small four-point profit, but bought back again two points higher in October at about 146.

The same sequence occurred in 1945. First, the October, 1944, purchases were sold on July 26, 1945, at about 163 for a 17-point profit. Just a month later on August 27, buying evidence coming in again indicated that the market should be re-entered at the 170 level — about seven points above the previous selling level. These last purchases of August 27, 1945, were carried up to February 13, 1946, when they were sold around 200 for a 30-point gain, and then repurchased on March 6 at about 190, thus taking advantage of the February, 1946, reaction to an extent which was all that could be reasonably expected. The March purchases were sold on July 16 again at the 200 level, as in February.

The 1946 Top

The period of January to July, 1946 — which represented the "distribution period" of the 1942-1946 bull market — is shown in Figure 3. It will be noticed that prior to the February "Sell", the "Buying Power" line was far above that for "Selling Pressure". For two weeks before the actual signal, it had been stated that if "Buying Power" broke below 181 — where it had held twice before — with Selling Pressure also increasing, it would constitute intermediate trend selling evidence in accordance with the Lowry rules under such circumstances. Also, it was pointed out that the overall picture in both Indexes suggested that "considerable distribution of stocks has been taking place under cover of recent market enthusiasm". When "Buying Power", therefore, did break the 181 level, sales should have been made on the following day.

The "Buy" shortly thereafter on March 6 was typical of what is called an "oversold" position. In fact, it was the same as that which occurred in May, 1942, although it cannot, of course, be inferred that all advances arising from such a condition will be of equal extent and duration. The Short-Term Measurement of Buying Power had dropped below 60 and then turned upward for more than six points, while at the same time, "Buying Power" and "Selling Pressure" suggested that their previous bearish trends were in the process of reversing. It may be noted here, however, that if "Selling Pressure" had increased above the high at 161 *after* the March 6 purchases had been made, these purchases would have been abandoned — at a loss, if need be — in accordance with the rules governing "safety controls".

The "Sell" on July 16 was of a different type than that occurring in February. It had been stated several times since May that if "Buying Power" declined below 160 and Selling Pressure increased above 161, it would call for selling. Such a crossing of the two Indexes as occurred in July (see Figure 3) is also a selling signal, and both developments occurred almost simultaneously.

An Illustrative Example

Although the following observation is outside of the actual Lowry rules, the period shown in Figure 3 is an interesting one, and affords an idea of the general function of the "Buying Power" and "Selling Pressure" indexes. Looking at the picture as a whole, it will be seen that the tendency of stock prices is upward, but that the trend of "Buying Power" (for the seven-month period) is generally down, while "Selling Pressure" inclines somewhat less markedly to the upside. This is just the opposite of what would normally be expected in a rising market if the latter were healthy. It suggested, therefore, that the market as a whole was less strong than the Industrial Average looked, and that most issues — the calculations being based on all round-lot transactions in common stocks — were finding the going rather heavy. More literally, the sluggish action of "Buying Power" — lower in May when the Average reached a new high than it had been in January and February — showed that even a heavy volume of trading was not able to move prices up very much. In other words, the market was meeting a ready supply of stock for sale. Thus, regardless of the rules for the specific timing of action, there did exist a background which could only be regarded with considerable suspicion.

Up to September, 1946, all long transactions since 1942 had resulted in a profit, and — as pointed out earlier — the investor had fared exceptionally well, despite the minor contretemps of 1944 and 1945. Now, however, the bull market was over, and prices were shortly to embark upon a sharp decline and then a period of highly irregular fluctuations. It is evident that no method of the Lowry type will fare as well under such erratic conditions as it does when there is a background of consistent trends.

Uncertainty of 1946-1947

What actually happened, therefore, was this. On August 1, 1946, purchases were signaled at 202 — two points higher than sales had been effected a couple of weeks before. These purchases had to be abandoned at a 14-point loss on September 3 at around 188, but were bought back at a 16-point advantage around 172 on September 12. What turned out to be poorly-timed selling evidence resulted in a second loss of nearly nine points being taken on October 30 at about the 163 level. Immediately afterward, on November 2, another whipsaw occurred, with purchases being indicated almost nine points higher at the 172 level. The subsequent erratic and narrow-range market of 1947 afforded just about the sort of irregular results which would be expected under such circumstances, buying and selling indications occurring at nearly the same price level, with small losses being taken on several occasions.

Full Record Since 1942

The intermediate signals of the 1946-47 period are included in the recapitulation below to June, 1948. In the "Gain or Loss" column, a plus or minus figure is shown for each change in position, thus indicating total results if short sales are assumed on sell signals, and otherwise showing the advantage or disadvantage at which a long position would have been reassumed. The Average price level shown is the opening on the day following the indicated signal.

Date	Dow-Jones Industrial Average	Signal	Gain or Loss
	1942		
May 2	96.25	Buy	
	1943		
June 22	138.52	Sell	+42.27
Nov. 30	129.62	Buy	+ 8.90
	1944		
April 19	135.64	Sell	+ 6.02
May 19	139.38	Buy	— 3.74
Sept. 11	143.77	Sell	+ 4.39
Oct. 27	145.81	Buy	— 2.04
	1945		
July 26	162.50	Sell	+16.69
Aug. 27	170.42	Buy	— 7.92
	1946		
Feb. 13	200.37	Sell	+29.95
Mar. 6	190.12	Buy	+10.25
July 16	200.24	Sell	+10.12
Aug. 1	202.18	Buy	— 1.94
Sept. 3	188.04	Sell	—14.14
Sept. 12	172.22	Buy	+15.82
Oct. 30	163.47	Sell	— 8.75
Nov. 2	171.99	Buy	— 8.52
	1947		
April 14	170.23	Sell	— 1.76
April 21	171.04	Buy	— 0.81
May 17	164.44	Sell	— 6.60
May 29	168.36	Buy	— 3.92
	1948		
Jan. 23	172.46	Sell	+ 4.10
Mar. 17	165.30	Buy	+ 7.16

Summary of Lowry Record

Obviously, nothing was gained from the end of the bull market in May, 1946, to early 1948. However, neither the "errors" of 1944 and 1945, nor the lack of progress from 1946 to 1948 detract from the basic merits of the Lowry approach. Both 1944-45 and 1946-48 were periods of confusion. In the first, it applied to the action of stocks as a whole, since at that time the market was highly selective. The impact of war on various companies had been uneven, while it was also clear that peace would not bear on all alike. Consequently, some stocks declined while others rose, but not for reasons ordinarily indicative of a broad area of distribution or accumulation. In 1947, the whole market was confused as evidenced by the several swings back and forth within almost exactly the same price range. In both cases, the Lowry analysis reflected the condition of confusion — which, indeed, must be the case by its very nature if it is to present clear evidence for the decisive trends when the latter do exist.

The record as given is based upon the Lowry organization's own interpretations as stated in their reports and other specific advices. There has often been other general comment on which an investor might have acted had he seen fit, as to shorter-term fluctuations, partial positions, etc. The record as given, however, refers only to the junctures when definite intermediate and/or basic buying and selling evidence appeared according to the specific rules set up in the Lowry "Manual".

MILLS' BUYING AND SELLING

The Mansfield Mills Co. uses a procedure similar to that of the Lowry organization. The most important difference, however, is that the two major indexes representing Buying and Selling are derived from the dollar values involved in price changes rather than the price changes themselves.

Thus, the total of dollar-value gains is computed for a given day by adding the points gained in each individual stock that advanced, multiplied by its volume of trading. (The gain for a stock advancing two points on 5000 shares is $10,000.) By the same procedure, the total of dollar-value losses is calculated, and then each is divided by the total volume of trading for the day, which gives the "gain-ratio" and the "loss-ratio" for that particular date.

These are placed on a moving-average basis for the final indexes of Buying and Selling. It is evident that such indexes will not be far away from the Lowry indexes of "Buying Power" and "Selling Pressure". Naturally, minor variations occur, as in the exact dates that the lines may cross or reverse direction, but the broad trends are necessarily the same.

The Mansfield Mills Co. method also uses a shorter-term moving average, but based on the loss-ratios and referred to as Short-term Selling Intensity. This is employed in much the same way as the Lowry Short-Term Measurement of Buying Power, but of course, works in reverse. That is, an "oversold" condition in the market after a sharp decline is likely to be registered when "Selling Intensity" rises above 100, whereas the Lowry Short-Term Measurement of Buying Power usually drops below 60 under similar conditions.

Method of Interpretation

In fact, the same general principles of interpretation hold for both approaches — as, indeed, it is only logical that they should. All the general remarks made earlier in the discussion of the Lowry Indexes may be taken to apply with equal force to those used by the Mansfield Mills Co. Both are sound and logical approaches. Occasional whipsaws and losses will inevitably occur, but by nature, they can never be seriously wrong on important trends.

The 1942-1948 Record

The Mansfield Mills Co.'s record of intermediate trend indications is given below on the same basis as that of Lowry's Investment Reports. Since the published interpretations did not begin until May, 1946, the previous "signals" indicated are those which it is assumed would have been used in accordance with the organization's stated policies. Although these policies are reasonably specific, there is still a slight element of interpretation which may be involved under certain circumstances. Hence, it cannot be said with absolute certainty that the buying and selling prior to June 24, 1946, would have been advised on the exact dates given, or that these represent all the points of action which might have been called. This hypothetical part of the record, however, may be regarded as substantially correct.

Date	Dow-Jones Industrial Average	Signal	Gain or Loss
	1942		
*May 2	96.25	Buy	
	1943		
*June 19	139.42	Sell	+43.17
*Dec. 11	135.06	Buy	+ 4.36
	1945		
*July 23	162.57	Sell	+27.51
*Aug. 6	163.09	Buy	— 0.42

1946

*Feb. 16	204.39	Sell	+41.30
*Mar. 9	193.96	Buy	+10.43
June 24	203.90	Sell	+ 9.94
Aug. 5	202.57	Buy	+ 1.33
Aug. 19	200.35	Sell	— 2.22
Sept. 16	174.33	Buy	+26.02

1947

Mar. 14	173.99	Sell	— 0.45
June 13	173.63	Buy	+ 0.25
Oct. 29	183.93	Sell	+10.30

1948

Jan. 23	172.46	Buy	+11.47
Feb. 13	165.96	Sell	— 6.50
Mar. 13	167.15	Buy	— 1.19

* Hypothetical record. Remainder given on the dates specified subsequent to the inauguration of published reports.

Natural Coincidences

As would be expected, a good many of these indications coincide approximately with those of Lowry. It will be noticed, however, that they are somewhat fewer, and the discrepancies thus lie primarily in action on the part of one approach against no action on the part of the other. Not many of the occasional conflicts which do occur are of great significance. The Mills record shows slightly fewer signals, largely because of the presumed inactivity during 1944. In 1946 and 1947, the Lowry selling signals tended to be later than those of the Mills method. The most notable difference during this period occurred in late October, 1946, when Lowry sold on an increase in "Selling Pressure" that did not show up in the Mills Index.

The loss whipsaw recorded there, however, was offset later by another one the other way around. On January 23, 1948, the Mills Indexes indicated buying, while those of Lowry suggested just the opposite. The Lowry signal was derived from the line of "Selling Pressure" crossing that of "Buying Power", whereas the corresponding action had occurred about a month earlier in the Mills Indexes. It was an apparent *reversal* in Index trends that caused the opposite Mills signal. Such conflicts are likely to occur only on rare occasions, however, and it will be noticed that both approaches were shortly thereafter "in gear". Both bought correctly during the early part of March, 1948 — just before the sharp market advance that was to follow.

SUPPLY AND DEMAND MEASURES
(LAMOTTE AND WHITMAN)

The Lamotte and Whitman "Cumulative Measures of Supply and Demand" are in the same general class as the Lowry and the Mansfield Mills indexes. They are, however, based on the price changes and trading volume of the stocks used in the Dow-Jones Averages only, rather than all round lot trading. Secondly, instead of showing one Index for the buying and another for the selling, results are combined into one measure for each of the Dow-Jones groups. Hence, there is one "Measure" for the Industrials, another for the Rails, a third for the Utilities, and still a fourth for the Dow-Jones 65-Stock Average, which is a combination of the three.

Method Used

The first step in computing a Measure is to segregate the gains and losses for the day in a given Average. As in the Mills' calculations, multiplication by the volume involved on each side gives the total dollar-value gain and total dollar-value loss. The difference between these is then taken, so that the final figure is either a net loss or a net gain for the day in the Average in question. This is then combined with the closing price level for a final figure, but the exact process is held as a "trade secret" by the Lamotte and Whitman organization. The "Measures" themselves appear as cumulative totals of these final figures.

Principles of Interpretation

Broadly speaking, the Measures move with the Average trends, although, as the construction implies, their movement is always gradual and never so erratic as the price and volume fluctuations themselves may be on occasion. In fact, interpretation of the Measures is little different from that of any reasonably intelligent interpretation of the movements of the Averages themselves. Being a more refined picture of what is actually going on, however, areas of supply and areas of demand are likely to stand out with far greater clarity, and there have been occasions when the action of a Measure has differed materially from that of its Average, thus indicating that the surface appearance of the Average was deceptive. This was true during the last half of 1943, for example, when stock prices were tending mildly down, but the 65-stock Measure remained in a persistent upward trend.

The reverse of this was largely true in the middle of 1946, and resulted in the first selling indications since a long position was signaled under this approach in July of 1942. Interpretations of the Measures were not published until March of 1945, although they are understood to have been in private use since 1939. Unquestionably, the principle employed is logical and sound, and affords one means of visualizing the forces of supply and demand in the market. Like other comparable approaches, however, it is naturally not perfect.

The 1942-1948 Record

The record of recent years is as follows, the published recommendations dating from March of 1945, when, of course, a Buy or Hold position was in effect. These prices again are the opening levels of the day following the signal.

Date	Dow-Jones Industrial Average	Signal	Gain or Loss
	1942		
*July 6	105.28	Buy	
	1946		
June 24	203.90	Sell	+98.62
Dec. 9	174.54	Buy	+29.36
	1947		
May 17	164.44	Sell	—10.10
Oct. 3	178.58	Buy	—14.14
	1948		
Jan. 22	172.65	Sell	— 5.93
Mar. 20	170.96	Buy	+ 1.69

* Not published.

MOVING VOLUME CURVE (QUINN)

Edwin S. Quinn (Investographs of Rochester, New York) is currently using two indexes which fall within the "character-of-the-market" classification. Both are based on trading volume, price entering in only to the extent that the implications of the volume analysis are considered in relation to the price trend.

The more important of the two is called the Moving Volume Curve, and is a six-weeks' moving average of the weekly volume of trading. This period of time is used in order to eliminate minor fluctuations and reveal the underlying trend of volume. (See Figure 4.) The action of the Moving Volume Curve is compared with that of the average price movement in accordance with the following "Principles and Interpretations" as evolved by Quinn.

GENERAL

Volume is the measure of demand in advance.

Volume is the measure of supply in a decline.

In a healthy market, volume will increase in intermediate advances and decrease in declines.

Such a market will continue to rise while volume and price are thus in gear.

In an unhealthy market, volume will increase in intermediate declines and decrease in rallies.

Such a market will continue to decline while volume and price are in opposing trends.

SELLING SIGNALS

In a major (bull market) advance, volume should increase continuously, more or less in proportion to price. The underlying condition is sound and justifies new investments as long as these two curves are thus in gear.

The moving volume curve will reach its peak some time ahead of the stock market, usually when about 75% of the major advance has been completed. But, because a long bull trend is in the nature of a moving force, its own momentum will carry it to its ultimate top despite inadequate volume support. For this reason, general sales should not be ordered on the first "weakness" formation, although new investment, thereafter, would entail considerable risk.

This first weakness formation has always taken the same form during all the major advances of the past 29 years. The moving volume curve declines *for four weeks or more*

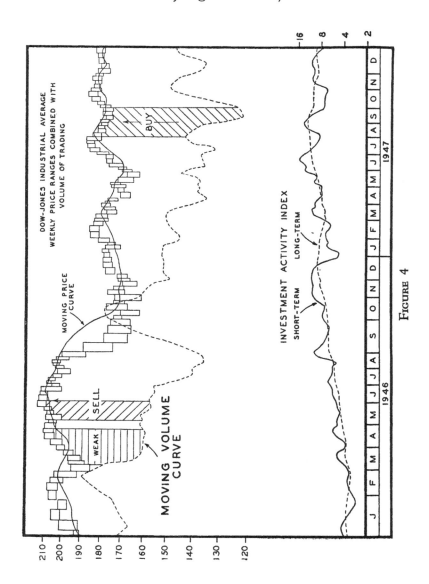

FIGURE 4

as prices advance. But, as explained in the preceding paragraph, no action is taken on this except to observe it as a warning. General selling is timed on the *next* negative pattern, which may take one of three forms and *which must continue for four weeks,* with action taken after the fourth week. These are:

1. The moving volume curve declines while prices advance,
2. The moving volume curve rises during a price decline,
3. After an intermediate reaction, price rises toward a previous high but the volume curve is so low (in terms of preceding price-volume relationships) that there is little prospect of penetration.

First weakness in a bull market is not always followed by a selling formation. When, instead, both volume and price later go into new high ground, first weakness is ignored.

BUYING SIGNALS

In a major (bear market) decline, the volume curve will usually move contrary to price; that is, when one is rising the other will be falling and vice-versa. While this condition prevails, no stocks should be bought.

In a major decline, volume should decline more or less proportionately with price.

When volume and price finally do fall into gear on the way down for not less than four weeks, and when the volume curve drops below a previous price reaction low point, a buying signal is given.

A Recent Illustration

Figure 4 shows the Moving Volume Curve for 1946 and 1947. In this chart, the rectangles represent from top to bottom the weekly high and low of the Dow-Jones Industrial Average. The varying widths are determined by the volume of trading for the week. Thus, price and volume are combined. This is not specifically a part of the method, but makes it easier to visualize the basic implications of changes in the volume of trading.

During the latter part of 1945, and just before the chart in Figure 4 begins, price-volume relationships had remained satisfactory. That is, volume increased continuously in proportion to price, so that no change in an invested position would have been indicated. It may be seen that this same condition prevailed through January and February of 1946, but that signs of trouble appeared immediately thereafter. As prices advanced in March and early April, the Moving Volume Curve dropped lower and lower, instead of climbing with the rising Industrial Average as it had been doing previously. To interpret it further, buyers had stopped bidding up for stocks.

The Curve at the 1946 Top

This fulfilled the requirements of "warning weakness"; i.e. that the Moving Volume Curve must decline for four weeks or more as prices advance. During the final May push to the ultimate 1946 top, the Curve again headed down. Following the first rule for selling after a weakness formation has developed, this indicated a time for selling (after the fourth week of divergence) which coincided very closely with the top in the Industrial Average. Notice that the picture in the first few months of 1946 had revealed the same under-surface deterioration in the market structure which was also apparent in the trends of the Lowry and the Mills indexes, even though the manner of approach is quite different.

At the same time, many Dow Theorists — necessarily basing their conclusions on the surface picture — were hailing the penetration of the January high as an indication of another substantial intermediate advance in a bull market which was actually close to its zenith. To quote one Dow Theory commentator directly on June 3, 1946 (virtually the exact top), "Such action designates the recent trading period as one of stock accumulation, with appreciably higher levels the eventual objective". As other methods showed and events proved, however, it had been a period of *distribution* and not accumulation.

Bull Market Behavior

From the May top on and, indeed, all the way up to late June of the following year (1947), it will be seen that the volume and price curves were just "fighting each other" and, therefore, afforded no new or useful indications. When prices were rising, volume was declining and vice-versa. But, in the final week of the advance to the July, 1947, top, volume meshed with price. Hence, purchases were indicated at the end of August under the last rule for "Buying Signals" given on page 79. As may also be seen in Figure 4, the Moving Volume Curve and the price trend remained in gear for the remainder of 1947, indicating that the market was to be regarded as in a long-term buying area.

This was statistical evidence of a fact noted at the time by many close observers of market behavior — that, although still in a "bear market" by Dow Theory definition, the character of the volume-action on advances and declines was much more like that of a bull market.

Corroborative Investment Activity Index

The other line at the bottom of Figure 4 is Quinn's "Investment Activity Index". This serves as a general guide in determining whether the character of investment support is clearly confirming the Moving Volume Curve. Although the Investment Activity Index uses volume rather than price, it nevertheless follows the classic procedure of segregating the action of a certain group of stocks, selected on the basis of investment (or speculative) quality, in order to compare it with some different group. (See the "Index of Confidence", for example.)

Quinn's actual procedure in computing the Investment Activity Index is to take a ratio of the volume of transactions in a group of investment stocks to total trading on the New York Stock Exchange. Thus, the ratio represents the percentage of investment transactions to total turnover. When high, the interest indicated in investment stocks is regarded as a factor of market strength. Conversely, if the ratio drops — suggesting that activity in speculative stocks is increasing — it is an element of weakness. The ratios are placed on moving average bases (one longer than the other), represented by the long-term and short-term curves at the bottom of Figure 4.

It will be noticed that when the Moving Volume Curve indicated buying in August, 1947, for example, the long-term Investment Activity Index had risen to a relatively high level, thus confirming the implications in the more important Index. On the basis of the record, it is apparently more valuable in the case of bottom turning points than top formations.

Characteristic Signs

Although the short-term Investment Activity Index is not used except as confirmation of the Moving Volume Curve, it will be noticed that sudden changes in its direction — which carry it abruptly and importantly above or below the long-term trend — usually bring about intermediate reversals in stock prices. For example, there was a bulge in the short-term curve above the long-term curve at the bottom in October, 1946. Conversely, it dropped sharply below at the approach to the February top in 1947, rose above it at the May low, and declined below again at the July and October tops.

Apparent Record of Moving Volume Curve

Since this particular research was not completed until 1947, there is no actual long-term record which can be adduced. However, by applying the rules quoted earlier to the past, a hypothetical record can be set up which shows excellent results. Since some interpretation is involved, it is impossible to be sure that the indications are exactly those which would have been given on a current basis. Nevertheless, the rules are reasonably definite, and hence the "record" should be at least substantially correct.

As the record since 1942 was given earlier in this Section for two other methods, it is interesting to compare Quinn's hypothetical record with them for the same period. This is as follows:

Date	Dow-Jones Industrial Average*	Signal	Gain or Loss
	1942		
May 2	96.44	Buy	
	1943		
Sept. 25	140.18	Sell	+73.74
	1944		
Apr. 29	136.23	Buy	+ 3.95
	1946		
June 7	212.28	Sell	+76.05
	1947		
Aug. 28	177.70	Buy	+34.58

* Closing prices.

Quinn has reconstructed the Moving Volume Curve for the whole period since 1919, and also the Investment Activity Index since 1935. The hypothetical record appears excellent throughout the whole 29 years, with two exceptions. One is a premature "Sell" in mid-1925, not followed by a countermanding "Buy" formation until a year later at about the same price level. The other is a purchase indicated in August, 1931, which would presumably have resulted in a loss being taken later in the same year on a resumption of bear market action. As the transactions for the 1942-1947 period suggest, the method is not one resulting in much activity — a fact which has little appeal to some investors, but a great deal to many others. There are only 25 signals in the 29-year period, and on more than one occasion the same position is maintained for two years or even longer.

Significance of Volume

Taken as a whole, the 1929-1932 bear market picture is a good illustration of the fundamental importance of trading volume. It is a market axiom that weakness is present when volume increases during an intermediate decline as an expression of "fear" liquidation, and similarly, when it (volume) contracts in a rise, as potential buyers thus express a preference for their cash as opposed to stocks at the prices which prevail.

The great bear market of 1929-32 thus progressed in a series of seven downward steps, the first six of which were marked by the characteristic of weakness in trading volume just cited. It was not until the seventh and final downward step in 1932 that volume dried up on a decline into new low ground, thus indicating a refusal on the part of stockholders to sell under such conditions. From the nature of the Moving Volume Curve, therefore, it can readily be visualized how it could not permanently get into gear with price until this stage was reached. The false signal mentioned above (August, 1931) occurred on a minor decline which held temporarily above the previous low, and was countermanded shortly thereafter by the increase of volume which accompanied a penetration into new low ground.

HOOD'S GROUP ACTION

The basic idea of determining market strength or weakness through analysis of its component sections has been carried out from a still different point of view by Oakman Hood. He uses his own price indexes of thirty-eight stock groups, such as steels, oils, rubbers, etc. Although primarily designed to show which groups are the best buys or sales at any given time, further refinements of group action have been employed in order to gain some indications of probable market action as a whole.

Comparisons with Average

Hood compares his groups with the Dow-Jones Industrial Average; that is, whether they are exceeding, or failing to keep up with, the pace of the latter. Since some groups, like the steels, habitually move more than the Average and others, such as the tobaccos, move less, the price change of each group is first adjusted for its normal volatility. Stated briefly, the theory is that if fewer and fewer of the groups on an adjusted basis are failing to keep pace with the Average, i.e., rising less or declining more, it is a sign of market weakness. Conversely, of course, underlying strength is indicated as a progressively larger number of groups perform better than the Average. The reason is that the Dow-

Jones Industrial Average is not a picture of the whole market, but represents the behaviour of thirty well-known investment and speculative favorites.

The logic of Hood's assumption will be immediately apparent to anyone familiar with market characteristics. It has been recognized, for example, that the very last stage of bull market is marked by rather spectacular strength in a few groups and individual stocks, under cover of which the majority of issues are sold or "distributed". The group analysis is really just another way of getting at the sub-surface conditions.

A Record and a Change

At the time the first edition of this book was published in 1941, Hood was using a particular formula for relative group strength or weakness. When this was plus or minus for four consecutive weeks, it was regarded as a definite intermediate Buy or Sell signal. As the original book pointed out, these intermediate signals had been remarkably accurate for the 1936-41 period — not only in the 1937 drop, but throughout the difficult time of 1938-1939, and also in calling almost to a hair, the top and bottom of the collapse when France fell in 1940. No "hindsight" was involved, the signals having been given at the times they occurred. Hence, the remark was made in the 1941 edition that they had been *"uncannily accurate — so much so, in fact, that it may be wondered whether the same degree of accuracy can be maintained in the future"*.

Perhaps, therefore, these particular indications are a good illustration of another remark that *"It almost seems to be a law in these matters that the better something has been in the immediate past, the worse it is likely to be in the near future"*. In any event, what happened was that an intermediate Sell signal occurred early in the 1942-46 bull market at about 137 in October, 1943, but the position was never reversed by a Buy signal until long after the 1946 top had come and gone — specifically, December, 1946. It may be that this particular usage will "click" again in the future as it did in 1936-1941, but with the intervening blot on the record, it would be impossible to feel at all sure that such will be the case.

Present Usage

In an attempt to correct the evident weakness in the former application, Hood has since attacked the problem from a slightly different angle. Recognizing that volatility characteristics of groups and/or individual stocks are subject to change, the volatilities of the basic 38 groups are analyzed each month for that particular period. Thus, the 19 most volatile and the 19 least volatile are determined. The relative actions of these two group classifications are compared not only with the Dow-Jones Industrial Average, but also with each other, the results being combined by a mathematical formula into a new Group Action Index. Figured back, the hypothetical record appears as follows:

Date	Dow-Jones Industrial Average	Signal	Gain or Loss
	1939		
May 3	129.76	Buy	—
Sept. 6	149.30	Sell	+19.54
	1940		
July 3	120.80	Buy	+18.50
	1941		
Mar. 19	123.99	Sell	+ 3.19

	1942		
Aug. 12	105.24	Buy	+18.75

	1946		
June 26	201.76	Sell	+96.55

	1947		
*May 21	163.88	Buy	+37.91

* Not hypothetical. Given on date specified.

Underlying Value of Group Action

Whether or not group action is thus reduced to a specific formula giving definite signals, the analysis of group action is an important and helpful indication of market "health". A good illustration was the "line formation" from mid-February to mid-March of 1948 which followed a sharp decline to around the old lows of 1946 and 1947, but was itself followed by an even sharper advance. While the line was forming, there were no indications on the surface of the direction in which it would be broken, although general majority opinion leaned heavily to the downside in reflection of the pessimistic sentiment then prevailing. There is a more detailed discussion of this particular juncture on pages 185 and 186.

Hood's analysis of group action, however, showed that strength was building up internally. For example, in the week ending March 3, 1948, 13 out of the 19 investment (or "least volatile") groups gained on the market, which was the strongest action in this respect seen for more than six months. The next week showed exactly the same performance. It was possible, therefore, to point out on March 17 — just prior to the sharp upmove which followed — that "the group action of the past three weeks indicates that the 164 support level will not be penetrated in the immediate future, with the probability of a considerable rally ahead".

Although this is just one form of approach, it is nevertheless an excellent illustration of what analysis of the internal character of the market can mean, as opposed to reliance upon surface indications of strength or weakness.

USE OF MARKET-BREADTH DATA

Certain summaries of the daily trading on the New York Stock Exchange which are published in the *Wall Street Journal* and other newspapers are often of great value in determining the character of the market. These are as follows:

1. Number of issues traded
2. Number of issues showing advances
3. Number of issues showing declines
4. Number of new highs for the year
5. Number of new lows for the year

New Highs and New Lows

By customary practice, the new highs and new lows are tabulated up to about the first of March in the second year before making a new start. Thus, these recordings on February 28 will cover the 14-month period since January 1 of the preceding year. The figures tabulated for March 1, however, would be for the two-month period since the beginning of that particular year.

As a marked illustration of the value of these data, Figure 5 shows an index of the new highs and new lows compared with the market in 1946, beginning in March when the price ranges for that year first came into use, and carrying up through August. The indexes are seven-day moving averages of the daily ratios of the number of new highs and lows to the number of issues traded that day. It will be

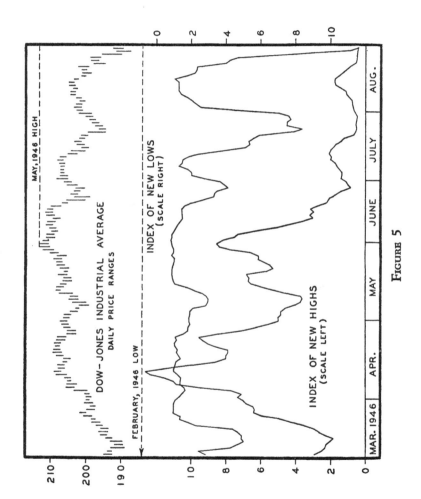

FIGURE 5

noticed that the index of new lows is shown on an inverted scale, and hence should characteristically move in the same direction as the index of new highs.

A Marked Warning

In general, the picture illustrates in still another way the progressive deterioration in the market price structure during the period covered. It has already been shown earlier in the Section how this was likewise apparent in some other methods of analysis. First, notice the Index of new highs at the end of May when the Industrial Average reached its peak. The Index is nowhere near as high· as it had been on the market advance culminating at a lower level in April. Hence, the apparent strength in the Average going into new high ground was deceptive. If the advance had been a healthy one with the great majority of issues participating, there should have been about as great a proportion of new highs in May as in April.

Then, during the next two months, it will be seen that new highs dropped off to almost nothing, despite the fact that the Average price level was closer to its high for 1946 than to the low which had been registered in February. Again, a healthy market in such a relative price position would have a good many outriders making new highs. Instead, just the opposite condition was apparent. The "outriders" were preponderantly on the downside, and it will be seen that on the July reaction, the Index of new lows dropped not only sharply, but also far below its previous bottom in March, even though the Average price level remained higher.

Surface Evidence Sufficient

Actually, it did not need a refined index to see this particular situation at all. The actual numbers of new highs and lows were as follows for three successive trading days in July while the Average price level was still over 200.

	New Highs	New Lows
July 12	9	61
July 15	8	111
July 16	5	97

At that time, the extreme range of the Industrial Average for the year was 213.36 to 184.05. On the three days cited above, it was 205.49 to 199.48. Obviously, a market which was thus considerably closer to its high than to its low in terms of that Average, could hardly be as strong as the latter looked when individual new lows were outnumbering new highs by nearly 16 to 1.

Qualifying Influences

These Indexes are not always going to show a "picture" week in and week out. Indeed, much of the time, they will simply be inconclusive. Nevertheless, they are particularly valuable in the broad areas when the major trend is about to change, because they then reveal the degree of underlying strength or weakness. For instance, just the opposite picture of that in Figure 5 appeared in the early part of 1942 when the trend was about to change from down to up. The Industrial Average dropped in April to 92.92, or about six points below its previous bottom in March, but the Index of new lows held higher at the same time, indicating that a majority of stocks were meeting support at a level above their earlier lows.

Another word of caution is necessary in connection with the use of these data. The tabulations include preferred as well as common stocks. (Preferred stocks represent about 30% of the issues listed on the New York Stock Exchange.)

Ordinarily, this is something that cancels out on both sides, but on comparatively rare occasions, a change in money rates may influence high-grade preferred stocks in one direction or another, and hence distort the new high and new low figures. This was very apparent in the fall of 1947, for example. A great many new lows were being registered, but examination of the detailed tables (given daily in the *Wall Street Journal*) showed that almost all of them were preferred stocks. The decline in this group had nothing to do with any investor qualms as to safety of dividends, but resulted purely from the slight stiffening of money rates which naturally meant that such issues should sell on a higher yield basis.

Advance and Decline Ratios

Similar indexes may be constructed by using the ratios of the number of advances and declines to the total issues traded for each day. It will be evident that these may also show underlying deterioration or improvement through their action in relation to that of the market. If, for example, the index of declines is increasing and that of advances is falling off while the Industrial Average is rising, the market as a whole is likely to be developing a sub-surface weakness which will later become general.

When these advance and decline ratios are placed on a seven-day moving average, they will be found to fluctuate around a center line of about 40 with extreme limits at approximately 20 and 60. Reaching such extremes is often an indication of an intermediate top or bottom, and sometimes the attempt is made to reduce such indexes to a rigid "system" with signals assumed to be given when the extremes are reached. That is a dangerous procedure, however, because there will almost inevitably be premature signals early in any really dynamic move. As in the case of the new highs and new lows, the advance and decline ratios should be used on an interpretative basis and regarded simply as one of the several approaches which are helpful in determining the character of the market.

CONCLUSION

It will have been observed that many of the techniques discussed in this Section depend upon a comparison of market action as a whole, and as analyzed by different methods, with the action of the Dow-Jones Industrial Average. Thus, the latter may look strong, but the analysis will show that the whole price structure is actually weak beneath the surface.

Use of Dow-Jones Industrial Average

The Industrial Average is valuable less as a picture of the whole market than as a picture of what people think the market is, since it is the oldest, the best-known, and the most widely disseminated. It is not, however, anywhere near as representative of the market as a whole as are some broader and perhaps more scientifically constructed indexes, such as Standard & Poor's daily Index of 90 stocks, or the same organization's even broader weekly tabulation of 402 issues. The Dow-Jones Industrial Average uses only 30 stocks, most of which are of the "blue-chip" variety. Hence, it is representative of such a group, but that is all. It is correct on the general trend, although sometimes accentuating such a trend — particularly around major turning points — in a rather deceptive manner as far as the great majority of stocks are concerned.

Relative price levels, however, may be highly deceptive. Anyone following stock prices closely realized, for example, that the majority of listed issues were lower in May, 1947, than they had been in the fall of 1946 (see Figure 6), but the Industrial Average managed to stay above that point, thanks to unusual resistance on the part of about half of its component stocks, particularly International Harvester, Chrysler, General Motors, and duPont.

It will be noticed from Figure 6 that the picture of the Standard & Poor's 402 Stock Index from the high of May, 1946, to the low of February, 1948, is quite different from that of the Dow-Jones Industrials. Not only did the broader Index more accurately show a new low level in May, 1947, but it also failed to make a new high for the year in July as did the Industrial Average. Again, it reached a final even lower bottom in February, 1948.

Thus, the whole period shown in Figure 6 is a typical picture of a bear market lasting for 21 months in the truly representative Index of 402 Stocks. According to the Dow Theory, on the other hand, the "bear market" was subsequently proved to have ended in May, 1947 — a technically correct assumption, perhaps, on the basis of the Dow-Jones Averages, but not on the basis of common sense in view of the more inclusive picture.

Sequence of Character-Group Movements

Nevertheless, another reason that comparisons of various broad analyses with the "blue-chip" stock Average are valuable lies in the usual sequences of character-group movements during the course of given market trends. There is a popular — but erroneous — notion, for example, that when "cats and dogs" (Wall Street's term for low-priced speculative issues) are occupying the center of the stage, it is a sign that an upward move is at an end. Actually, it is just the opposite. Whether a major or intermediate upswing,

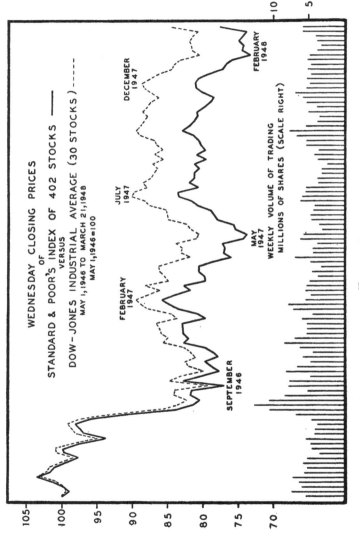

FIGURE 6

the sequence is usually initial interest and activity in the investment-grade issues, following which the "cats and dogs" have their day. But once again, in the final stage when the ultimate top is reached, the investment stocks come in, while the formerly active speculative issues do little. This is when the market looks stronger than it actually is, and investors — reassured by the "good investment buying" in the blue-chips making up the Industrial Average — mistakenly purchase the speculative stocks which are assumed to be "behind the market".

Hence, the Dow-Jones Industrial Average is a better comparison to use in connection with character-of-the-market methods than a broader and truer index, although the latter has more value for other purposes. The aim of such methods is to probe beneath the surface appearance, and the surface appearance is what the Dow-Jones Industrial Average depicts. Moreover, it is the medium in which most investors think of the market as being weak or strong.

FORMULA PLANS

It should be understood at the outset that formula plans are not potentially productive of as large profits as are the methods discussed up to this point. Reasonably accurate "forecasting" will give much better results, but the proponents of formula plans are convinced — or assume — that such forecasting is impossible. They feel that there is a certain analogy with Aesop's fable of the race between the tortoise and the hare. The hare could have won easily, but his unreliability caused him to lose. On the other hand, a good formula plan — like the tortoise — is slow and plodding, but sure.

There is a story — perhaps apocryphal — that when the elder J. P. Morgan was asked what he thought the stock market would do, he replied that he believed it would continue to fluctuate. That is exactly the frame of mind in which the user of a formula plan approaches the investment problem. His purpose is to take advantage of the fact that stock prices do fluctuate without ever attempting to forecast the direction of the trends.

Profit Assured in any Cycle

The profits under a formula plan may not be spectacular, but there always will be a profit when the price travels through any cycle and hence comes back to the same level from which it originally started. Granted, then, that the market does not cease to fluctuate or that stocks do not become permanently worthless, a logically constructed formula plan guarantees that there will be no loss and moderate profits over a sufficient period of time. The criticism has been made that in a "permanent new era" of prices, formula plans would keep the investor out of the market. Although this is true of many such plans, it will be seen that it is not true of all.

At the time the first edition of this book was published in 1941, the term "formula plan" was relatively unfamiliar. In fact, the one method in this category (Burlingame Plan) originally discussed, was not designated as such, and appeared under the "Miscellaneous" heading. During the past few years, however, formula plans have received considerable publicity, while new material and later records available call for a more extensive treatment.

The most basic and exhaustive research on this whole subject appears in the 1947 book "Successful Investing Formulas" (Barron's) by Lucile Tomlinson. Readers who wish to pursue the subject further will find her performance tables for different well-known plans and the whole book of considerable interest. This Section also includes some special adaptations of formula principles which do not appear in "Successful Investing Formulas", and are designed more for the individual than the institution.

Automatic Functioning

Employment of a formula plan assumes that forecasting — with worth-while accuracy, at least — is impossible. In essence, it aims merely to take advantage of the fact that stock prices fluctuate, by selling (on a scale up) in "high" areas and buying (on a scale down) in "low" areas. It differs, therefore, from a trend method in that, at times, it will be bucking an apparently established trend. Neither, of course, does it attempt to pick points of reversal by analyzing the character of the market, although conceivably, selling points could coincide with trend reversals.

In explaining the adoption of a formula plan for a large college endowment fund, the treasurer said that the main object was "to set up some plan which works automatically and is not dependent upon the judgment of one individual or group of individuals." The implication seemed to be that this requirement was satisfied only by a formula plan. This is not necessarily true, since most trend methods are likewise automatic and do not involve any judgment. Refer to the "Ten Percent Rule", for example, (Page 31), and also the Dow Theory if the latter is used on the basis of Moment's rules and not on the more common interpretive basis. Even some of the character-of-the-market methods come close to being completely automatic, or could be so made if desired.

A Predetermined Basis

The chief difference in manner of operation between such methods and formula plans is that the former mean going whole-hog, whereas a formula plan proceeds cautiously. If a trend method, for example, indicates that sales should be made, at least all holdings must be sold, and perhaps a short position taken at the option of the individual, in order to adhere to the principle involved. On the other hand, a formula plan operating on predetermined percentages will sell initially only a part of its holdings, then more as a higher level may be reached, and so on.

Obviously, the basis of a formula plan must be some criterion for determining what the initial position shall be and also for calculating ahead of time where scale selling or additional buying will begin. This is where the various types differ.

VASSAR PLAN

A simple illustration of one class is the Vassar Plan, adopted by the college of that name in 1938 for the management of part of its endowment. At that time, it was calculated that the median level of the Dow-Jones Industrial Average was approximately 135 on the basis of its fluctuations during the past few years. At this "normal" level, the fund allocated to operation of the Plan was to be 50% in stocks. As such plans operate in practice, the other 50% is ordinarily allocated to bonds because of the pressure for constant income. The assumption is that the bond section will remain unchanged in value, although in reality, even high-grade bonds are subject to a certain amount of fluctuation which may be advantageous or otherwise, depending on money rate conditions or even the degree of a general deflation. For the purpose of the discussion in this book, the stock position is the only important factor, and whether the remainder of the fund is considered to be in cash or invested in bonds is an irrelevant detail.

Should the price level decline substantially from 135, more stocks in equal percentages were to be bought by the Vassar Plan at 125, 115 and 105. At the 105 level, the fund would be 100% in stocks where it would remain regardless, until the 150 level was reached at some point in the future.

Selling was then to begin, reducing the position to only three-eighths in stocks. Additional and equal percentage selling was also to be carried out successively as the 165, 180 and 195 levels might be reached. At 195, the last remaining stocks would be sold, not to be repurchased until some further decline carried down to 135 — or whatever the median level might then be — when the original 50%

position would again be taken. The median level is determined by a ten-year record of the Dow-Jones Industrial Average, although in practice, the managers of the Vassar Plan have been prepared to modify the figure if their judgment so dictated.

Assumption Works Out in Practice

In any event, the Plan assumed at the time it began that 125-105 was to be regarded as a below-normal area in which stocks were to be bought and 150-195 as an abnormally high one in which they should be sold. These limits, however, represented an arbitrary exercise of judgment, and some other individuals might just as well have set the extremes at 75 and 250. To this extent, the Vassar Plan is not a pure formula plan, because it proceeded originally on an assumption that was essentially a forecast, i.e., that stock prices would continue within the cyclical limits suggested by the fluctuations of the immediately preceding years. Carry such a "forecast" to its logical conclusion, and it would imply that stocks were considered a buy at 105 and a sale at 195. The percentages at levels in between represented, in effect, a hedge against the probable inaccuracy of such a categorical assumption.

As it happened, however, the basis of the Vassar Plan was quite close to the mark for the succeeding eight years, the price range being approximately 93 to 212. Thus, the fund became entirely invested in common stocks shortly before the low in 1942. Similarly, it was entirely out of stocks by the latter part of 1945. At the end of that year, the fund showed a gain of 38.4% versus 44.1% in the Industrial Average (from June 30, 1938), but naturally held on to its advantage in 1946 when the Average dropped to a point only 32.4% ahead of June 30, 1938.

In 1947, the median level (subject to change) was taken as 145 and no stock purchases were to be made until that level was reached, the next buying points being 130, 117 and finally 105, this last as in the original setup. If enabled to make these purchases, sales were scheduled for 160,176 and 194 in equal thirds. Notice that the buying and selling levels are at 10% intervals — a slight change from the original scale. Another change was made in early 1948 as to determination of the median, but since this discussion is intended to be illustrative of the basic principle of formula plans, the details are not important.

YALE PLAN

Instead of setting up a semi-fixed price range for its operations, the other major university whose name is most often associated with formula plans, adopted the second broad class of such methods which use stock percentages as a primary base.

Thus, when Yale began its formula plan in 1939, it was arbitrarily decided that — under the then existing circumstances — a stock position of 30% of the entire investment portfolio was all that satisfied the various requirements of the fund.

The amount in stocks would, however, be increased or decreased according to the following conditions. If stock prices rose to an extent bringing the University's stock-holdings up from 30% to 40% of its total portfolio (actually equivalent to something like a 55% gain in stock prices as a whole) enough would be sold to bring it down to a 35% stock position. The process would be repeated at any time that a further rise brought the remaining stocks up to a point where they again constituted 40% of the whole.

Conversely, if stock prices declined to an extent whereby the original 30% in stocks came to constitute only 15% of the entire fund (representing a drop of nearly 60% in the average price level) enough stocks would be bought to bring the position up to 20%. This process would likewise be repeated on a further sufficient decline. Yale has since raised the original percentages, however, so that whenever stocks drop to 20% of the total, purchases are made in order to raise the figure to 25%.

CONSTANT-RATIO SYSTEM

Constant-ratio (or equalizing) plans are straight formula, pure and simple, the Yale Plan being a slightly more elaborate variation. They may be started at any point without attempting to judge whether the price level is high or low.

The "constant ratio" is often 50-50 which might be taken to imply complete neutrality of judgment; i.e., 50% in stocks and 50% in cash (or bonds if the desirability of interest income is placed ahead of the risk of possibly disadvantageous minor price fluctuations). Having assumed the 50% stock position at the X-level, sales or additional purchases are then made on a predetermined logarithmic scale to bring the fund back to a 50-50 position. However, 40-60 or any other ratio that seemed to fit the particular circumstances could just as well be used.

The scale may be built on different percentages. The smaller the percentages, the greater the activity. It is impossible to say that one percentage will necessarily be better than another, because the results will depend upon the amplitude of the fluctuations encountered. A small percentage will be better for small fluctuations and a larger one for correspondingly larger price movements.

An Arbitrary Illustration

A good average figure for purposes of illustration, however, would be 20%. Starting with a logarithmic table at 40 (lower than the extreme low of the Dow-Jones Industrial Average in 1932) would give the following "action points" in the price range of more recent years. Notice that each figure is 20% above the preceding one.

82.9
99.5
119.4
143.3
172.0
206.4
247.7

Beginning at any point on this scale, which can, of course, be extended in either direction, the fund is readjusted to a 50-50 position (or whatever ratio may have been elected) by sales or additional purchases as the higher or lower points may be reached.

Suppose a start is made at 143.3 by allocating $10,000 to the plan. This results in the following position.

Stocks Bought	*Cash (or Bonds)*
$5,000	$5,000

The price level advances to 172 or 20%, so that the position is as follows:

Stocks	*Cash (or Bonds)*
$6,000	$5,000

Total Fund — $11,000

Stocks must, therefore, be reduced to $5,500 (50% of

$11,000) by the sale of enough shares to raise $500 ($6,000 minus $5,500).

More sales would similarly be made if prices advanced further to 206.4, or there would be repurchases if stocks came back to 143.3 and still more if the decline continued to 119.4. Thus, the fund is *always* approximately 50% in stocks, regardless of the extent to which prices may move in a given direction.

CONSTANT-DOLLAR METHOD

This is very simple and very similar, the idea being always to keep the same dollar amount in stocks rather than a given percentage. Suppose operations are to be confined to one stock, beginning with 100 shares at a price of 50, or an investment of $5,000. If the price rose to 60, making the value $6,000, ten shares would be sold, bringing the dollar value in stock back approximately to $5,000. This assumes that it has been decided to act on 20% price changes. More would be sold on a further 20% advance to bring the fund back again to the predetermined level.

Conversely, on a decline, additional purchases would be needed as, for instance, 25 more shares on a 20% drop to 40. In actual practice, such rebalancing would best be carried out at fixed time intervals—perhaps every six months or every year, but only if the required degree of price change had likewise occurred.

It will be noticed, too, that enough cash would necessarily have to be held out at the start to assure being able to make the required purchases in the event of the most serious decline believed possible. The complete simplicity of this plan, however, commends itself to some investors. Long-term tables of results may be found in the book mentioned earlier in this Section (Successful Investing Formulas).

KEYSTONE SEVEN-STEP PLAN

This plan was worked out by the Keystone Company of Boston, distributors of the Keystone Custodian Funds. The latter are open-end investment funds always fully invested in particular classes of securities ranging from high-grade bonds to speculative stocks, and which can be logically employed as mediums in the operation of a formula plan.

The Seven-Step Plan belongs to the same family as the Vassar Plan, since it assumes a "normal" or median level for stock prices, above which scale selling is done, and below which scale buying is in order. This normal level is determined by the pattern on a logarithmic scale of the Dow-Jones Industrial Average for the past fifty years (since 1897). If the extreme high of 1929 and the extreme low of 1932 are excluded, prices have fluctuated for this fifty-year period within a gradually ascending channel, the top and bottom lines of which are parallel.

Operational Zones

This channel is arbitrarily divided into five equal zones by other lines parallel to the top and bottom and the areas above and below make a total of seven zones. The center one is regarded as the median price zone (comparable to the Vassar Plan's original 135 level) and when prices are within this zone, a 50% stock position is held. Three plans are then suggested. Under the most aggressive, if the price level rises to the next zone above, stocks are reduced to 35%, then to 20% and finally to 10% if the topmost zone is reached. The least extreme of the three plans would — under such circumstances — reduce the stock position to only 30%, and conversely, not assume more than a maximum 70% stock position on the downside.

The same proportions are applied in reverse in a major

downtrend with stocks being increased (under the most aggressive plan) to 65% and then 80% in the two lower zones, and finally to 90%. Whenever prices may happen to remain in the extreme zones outside of the channel, the Seven-Step Plan would not be completely inoperative, since the maximum or minimum stock position would be maintained as if it were a constant-ratio plan in the event of even further decline or advance.

Some Refinements

In order to avoid possible whipsawing if prices happen to fluctuate back and forth at some period around one of the zone lines, an account operated under this plan is rebalanced only at 90-day intervals from the start. Moreover, even though prices may remain within the same zone (a zone may cover a range of 20 to 30 points) the proportions of the account itself can be changed enough by fluctuations within the zone to require rebalancing at one of the fixed points of time.

A second modification employed under certain conditions is a delay in rebalancing to the proportions called for by a change in the price level from one zone to another. That is, if an 80% or 90% stock position has been taken as the result of a decline to or below the lowest zone of the normal channel, it is not reduced to 65% on a rise to the zone calling for that proportion, but is held until the zone calling for a 35% stock position above the median is reached. Conversely, if stocks have been reduced to 20% or 10%, holdings are not increased until prices have declined to the zones where a 65% stock position is indicated. Because of the momentum of major price trends, this will usually be an advantageous modification as long as prices remain substantially within the "normal" channel.

F. I. DUPONT INSTITUTIONAL PLAN

This variable-ratio plan has been provided by the New York Stock Exchange firm of Francis I. duPont & Co. as a "sample" for institutional investors, although it is equally well adapted to the highly conservative individual.

As with the Vassar Plan, the median line is determined by the ten-year record of the Dow-Jones Industrial Average — specifically, a 120-month moving Average of the monthly mean prices as shown in Figure 7. duPont & Co. remark about this: "Recognizing the fact that actual prices determine the average (median line), we find it possible to accept the average as normal without thereby implying any opinion as to the future course of stock prices".

When the price level is at the median line, a 50% stock position is held. Sales are made above and purchases below in accordance with the following scale which can be extended further in either direction.

Percentage of Median Price	Percentage in Stocks
150.0	29.5
140.0	32.8
130.0	36.5
120.0	40.5
110.0	45.0
100.0	50.0
90.9	55.0
83.3	59.5
76.9	63.5
71.4	67.2
66.6	70.5

A True Formula

Since each step reducing holdings is by 10% of the previous proportion held, stockholdings can never reach zero, no matter how high the market goes. Conversely, a fund

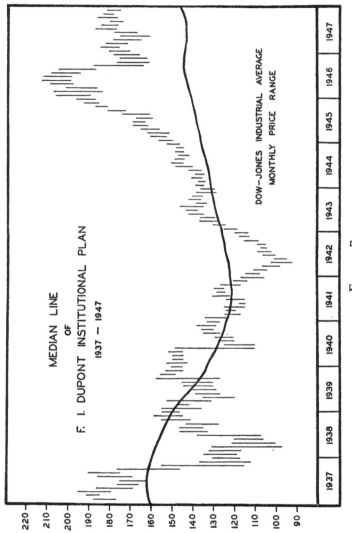

MEDIAN LINE
OF
F. I. DUPONT INSTITUTIONAL PLAN
1937 — 1947

DOW—JONES INDUSTRIAL AVERAGE
MONTHLY PRICE RANGE

FIGURE 7

operated under this plan never reaches a completely invested position in common stocks. In this respect, it is quite different from the Vassar Plan and is more of a true formula, since the element of "forecast" involved is much less.

Under no circumstances are stock purchases made above the median line or sales below it except, of course, as this might be necessary with a cash fund when the Plan was initially adopted, in order to get in line with the position then called for. When the price level reached calls for action, nothing is done until the actual monthly mean price at the time rises above the similar price of the preceding month or falls below if sales have been signalled. This modifying rule stems from the established fact that there is a certain momentum to price trends. From the record, it is estimated that if the market has risen or fallen in any given month, the chances are five out of eight that it will continue in the same direction for the succeeding month.

DOLLAR AVERAGING

This is perhaps the simplest of all "methods" and although not strictly a formula plan, it belongs to the same family. It employs one of the principles which always enables a formula plan to beat a straight purchase over a complete cycle — namely, that the same amount of money will buy more shares when the price is low than when the price is high.

Its most practical application is for investors who can set aside steady savings from steady income, although spreading the investment of a principal sum over a sufficient period of time would also achieve the same result.

Dollar averaging is simply the buying of equal dollar amounts of a given stock (or stocks) at predetermined regular time intervals. Over a long period, the investor will have bought at the highest prices, but also at the lowest. However, he will have been able to buy so many more shares at the lowest prices that his average cost is always lower than the average price of the stock. Suppose, for example, that the unit of purchase is $1,000. The first purchase is 10 shares of stock at 100, the second 20 shares a year later at 50, and the third 40 shares in still another year at 25. The average cost of the 70 shares is then less than 43, whereas the average price is over 58.

Over the course of a complete cycle which might take eight or ten years, the result will inevitably be a low-cost position in stocks.

INDIVIDUAL STOCK FORMULA ADAPTATIONS

The foregoing plans were treated quite briefly, because the primary purpose of their inclusion was to illustrate the basic types. To give complete details would simply be to repeat the information already available in the book mentioned earlier — "Successful Investing Formulas". The following plans, however, are individual stock adaptations of formula principles referred to on page 99, and which are not covered in Miss Tomlinson's book.

There is one important difference in ordinary practice between these plans and the usual institutional procedures. The latter are seeking both preservation and long-term growth of principal. Income is important, but only that received in the form of dividends and interest is ordinarily withdrawn for use. Capital gains are simply added to the total fund.

With these adaptations, however — which are applied only to individual stock issues — it has often been customary to withdraw capital gains, treating them as the income which the Bureau of Internal Revenue likewise assumes them to be. There is no reason, of course, why such gains cannot be plowed back into principal for long-term growth if so desired. Nevertheless, there is an appeal in these plans to the individual looking for a reasonably assured higher average return than he could get by orthodox investment for income.

Actuarial principles are involved in the whole formula procedure, so that if the record shows that a certain plan has averaged a combined return of, say, 9% from regular income and from capital gains through the fluctuations in a group of seasoned stocks over a period of time, it is a reasonable presumption that the same average result will continue in the future.

The figure is, however, an average. In some years, the return might be only 3% and in others 15% or 20%, depending upon the percentage invested in stocks and the amplitude of price fluctuations. Hence, it is often the practice to draw regularly upon the fund at the assumed average rate of return, which will be less than the total "income" in some years but more in others.

BURLINGAME PLAN

This first individual stock adaptation is the one "formula plan" discussed in the 1941 edition of this book. It is quite different and also more complicated than the plans outlined up to this point, which is one reason for the fact that it seems better adapted to the individual investor than the institution. As implied above, the Burlingame Plan begins with individual stocks rather than using the latter on the basis of some particular Average as do most other well-known formula plans.

There is a definite advantage in this, because, in order to profit from price fluctuations, there must be such fluctuations, and — mathematically speaking — the sum of the movements in the individual stocks making up an Average is greater than the sum of the movements in the Average itself. There is no reason, however, why other plans could not also be applied to individual stocks. With the F. I. duPont Plan, for example, the same median and the same buying and selling scales customarily applied to the Industrial Average could be used for each stock held.

Each Stock Has Own Formula

The "formula" — to call it that — for each stock is, therefore, naturally different, being based on its own record of price fluctuations under definite mathematical rules and tables worked out by Warren F. Burlingame. Although the basic "formulas" remain the same, the scales on which buying and selling take place may change as the fluctuation record develops.

Thus, starting with an initial commitment under the Burlingame Plan in a certain stock today at a price of 50, the next lower level for scale-down purchasing might be 20% below at 40, but that percentage could be different at a future date. The buying levels are on a logarithmic (equal percentage) scale.

The second important difference in the Burlingame Plan is that buying can take place on a scale up as well as a scale down. The percentages for scale-up purchasing, however, are ordinarily smaller than those for scale-down buying.

In principle, the Plan operates as follows: It may be applied at any time and at any price, the first step — except under one very extraordinary set of conditions — always being to purchase at the market an amount of the stock which will use 25% of the total fund allocated to that particular issue. From there on, the buying scale percentages control further purchases.

Procedure in Unbroken Decline

In order to illustrate how all contingencies are met, the very unusual example of a stock immediately losing most of its market value after the first purchase, and without any worth-while recovery during its decline, will be used. Let us call the stock X which is selling at 50 at the time the Plan goes into effect with an allocated fund of $4,000. The first move would be the purchase of 20 shares for $1,000 or one-fourth of the money available. It is assumed that the fluctuation record of X is such that the purchase scale on the way down is on each 20% decline. Therefore, the second lower buying level is at 40 which results in the purchase of 25 more shares at that price, again costing $1,000. The third and fourth buying units of $1,000 each then purchase 31 shares and 39 shares at 32 and 25½, respectively. A total of 115 shares would finally be held, and the fund would be fully invested.

Supposing still further decline, however, a course of action would be called for under the Burlingame Plan which is again totally unlike any of the other formula plans. On a fifth 20% decline from 25½ to around 20, it would sell at a loss 29 shares of X, or one-fourth of the total held. Proceeds of this sale would then be reinvested on a sixth 20% decline in 36 shares at about 16, making an average cost of 32¾ for 122 shares. Further operations would then await a return above that price which would be presumed to occur sooner or later. If not, it would illustrate the risk of a stock going down and staying down permanently. In that case, there would be an irretrievable loss, to be sure, but it would still be less than if a fully invested position had been taken in the beginning. Probably nothing like that would occur once in a hundred times, but this extreme example has been used to show how the Plan would function under the most adverse circumstances.

Meeting an Extraordinary Advance

Now, assume the opposite set of conditions where the price rises steadily after the initial one-fourth commitment of 20 shares at 50. The procedure in such a case also sets the Burlingame Plan off from the orthodox formula plans because of the fact that it can buy as well as sell on a scale up.

When the original purchase was made at 50, two orders would actually have been entered immediately afterward. One would have been the order to buy 25 additional shares at 40 which was assumed to have been executed in the first illustration of X dropping steadily. The second order would have been to buy 17 shares at 60 "on stop", meaning that the order would be executed at the market when the price touched that figure on an advance.

In taking the next higher buying level as 60, or 20% above the starting point at 50, it was arbitrarily assumed for the sake of convenience that the percentage scale on the way up was the same as on the way down. As previously pointed out, however, it is usually smaller in actual practice, and not likely to be much more than half.

Now assume that this order to buy 17 shares on stop at 60 is executed. This automatically calls for the cancellation of the lower order to buy at 40. Another difference between the Burlingame Plan and most formula plans enters in at this point, because — unlike purchases made on a scale down — each commitment made on a scale up is regarded as a separate unit in itself.

Thus, at the time that the second order to buy at 60 was executed, a profit-protecting order would be entered to sell on stop at perhaps 57 the shares bought at 50. Similarly, the second unit bought at 60 would receive a protective stop order at, say 68, after the price had advanced another 20% to the third buying level at 72. There would also be additional one-fourth purchases on a further advance as, in this case, 14 more shares at 72 and 12 more at 86.

The stop orders are figured on a definite scale linked to the buying levels, and are raised proportionately as the price may advance between such points. Stop orders are not ordinarily adjusted to compensate for a stock being ex-dividend or ex-rights (rights would always be sold) which is contrary to usual brokerage practice on limit orders. On a straightaway advance, therefore, from 50 to 86, the result would be a fully invested position with 63 shares at an average cost of about 64½. No matter how high the price might go, the profit-protecting orders to sell each unit would be raised each time that the price advanced another 20%.

This effectively disposes of the charge mentioned at the beginning of this Section that *all* formula plans will "eventually get the investor out of the market" and a "new era" of prices. The reasons are that the Burlingame Plan can buy on a scale up and that profit-realizing sales take place only on stop orders rather than at predetermined top limits as in the case of most formula plans.

Normal Operations

In the two examples used so far, very extreme cases have been taken in order to illustrate the principles involved, and it has been assumed that the price continued in the same direction without even temporarily reversing — obviously a very unlikely type of movement. During either a decline or an advance, temporary reversals of sufficient extent would change the operations.

For example, go back to the first two steps on the scale-up purchasing of X — 20 shares at 50 and 17 at 60. Assume that instead of continuing on to the third point of purchase at 72, the price movement reversed itself at 63 and began an important decline. In that case, the first unit bought at 50 would be sold on the stop order at 57, while the second unit of 17 shares bought at 60 would become the first quarter of a new purchase plan for 21 shares at 48, 26 shares at 38½, etc.

Stock so purchased on a scale down is regarded as a unit. That is, in the foregoing example, if the third purchase at 38½ were made, the total of 64 shares then held would be subject to one profit-protecting stop order on the average cost, placed whenever there might be an execution on the next higher buying order entered after the 38½ purchase. Thus, at all times, there are orders placed to meet virtually any contingency that may arise. An actual record taken more or less at random from recent operations will show how the Plan is likely to work in practice on an active stock with fairly wide fluctuations like Flintkote. The period covered is February 14, 1945 to October 28, 1947 when Flintkote rose from a starting point of 29¼ for the Plan to 45⅞ in 1946, dropped back for scale-down purchases to 25⅛ and rose to a last point of commitment at 38½.

Since the price trend was generally upward for fifteen months after the start, three scale-up commitments were made. The first two of these and the initial purchase were stopped out at a profit, while the ensuing scale-down purchases at a low average cost finally went out at a profit on the subsequent recovery.

Pertinent factors and details of the results are as follows.

1. There were seven purchases and four sales, stock purchased on the way down being sold as a unit.
2. Average percentage of capital invested in stock was 55%, although a completely invested position was held at one time for four and one-half months. Uninvested funds held in cash.
3. Capital allocated to operation — $4,000.
4. All dollar figures below are net after broker's commissions and similar expenses.
5. Incidental dividends received totaled $175.80.
6. Dividends and realized profits were withdrawn; there was no reinvestment of profits.
7. Of realized capital gains, $499.60 was long-term from a tax standpoint, and $182.34 short-term.
8. Combined capital gains and dividends taken out for the period February 14, 1945, to October 28, 1947, were $857.74 on the $4,000 of capital, or an average annual return of approximately 8%.

The example might be a better one if the price of Flintkote happened to have returned to the starting point at the end, so as to show results over a complete cycle. In that event, the actual realized return would have been just the same, although there would also have been a paper loss of $231 at that particular point.

The selection of this example was made, however, because the result was closely in line with what has been demonstrated to be average experience. For example, a study of actual results on 57 different issues for the erratic 1939-1944 period showed a return of 8.3%. It should be noticed, however, that brokerage commission rates were then much less than they are now, so that results are somewhat overstated on the basis of present-day circumstances.

HOWE METHOD

Basically, the Howe Method is a variable-ratio type of formula plan which — like the Burlingame Plan — is applied in practice to individual stocks only. It has been mentioned before that there is no reason why any of the variable-ratio plans using a stock Average as a basis, could not just as well be applied to individual stocks. To do so, however, has simply happened not to have been customary — perhaps because the more frequent buying and selling involved is foreign to usual institutional procedure.

To understand the principles of the Howe Method, it is helpful to go back to the Vassar Plan. The 1947 basis of the latter, for example, was a low limit of 105 in the Dow-Jones Industrial Average, at which point (if reached) it would be fully invested, while the subsequent high limit was 194, where it would be entirely out of stocks. These limits under the Vassar Plan were determined first by the selection of a median level (145 on the way down for a 50% stock position) and then successive 10% changes in the price level.

Judgment Used

The Howe Method sets up comparable high and low limits for each of the individual stocks selected as suitable candidates for operations. Only conservative issues sub-ject, nevertheless, to fairly wide fluctuations, are chosen, and the limits are set by judgment to a considerably greater extent than in the case of the Vassar Plan.

The price level of the stock in relation to this estimated range determines the amount of the initial commitment. If, for example, the range has been estimated at 10 to 50, and the price should happen to be 10 when the Method went into effect, the operating fund would take a fully invested position in that stock. Conversely, if the price were 50, no stock at all would be purchased, and the fund would remain in, or purchase, high-grade bonds (usually U. S.

Treasury issues), since — contrary to the Burlingame Plan — a policy of not holding cash is followed in practice.

The initial percentage stock position is determined essentially by the level within the estimated range. Mathematically, it would be 75% at the 20 level on a range of 10 to 50; 50% at 30; 25% at 40, etc. In practice, however, the amount initially committed is not always exactly proportionate to the distance between the price and the high and low limits. Here again, some judgment enters in, although the actual amounts would never be very far away from the indicated percentages as in the preceding mathematical illustration.

After the initial commitment in any amount is made, it is further divided into blocks for possible sales on a scale up, with the last block going out at the high limit. Similarly, the remaining bond reserve is also divided into blocks to be liquidated for possible additional stock purchases on a scale down, with the last one at the low limit. Judgment is used once more at this point, since the divisions are not made according to an exact formula in all cases. Any blocks sold at a profit on the way up are repurchased (when and if possible) at a predetermined number of points under their selling prices. Conversely, if additional purchases are first made on the way down, these are sold (in the event of a later rise) at a specified number of points above their original purchase price.

Illustration

The principles involved may, at least, be illustrated by the following example, where it is assumed that a start is made at a price of 30 with a stock having an estimated range of 10 to 50. During the period covered, the price first drops from 30 to the low limit of 10, rises to the high limit of 50, and falls back to the starting point of 30 again. In this illustration, 60% rather than 50% is the initial commitment. Capital of $1,000 is assumed.

Initial Commitment	(A)	Bought 20 shs. at 30
Second Commitment	(B)	Bought 10 shs. at 20
Third Commitment	(C)	Bought 20 shs. at 10
		Sold 20 shs. at 20(C)
		Sold 10 shs. at 30(B)
		Sold 10 shs. at 40(½A)
		Sold 10 shs. at 50(½A)
New Initial Commitment		Bought 10 shs. at 40
New Second Commitment		Bought 10 shs. at 30

It will be noticed that the position at the end is the same as at the start; i. e., 20 shares held when the price is 30. On 10 of these shares (bought at 40) there is a paper loss of 10 points or $100, but gross profits of $600 have been realized during the price movement from 30 to 10, to 50, and back to 30 again. In practice, such uninterrupted swings would not be likely to occur so obligingly, and the example is illustrative rather than indicative of actual results in operation.

Theoretical Record

The Howe Method has not been in operation long enough to have established a black and white record, and since there is not a fixed formula applied with mathematical precision at all times, the record as worked back cannot be taken literally to the last decimal point. However, the computations for the past — which are believed to have been worked out as fairly as possible — show an average net 9.79% return from dividends, interest and capital gains for a 21-year test period from January 2, 1926 through December 31, 1946.

In arriving at this figure, 1% of the amount involved in each purchase and sale was deducted to cover brokerage commissions and transfer taxes. Also, 1% of the account value at the end of each year was allowed to cover advisory fees, custodian expenses, etc. The fact that the average return is a little ahead of the comparable Burlingame figure may be accounted for by the bond interest allowed on the reserve portions of the fund.

Because both the Burlingame Plan and the Howe Method appeal to the individual interested in a good average return, capital gains are ordinarily withdrawn in order to augment "income". On this basis, then, they cannot be compared with the long-term results of the "institutional" plans which draw out only interest and dividends, plowing back capital gains into additional investments.

A calculation assuming the reinvestment of capital gains was made, however, on a group of stocks under the Howe Method. On this basis, the average percentage growth in the 21-year test period referred to above, was 366% with a natural disparity of results as between individual issues. For example, General Motors showed an appreciation of 569%, Loew's 545%, General Electric 335% and Kennecott Copper 325%.

U. S. Steel did not happen to be included in this group, but has been tested for the same period under the Burlingame Plan on the same basis of reinvesting capital gains. The result was 462% which suggests that both approaches would not be far apart over a period of time.

The longer the period of time involved with these — or any other formula plans — the more impressive such calculations look, since the principle of compound interest enters in. A gain of 640% in a 21-year period, for example, is an annual increase of only 10% compounded.

NEW ENGLAND PLAN

This recently developed Plan was designed from the standpoint of flexibility. The comparative future results of almost any application of the formula principle will depend upon how future circumstances happen to be adapted to its particular operational requirements. For example, if the arbitrarily assumed high and low limits for each stock under the Howe Method prove to be the actual limits of the future, it will do extremely well in this particular class.

The catch, of course, is always how well the facts will jibe with the suppositions. It will be recalled that one of the criticisms often heard of formula plans in general is that they would keep the investor out — or largely out — of an extraordinary inflation in stock prices such as that which occurred between 1927 and 1929.

Flexibility of Operation

The Burlingame Plan, however, is able to cope with such a possibility by its scale-up purchase provisions, and the New England Plan employs the same principle in order to obtain the desired flexibility of operation. Unlike the Burlingame Plan, however, the latter does not make a partial sale at a loss in the event of a decline below the final purchase point, while the size of each commitment is also subject to considerably more variation, thus providing another element of flexibility in meeting the abnormal.

In this latter respect, it is more like the Howe Method, although it does not borrow entirely from that particular approach, since any variable-ratio plan — to which broad class all these individual stock adaptations belong — starts with relatively large commitments at what are presumed to be low levels and vice versa. Profit taking on scale-down purchases is also handled differently than under either the Burlingame Plan or the Howe Method.

Blue Chips Most Suitable

It has been pointed out before that application of any plan to the individual stocks in a group is likely to give better results than if the group is used as an average and as a basis for collective action. A corollary here is that the choice of the individual stocks to be used is of major importance in the results. The best all-around mediums are issues which have not been individually erratic in the past and — as nearly as can be foreseen — are not likely to be erratic in the future.

Amplitude of fluctuations is not so important, since the percentage purchase scale is automatically adjusted to the characteristics of the price movement in each individual issue. Consistency of fluctuation in relation to the market is, however, important. In practice, dividend-paying issues in the "blue chip" class are — generally speaking — found to be the best mediums. Not all in that category are the most desirable, because the character of the price fluctuation is most important, and there are some "blue chips" which have been highly erratic.

Determining the Low

The first thing to be determined is the "expectable possible low". This may be defined as the lowest point which the stock might be expected to reach under depressed business conditions or some other background causing a bear market of major proportions. Among comparable plans, the Howe Plan uses judgment to determine this point, and it is understood that the Burlingame Plan employs the last major low point in the market. In order that the New

England Plan may be more of a formula, a median line is first calculated by a moving average of ten years of price fluctuations. The "expectable possible low" is then determined by the relationship of previous cyclical low points to that line. Hence, if the stock being used is definitely in a long-term uptrend, the "expectable possible low" would be higher than the last major bottom. Conversely, it would become lower in the event of a secular downtrend developing in the stock.

The scale of purchasing is determined initially by the distance between the price when the plan is started and the "expectable possible low". In the event of a rise, scale-up purchasing also takes place, and as in the Burlingame Plan procedure, this is linked to the downside intervals.

Variable Purchase Units

The amounts of the unit purchases are variable rather than fixed, somewhat on the same principle as the Howe Method, but less subject to change. The Burlingame Plan units, for example, are always 25% except under very extraordinary conditions that have not arisen since 1929. It will be recalled, however, that under the Howe Method, the nearer prices may be to the predetermined high limit, the less the size of the initial commitment, and vice versa.

The New England Plan uses this principle, but to a lesser degree. Employing the same median line which — adjusted to other points — determines the "expectable possible low", three zones are calculated from its relationship to previous cyclical highs and lows. In the middle zone, unit purchases of 25% are used. In the below-normal zone, the initial commitment is 40%, followed by 30%, 20% and 10%. It could be argued that this last would result in a higher average cost than equal commitments if the "expectable possible low" were reached. That is true, but the latter might just as well *not* be reached, and the initial larger commitment is justified on the basis of the record and the fact that the price is in the below-normal zone. Thus, if a change of major trend occurs before the "expectable possible low", is reached, a 70% or 90% invested position could still be held at a low average cost.

The initial purchase percentage is reversed for a similar reason if a start is made in the above-normal zone; i.e., only 10%. Should the price level then continue to rise, the amount of any scale-up purchases indicated by the formula would continue to be limited to 10%. On the downside from that initial point, however, the unit purchases would continue in reverse — that is, from 10% to 20%, to 30% and finally to 40% at the "expectable possible low". Should a start with the Plan be made at a time when the price is at or below the assumed low point, a fully invested position is taken as under the Howe Method. This is only logical, since such a price is the starting point for the whole method of operation under any circumstances.

At any time that all profit-protecting stop orders may be executed, thus resulting — in effect — in a fresh start, the subsequent purchase units are made in the amount indicated by the zone in which the price may then be. This procedure affords an unusual degree of adaptability in meeting all possible conditions, although by the same token, it lacks the simplicity of some other formula plans. Nevertheless, simple requirements are usually also rigid ones, and this is often an undesirable attribute. At the present time (1948), for example, some of the better-known formula plans have been out, or nearly out of stocks for three years or so, and cannot buy unless and until there is a rather drastic decline.

Logic of Procedure

Because of traditional methods of investing, i.e., buying 50 or 100 shares of a stock because it appears attractive, some people recoil instinctively from the odd amounts called for by some formula plans and particularly these individual stock adaptations. One hundred shares is regarded as a good round amount, but such lots as the 27s, 34s, etc. which may be needed seem — as one investor expressed it — like too much "monkey business".

The odd share amounts, however, are dictated by uniform dollar amounts. People are simply habituated to paying changing dollar prices for the same physical amounts of goods rather than paying a fixed amount of dollars for a variable supply of goods. The housewife says that eggs have gone up from 84c to $1.20 a dozen instead of saying that her dollar will now buy only 10 eggs instead of 14. It is only in rare cases that people are accustomed to uniform money amounts for goods, and often without realizing it. A chocolate bar may remain at a retail price of 10c year in and year out, but the manufacturer will vary the number of ounces it contains in accordance with his costs.

There is nothing esoteric or illogical in buying the odd amounts of stock which are called for by even amounts of dollars. In fact, there are several reasons why it is even more logical, and only custom and habit stand in the way.

Similarly, the use of stop orders (instructions which become orders to buy or sell at the market price when a specified level is reached) seems highly complicated to some, although here again, it merely represents an easy way of being sure that action will be taken under certain circumstances that may arise without the necessity of following price changes every minute of the day. The orders to buy on stop represent protection against a change in trend before a lower buying level is reached. The profit-protecting stop orders are insurance against the chance of a profit turning into a loss, or of a large profit evaporating.

In fact, the New England Plan really employs two of the recognized precepts for successful trading (1) Never let a profit become a loss and (2) Let profits run. The first is taken literally after a specified percentage profit has accrued, either on a scale-up unit purchase or on the average cost of scale-down purchases. If an initial stop order is caught, the profit realized will be negligible, but the commitments will never result in a loss. The second is a potential not realized too often, since there is always a good possibility of the stop being caught somewhere along the way. Nevertheless, without the necessity of employing judgment, it offers the chance, at least, of riding a big upswing and securing a large part of the total move.

A Specific Example

Figure 8 shows the specific purchases and sales which would have resulted from application of the New England Plan to General Motors between 1937 and 1947. The Plan itself, of course, was not in actual operation during this period.

In order to illustrate the long-term growth possible under such a plan, it was assumed in this example that capital gains were held available for new investment, only dividends being withdrawn. Hence, the amounts bought and sold in the later stages are larger than if capital gains were taken out as they accrued. Results under the latter procedure will be given later.

The starting point is January 2, 1937, at a price of 63 — close to a peak for General Motors which was not reached

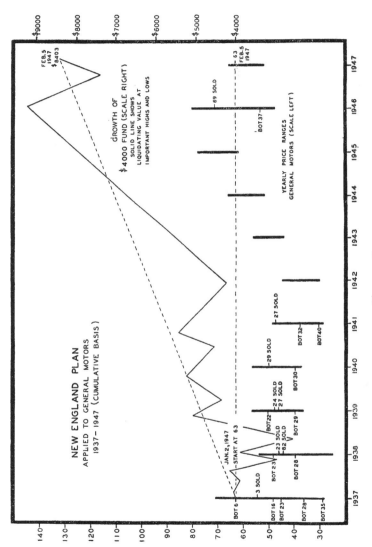

FIGURE 8

again until 1944. The finish point is February 5, 1947 — about one month more than an exact decade — because the price was then just the same as at the start. It will be noticed, however, that the Plan succeeded in more than doubling the original principal ($4,000 to $8,403) during the same period of time.

Calculations Exact

All calculations were exact, and used 1948 brokerage commission rates throughout. These are considerably higher than those actually prevailing during most of the period covered. However, the purpose was to get some idea of future expectancies under a similar degree of price fluctuation, and commission rates are hardly likely to be decreased.

Taxes on realized capital gains were not included, however, since they are a variable with the individual. These were almost entirely in the long-term category, however, since the "first in — first out" rule applies in the operation of such a plan. That is, unless a stock certificate is specifically identified, stock sold is assumed to have been the earliest purchase when one or more units are held and a partial sale is effected.

Activity Differs

One obvious phenomenon in Figure 8 is the activity from 1937 to 1942, and the relative lack of activity thereafter. This reflects the different character of the market in those periods. Price swings were very sharp and erratic in the earlier years, thus resulting in many more executions of orders placed.

On the other hand, the rise after 1942 was unusually slow and gradual which afforded a chance to follow up the trend with successively higher profit-protecting stop orders, none of which was caught until the last one at 71¼ in 1946.

Initial Steps

It will be noticed that the initial transaction was the purchase of only six shares. This was because the median line method of determination at the time showed General Motors to be in an "above-normal" zone, so only 10% of the $4,000 fund was used for the first purchase. At that time, the "possible expectable low" was figured at 29. On the distance from 63 to 29, the scale-down percentage is 23% (63 less 23% is 48½; 48½ less 23% is 37⅜; and 37⅜ less 23% is 29). Hence the next purchase was 16 shares (20% of the $4,000) at 48½.

This made 22 shares at an average cost of 52½. The 12½% arbitrary gain allowed for scale-down purchases occurred when the price then reached 59, and a profit-protecting stop order was hence entered halfway between at 55¾. If another 12½% gain had occurred from 59 to 66⅜, the stop would have been raised to 59 the second time. In this case, however, the first halfway stop was caught. This was an unfortunate occurrence from the standpoint of an ideal operation. The best thing that could have happened would have been a continued decline without the rally which called for the stop order, so that the 30% and 40% purchase units might have been bought.

The amount sold on stop, however, was only 3 shares for the following reason. If the 22 shares were sold, the fund would be all in cash and it would be necessary to start over again at the market price. This would mean the purchase of 19 shares at around 55¾ — a price just within the "normal" zone, and therefore requiring a 25%, or $1,000 commitment. Hence, instead of entering an order to sell

22 shares on stop and then buying 19 if it was executed, the order was entered to sell only 3 shares.

Shrinkage at Low Point

It would be tedious to follow details of all the later transactions, but the procedure is always similar. Scale-up purchases are made at 60% of the downside percentage interval at any given time, and are protected at 40% of the distance from cost to the next scale-up point whenever the latter is reached.

The fund was fully invested at the end of 1937 which is the reason that no purchases show up around the extreme low levels of 1938. In fact, when the price of General Motors was down to 25, a shrinkage to about $2,600 in the market value of the fund was suffered. This was substantial, but on the other hand, nowhere near as much as if a straight investment had been made at the starting point of 63. Such an investment would have shrunk to only $1,500 market value at the low point.

In any event, notice that the fund was back above water later in the same year (1938) and never again went below the starting level, even though it was seven years before the actual price of the stock reached an equivalent basis.

Not Fully Invested

There is one other point of interest in connection with the record shown in Figure 8. On the decline of 1941-42, the fund never became fully invested, because the "possible expectable low" was then 24½ — a price not reached. Despite this handicap, however, results were still quite satisfactory for a plan of this type.

Final Results

Under a procedure of reinvesting capital gains, 65 shares were held at the end of the illustration worth $4,095 at the market price, plus cash or equivalent reserves of $4,307.90. In other words, the position was approximately 50% in stock. If capital gains had been withdrawn as they accrued, the position would likewise be 50%, but only 33 shares would have been held with reserves of about $2,000. Under this procedure principal is always roughly a constant except as paper losses or paper profits may exist at any given time.

Return Averages 10.73%

In this particular example, capital gains if withdrawn would have totalled $2,738.60 for the ten-year period, with the bulk of this amount realized on the 1946 sale. Incidental dividends received would have totalled $1,589.75, or a total of $4,328.35. Allowing for the extra month in 1947, this would be an average of $429.26 per year, equivalent to a 10.73% return. If short-term Treasury issues were used for the reserve portion as under the Howe Method, the figure would presumably be slightly larger.

As a matter of interest, dividends would have totalled $3,183.75 under the procedure shown in Figure 8 of reinvesting capital gains.

Patience Required

Under either option, however, the illustration shows clearly the one essential in the use of formula plans — that is, the necessity of patience and sticking to it. Results did not amount to much for several years in this case, although still much better than a straight investment in General Motors, and the greatest advantage was not reaped until the 1946 sale.

Flexibility at Different Points

Started at different points, there would be all sorts of different results. For example, suppose the start was at the 1942 bottom of 30. The "possible expectable low" was then 24½, so there would have been no scale-down purchases. However, the scale-up provisions would have resulted in a fully invested position fairly early in the subsequent long rise, and instead of selling on a scale up as would most formula plans, the position could have been carried in full a long way.

This again demonstrates the outstanding characteristic of this particular plan; i.e., flexibility in meeting all possible price patterns.

"Breaks" Are Variable

At the present time, not enough experiments have been made to say whether the General Motors illustration represents a fair average. Some other stocks have been found better, and some worse. It is inevitable that with a plan of this type, there will be good "breaks" in the price patterns of some issues and bad ones in others.

General Motors provided a good break in not catching any of the profit-protecting stop orders during the 1942-1946 rise, but it failed to reach the possible low before that and also brought about a fully invested position too early in 1937.

SUMMARY OF FORMULAS

It will have been seen from the descriptions in this whole Section that there can be endless variations in minor detail on formula plans, and many have been worked out. Most have taken the form of introducing additional "controls" over some basic plan such as the Seven-Step Plan's entirely valid idea of rebalancing at 90-day intervals only, and delaying the action called for by zone changes under certain conditions.

Constant-ratio plans have even been modified by introducing so extraneous a factor as the Federal Reserve Board Production Index, the action called for by the basic plan being taken only if the Production Index shows a certain pattern at the same time. The objection to such variants as this one goes back to the discussion on market methods in general on pages 11 and 12. That is, they are likely to be introduced only because it is found that they would have been an improvement on the basis of the past record which is no guarantee of the future. Moreover, they depart in rather radical fashion from the essential theory of formula plan investing.

Two Broad Classes

An initial choice, however, must be made between the two broad classes of formula plans: i.e., those where changes are derived from the proportions of the account itself (parent constant-ratio plan) or the variable-ratio plans where the past record in some way determines what shall be done (Vassar, Seven-Step, duPont, or the three individual stock adaptations just discussed).

There are more widely diversified sub-approaches in this second group than in the first. Broadly, these might be classified as rigid and flexible. A rigid approach will proceed on an assumption — essentially a forecast — that prices will fluctuate within a certain area. In its simplest form, it could be assumed, for example, that prices would continue to fluctuate between approximately 100 and 200 in the Dow-Jones Industrial Average as has been the case for the past ten years, buying and selling on a scale within that range.

A constant-ratio or constant-dollar plan avoids the rigidity of an assumed normal, but by nature, is not potentially productive of as good results as may be obtained with the plans operating on a flexible sliding scale. To use a median price level derived from a moving average in a flexible plan, for instance, helps in adjusting for the fact that the future "normal" may be higher or lower than the past normal.

Common Characteristics

There are some characteristics common to all formula plans because of their very nature. (1) Started just before the rising trend of a bull market, they will result in considerably less appreciation of the fund (on paper, at least) at the peak than if a fully invested position in stocks had been taken, but conversely (2) they will show less shrinkage if started at the beginning of a bear market than a completely invested fund; and (3) over the course of a complete cycle — that is, a bull market followed by a bear market completely retracing the advance, or the reverse picture of a bear market followed by 100% recovery — formula plans will inevitably show a fair to excellent profit depending on the plan used, the way in which the latter happened to fit the fluctuations of the particular period covered, and the mediums of investment selected.

Comparable to Growth Stock Investing

It might be said that the use of a formula plan over a period of time is very much the same in results as a long-term investment in a well-selected growth stock. The value of the fund will slip back somewhat in a bear market, but should go ahead to new highs in each successive upswing, even though the medium employed stays within the same price range.

Unless stock prices move in one direction only for an indefinite period of time or cease to fluctuate entirely — either supposition being hardly conceivable — a good formula plan is absolute assurance of at least moderate investment success over a period of some years. Just as was stressed earlier in connection with trend methods, however, the *sine qua non* of success is the willingness to stick with the plan, come hell or high water, at least until one has passed through both a major bull and major bear market. It should also be realized that formula plans are not directed toward attainment of large or quick profits, and the speculative temperament, aiming high, will probably consider their goal unsatisfactory.

Basic Advantage

Obviously, no formula plan can beat reasonably accurate "forecasting". Indeed, the adoption of a formula plan by an individual implies that he believes such forecasting to be impossible. That, however, is a moot point, although formula plans do have in their favor — for some investors — the fact that they entail little worry and little work, whereas "forecasting" in the ordinary sense means a great deal of both. Neither are formula plans very exciting, although as their proponents are fond of pointing out, they automatically combat the natural tendency to become bullish after prices have risen and vice versa.

And certainly, for institutional investing, formula plans have even more in their favor. Entirely aside from possible errors in judgment, they eliminate the difficulty all fund managers or co-trustees experience in getting a decision to act from a committee of several men, no matter how able the latter may be individually. There is wry truth in the supposedly humorous definition of a committee as a group of important people who, individually, can do nothing, but collectively, can meet and decide that nothing can be done.

Comparative Results Subject to Conditions

It is natural to wonder at this point which class of plan and which plan in that class — is "best". A great deal there, however, depends upon the purposes. A private investor, for example, can logically use an active individual stock plan that would not be suitable for a college endowment fund. Actually, there is no real answer to the question, despite the fact that "records" for some plans can be worked out on the basis of past fluctuations. The Vassar Plan has been much "better" than the Yale Plan during the period since both were started, because stock prices have fluctuated largely within Vassar's predetermined range of operations. On the other hand, the Yale Plan is designed to fit much wider fluctuations than have happened to occur in the 1938-1946 period.

If both had started on their present bases in 1926, Yale would thus have fared much better during the next decade than would Vassar. Perhaps it will again, but the point is that it is impossible to say that one is "better" than the other unless the statement is applied to past performance during one specific interval of time. Since Yale is more or less on a constant-ratio basis, while Vassar works with a variable-ratio, it follows that the same thing is true with respect to these two broad classes. It can be said, however, that variable-ratio plans are potentially more profitable than the constant-ratio schemes as long as price fluctuations happen to fit the particular premise reasonably well.

Qualification of Records

To make comparisons based on past hypothetical results

affords some interesting data, but it is not of much value in attempting to determine which formula plan may be most advantageous *in the future*. Being a relatively recent development, twenty- or twenty-five-year records of actual operations are not available. The oldest are those of the Burlingame Plan where operations began in 1935, although in that particular case, it does not make any difference whether results are actual or hypothetical, because the rules are fixed and no "hindsight" can be involved.

On the other hand, it would not be entirely fair to make comparisons with a variable-ratio plan using the 150 level as a median with upper and lower limits of 200 and 100 for the 1937-1946 decade. It is known now that such a premise was almost ideal for that period, but whether it would have been selected in 1936 is a different story. In any event, such a plan would show excellent results for that particular time, but as far as the unknown 1947-1956 is concerned, one can only say it will continue to do so *if* prices continue to fluctuate within the same approximate limits.

If conclusions are to be drawn with perfect fairness from results as worked back, the tests should be confined to plans which could logically have been set up at any time in the past on the basis of the data then prevailing, and as they would have been set up at the time. This would be true, for example, of the F. I. duPont Institutional Plan since the median used is always slowly conforming to changed conditions, and no rigid range based on the past is assumed.

Moreover, the pattern of the market during the period of time involved is highly important. Started in what proved to be the middle of the subsequent price range, a simple constant-ratio plan might show up as well or even better than some more complicated method, but begun at some point of extreme, would probably suffer by comparison.

Adaptability Desirable

Perhaps, therefore, a more practical approach for determining desirability — in relation to the individual's aims — lies in estimating future results for various plans under the possible different price patterns. If, for example, prices fluctuate for the 1947-1956 decade between the upper and lower limits of the "Seven-Step" Plan's ascending channel, it will be difficult to beat its results. But, a new high inflationary plateau or a new low price range (in the event of war, perhaps) are at least conceivable.

It seems logical, therefore, to conclude that a desirable attribute of any plan is its ability to meet all possible contingencies, including the abnormal as well as the normal. For the individual, it will be noticed that the Burlingame and New England Plans are the only ones which would not necessarily cut down to a minimum position in the event of an extraordinary rise.

Under the opposite set of conditions, i.e., a drop to extraordinarily low levels, it is more difficult to predict performance for these Plans, because it would depend on *how* the drop occurred — whether all at once or whether interrupted by fairly substantial temporary reversals. It would also depend on the point from which the decline and also the operation started.

The investor can, however, be reasonably certain of *ultimate* good results with almost any formula plan, and which is "best" will always be an arguable point.

CYCLE FORECASTING

CASE FOR ECONOMIC RHYTHMS

It was remarked in the Introduction that this Section might be skipped by the hard-headed and practical investor. The discussion is given for just what it is, and the author affirms neither his belief nor his disbelief in the premises.

Forecasting stock market moves by means of observed cyclical rhythms is the exact opposite of using formula plans to deal with price fluctuations. In fact, to proceed on the basis of repetitive cycles is one of the few forms of true "forecasting," because it involves laying out a pattern of the future which includes both the time and the extent of forthcoming moves. Since formula plans deny any ability whatsoever to forecast, it is evident that here are the two opposite ends of the scale.

In the 1941 edition of this book, cyclical forecasting was touched on only briefly under the heading of "Natural Rhythm Methods." The term "cyclical forecasting," however, has since become much more familiar, particularly as a result of Henry Holt and Company's 1947 publication "Cycles (the Science of Prediction)," by Edward R. Dewey and Edwin F. Dakin. (Mr. Dewey is the director of the Foundation for the Study of Cycles.)

There is some question, perhaps, whether the cyclical approach to the problem of stock market price changes can properly be classified as a "method." Even the individual accustomed to reasoning from economic cause to effect, will readily concede the logic of a technical market method which defines and goes with the trend, or attempts to analyze elements of latent strength or weakness in the price structure, indicating a change of trend. To make the mental leap necessary to accept a cycle theory, however, is something else again, since it must then be assumed that the trend — down or up — will come to pass anyway, and that the apparent "causes" can only be discerned after the event itself.

It is not surprising, therefore, that the most common query is whether there is — or can be — "anything to this cycle stuff." The answer seems to be "yes" — that it cannot be dismissed as pure fantasy or the result of just "happenstance." The evidence is too strong the other way. On the other hand, cyclical forecasting cannot lay out the stock market patterns of the future with demonstrable mathematical precision, or it would be a simple problem, indeed.

Cycles in Nature

No one has ever denied the existence of reasonably regular cycles in the many manifestations of nature. Leaving out the results of modern research, it will be recalled that Joseph, for example, advised the Biblical Egyptians to prepare for an inevitable period of seven lean crop years following the fat. Joseph was merely cognizant of the cyclical tendencies in weather conditions. Modern study has shown that there are long swings at fairly regular intervals from extremes of cold or moisture to extremes of heat and drought, and back again. It has likewise been observed that sunspots break out, increase and disappear over approximate eleven-year intervals. In fact, the correlation between the sunspot cycle and long-term changes in weather or climate has been sufficiently well-established to have gained acceptance in the most conservative scientific circles.

The Necessary Link

The foregoing is a far cry from the stock market, and yet the link is not too hard to accept. If there is a definite rhythm in natural phenomena, why should there not also be a definite rhythm in the activities of man in the mass, man himself being subject to natural laws in many respects? Certain physical rhythms in man are self-evident, and the results of some research strongly suggest the existence as well of psychological rhythms.

Dr. Harlan T. Stetson of the Massachusetts Institute of Technology and Director of its Cosmic Terrestrial Research Laboratory mentions an important banker whose experience had "convinced him — like many others — that there were periodic changes in our economic cycle that suggested the possibility of some unknown factor that might be related to some fundamental cycle in nature of which we are not yet intelligently aware." Part of the conclusion of Dr. Stetson's book, "Sunspots in Action" is likewise worth quoting.

> "Science, perhaps, has been altogether too slow in apprehending the significance of the earth's cosmic environment as an important factor in the geophysics of our planet. Moreover, we are becoming increasingly aware that *man himself* (italics ours) is a highly articulated organism, whose activities, and even whose metabolic processes, are quite dependent upon the quantity and quality of the sun's radiations and other factors in his terrestrial environment. The mysterious electron, that fundamental building block of matter which dances in our radio tubes to the tune of our favorite orchestra, dances likewise in the atoms of

the distant stars, in the vast interstellar spaces, and even in man himself. We are entering upon a strange new world of thought in science, perhaps as strange as was the Copernican doctrine of a heliocentric universe to the medieval mind of three hundred years ago."

This same statement may likewise apply to the study of cycles in mass psychology. There is something there, but it defies reduction to an exact formula. Capitalism, or business as we know it, is a man-made activity, and the business cycle — from prosperity to depression and back to prosperity again — has long been taken for granted. The suspicion that its timing also might be due to more than just the immediate circumstances, is not a new idea by any means, as will be pointed out later. In any event, since the major tops and bottoms of stock prices are primarily a reflection of economic and business conditions, approximately the same periodicity should be found in both. Or, if the existence of regular rhythms in mass psychology is accepted, the stock market would be a very obvious expression of degrees of optimism and pessimism, whether over the long term and thus applying to business as well, or whether in its shorter term fluctuations which often seem to occur with or without apparent cause.

Rhythm in Emotions

Emotional rhythm in individuals has been a subject of medical psychiatric study and the persistence of such rhythms appears beyond dispute. Indeed, almost any individual realizes from his own experience that on one day he may feel confident and cheerful, while on another — with no recognizable change in his background — he may feel inadequate and gloomy. The natural tendency, of course, is to attribute such emotions to "being up too late," "indigestion", etc., but the chances are that on numerous other occasions, he has stayed up much later and eaten more indigestible food without any deleterious effect. The individual may not even be so specific; he may merely say that he "got out of bed on the wrong side." What he seldom realizes, however, is that a record of his emotional changes would show the extremes of despondency and cheerfulness occurring at reasonably regular intervals.

Translate this to people in the mass, and even though not completely understandable, it nevertheless *explains* certain phenomena which have no rational explanation other than a state of mind. Thus, the 1928-1930 period represented an extreme peak of emotional optimism in business-men and investors. Stocks sold at prices far above any reasonable value, because it was assumed that a "new era" of business was at hand, that prosperity was permanent and that profits would keep expanding indefinitely. The theory was not rational in the light of all experience, but it was nevertheless almost universally embraced.

To the extent that all this may be accepted in connection with the stock market, the orthodox belief that there are always specific "reasons" for every rise and fall, must be scrapped. As Dewey and Dakin point out in this connection, "It was one of Freud's greatest contributions . . . that he showed how we do what we feel subconsciously impelled to do, and then satisf our conscious mind by devising adequate 'reasons'."

The columns of financial comment are one proof of this contention, since the action of the market is invariably interpreted in terms of current happenings. Thus, at one time, certain happenings will be used to "explain" a fall, while at another, they will be offered as the "explanation" for a rise. During World War II, for instance, military successes of the Allied Powers were first put forth as a reason for sudden drops on the ground that the end of the war meant the cessation of war production. Later on, similar developments were used to "explain" advances, because peace meant an end of excess profits taxes and tremendous production to fill pent-up civilian demand. In one way, however, these explanations were correct, because they were *reporting* psychological responses which were entirely different at different times, despite the existence of the same set of circumstances.

This is entirely analagous to the fluctuations of individual psychology without recognizable cause. A "cause" is always sought, but it is usually just as superficial in the case of mass action influencing stock prices as in that of the individual and his daily life.

Facts in Cycles

If the validity of the "cycle theory" is accepted, the economic "causes" of booms and depressions are more apparent than real. The cycles in steel production, in building, in stock prices, and in other man-made activities, will recur periodically according to natural rhythms in mass psychology induced by influences not completely understood. Building activity, for example, has been shown from the records to proceed according to a fairly well-defined 18⅓-year cycle, although *why* this should be so cannot be satisfactorily explained. Such observed cycles may be modified by variable factors during any given period — but not changed materially in basic length by wars, inventions, political changes, or similar unpredictable developments.

Conception Not New

It has been mentioned that the basic idea is not new. Not only has it long been recognized, but there have often been attempts at rationalization. The English economist, Jevons, put forth some 70 years ago what seemed to him a logical theory (for his time) that sunspots affected weather conditions, weather conditions affected crops, the state of crops affected business, and business conditions were reflected in stock prices. Hence there was an established relationship between sunspots and stock prices.

More recently, the theory has been advanced that since sunspots are accompanied by increased ultraviolet radiation which produces more Vitamin D in human beings and "keys them up," there is a logical connection between the coincidence observed of sunspots being at a maximum around the top of business booms and at a minimum around the bottom of depressions. Although such a fairly close correlation has existed during the past twenty-five years, it is not found over a much longer period of time. Curiously, however, the "rate of change" in sunspots shows a much closer relationship, but it still appears a somewhat tenuous basis for cyclical forecasting.

An Early Prophet

Every so often the story is reprinted of an old chart showing the business cycles from 1800 to the year 2000 which — according to different accounts — was originally found in a variety of places. One placed it in an old desk at the U. S. Steel Corporation in 1902. Another report says it was discovered in 1885 in an old distillery, pointing out that since whiskey must be aged, to have a knowledge of future business conditions would be of great help in estimating in advance what output should be.

There is no doubt, however, that the chart had its origin in a book published in 1876 by Samuel Benner, self-styled as an "Ohio Farmer." It was called "Benner's

Prophecies of Future Ups and Downs in Prices," and was based on the cycles which Benner had observed in pig iron prices, hog prices, corn prices, cotton prices, and business panics. His thinking was, perhaps, somewhat ahead of his time. To quote directly — "We have had to hunt down Price Cycles by establishing periodicity in high and low priced years; the length of the different periods in which they have repeated themselves, and by indisputable dates, facts, and figures, demonstrating their regularity. The cause producing the periodicity and length of these cycles may be found in our solar system. The writer does not claim a knowledge of the causes and conditions under which they occur, and the reasons why they occur . . ."

The curious point is that although Benner arbitrarily announced cycles for which it seems he had quite insufficient evidence in 1876, more scientific modern research has come up with some of the same answers, further reinforced by the experience of another seven decades. Benner had, for example, the nine-year rhythm in pig iron prices, which has been evidenced quite clearly since he wrote. He also stressed the long 54-year cycle in wholesale prices and general business which Dewey and Dakin believe to be one of the clearest and most important.

In the alternations between business booms and depressions, Benner claimed a cycle of 18 years in panics, with variations of two years one way or the other. He felt, however, that the variations were significant, because they also occurred in an ordered sequence with "panics" every 16, 18, and 20 years, and repeat.

Thus, the old chart referred to earlier, showing the business cycles from 1800 to the year 2000, is based on the supposition that booms reach their peaks in cycles of

8, 9, and 10 years, and that panics come in cycles of 16, 18, and 20 years, with some intervening smaller cycles of "hard times," at 7, 9, and 11 year intervals. It has not been too far off in subsequent experience, 1928 being a boom top and 1932 a panic bottom. 1948 is again slated as an important top and 1951 a bottom. The minor cycle in between called for 1938 as a high point and 1944 as low, which is not, however, a close correlation with the facts.

Latest Studies

When Dewey and Dakin's book "Cycles" was first published in the spring of 1947, it threw a chill over many investors. What this suggested was (1) that the 41-month cycle (regarded as one of the most definite and important) called for a top in early 1947 and hence would be down until late 1948 with another low (after an intervening upswing) in early 1952; (2) that an observed 9-year cycle in stock prices reached a peak in 1946 with its next bottom due in 1951; (3) that the 18⅓-year building cycle would be downward until 1953; and (4) that the 54-year cycle in wholesale prices and general trade was due to reach bottom around 1951-1952. Recalling also that the old chart based on Benner's cycles has a 1951 "panic low," cyclical forecasting seems to be approaching an important test period. If the theory is correct, the trough of a serious depression will be witnessed somewhere between 1951 and 1953.

Although such a confluence of observed cycles at that particular time leaves little room for change or modification, shorter term predictions are much less precise. The real difficulty, perhaps, is that there are cycles and cycles. The method used in isolating such rhythms from the records also may be important. Some processes will conceal certain periodicities while emphasizing others. Moreover, some research suggests that the major cycles are not simple waves, but are rather extraordinarily complex, and made up of a nearly complete series of harmonics. It is certainly a field where no one yet "knows all the answers," although another important contribution is expected in a book now in process of preparation by Mr. Robert D. Edwards of the Stock Trend Service in Springfield, Mass. There are, however, some special studies along this line which have been carried far enough or which have enough points of interest to warrant a specific presentation.

SMITH'S DECENNIAL PATTERN

The "Decennial Pattern" is the name given by Edgar Lawrence Smith (author, among other books, of "Common Stocks as Long Term Investments") to his observation of the apparent tendency of stock prices to show similar characteristics in successive decades. Thus, it is distinguished from a simple ten-year cycle which, however, is one of its components. The other two are the approximate 40-month cycle (one of the most widely observed rhythms), and the seasonal, or 12-month cycle.

If a long-term chart of stock prices is cut into ten-year segments, and these segments are then placed one above the other, it may be seen that there is a tendency toward the formulation of a recurring pattern. Despite the extreme divergence from such a pattern in 1926-1930, the preponderant similarities over a 70-year period seem too marked to be dismissed as the result of chance. Certain years have been habitually associated with declining or advancing prices. The "Five" years (1945, 1935, 1925, 1915, etc.), for example, have shown consistently rising trends, and the same is true of the "Eight" years and the greater part of the "Nine" years. Conversely, the "Three" years, the "Ten" years, and often the "Seven" years have ordinarily been periods of falling prices.

Such a brief statement of the "Decennial Pattern" is an oversimplification. Actually, gradual changes seem to be taking place in the segments of time involved. In other words, the pattern is being gradually modified decade by decade, because (1) the 40-month and ten-year cycles are not of those *exact* lengths, (2) other cycles (particularly the well-known 9-year rhythm) impinge upon them, and (3) shorter cycles affect the interplay of the approximate 40-month and 12-month seasonal cycles. Hence, Smith regards the Decennial Pattern as outlined above purely as a preliminary approach to be modified by other factors.

Influence of Weather Conditions

In view of the general cyclical discussion in the first part of this section, it should be pointed out that the "Decennial Pattern" in stock prices is viewed simply as an expression of changes in mass psychology induced by environmental changes of a cyclical nature. In Smith's view, solar conditions (not limited to sunspots alone) have a bearing upon weather conditions, using the term "weather" in a broad sense. That is, there are types of environmental change, such as the fluctuations of ultraviolet rays in solar radiation, which are not usually classified as weather, but which often accompany certain types of weather change.

Secondly, some medical research has indicated that a great majority of the population responds physically and emotionally to current changes in its environment. (See "The Patient and the Weather" by Dr. William F. Petersen, published by Edwards Bros., Ann Arbor, Michigan,

1938). Hence, the actions of man, as expressed in various economic series, may spring from subtle psychological changes, having their roots in cyclical cosmic phenomena. It is interesting to recall Benner's remark in 1876 that — although he did not understand the "whys and wherefores" — the cause of the "periodicity and length of these cycles may be found in our solar system."

Perhaps, therefore, Smith's most important contribution has been his research on certain characteristics of weather change which has revealed a "Decennial Pattern" paralleling that found in stock prices. Figure 9 is a reproduction from one of his studies on "Basic Economic Cycles." It compares stock price changes for 70 years (averaged by decennial year-groups) with similar changes in temperature and rainfall, combined into a single index.

As may be readily seen, there is a close parallel — a little closer than either temperature or rainfall would show alone. As Smith points out, this supports the belief that "each of the two weather indices is a measure of some third force, or condition. Any idea that the relationship between single environmental measurements and economic change is accidental, is not tenable. The combination of two accidental series could not produce such a result within the realm of rational probability."

By using such relationships, Smith has found that a deviation from average pattern in weather can furnish valuable clues to probable deviation from average pattern in economic series, such as stock prices, pig iron production, retail sales, etc. Since it is impossible to do full justice to the subject here, reference is made to Mr. Smith's series of special studies appearing currently as a part of the "Brookmire Economic Service." It is planned to assemble these later in book form, superseding his 1939

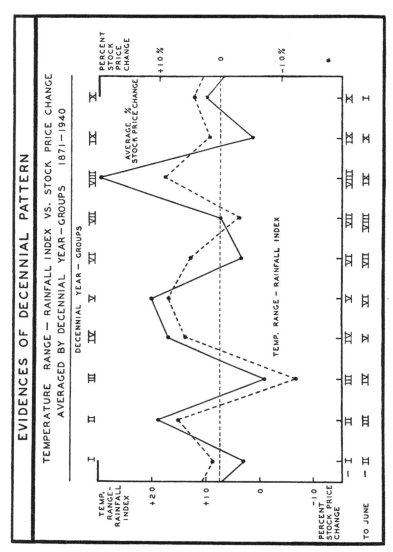

FIGURE 9

Macmillan Co. publication, "Tides in the Affairs of Men," now out of print.

SIDEREAL RADIATION AND THE STOCK MARKET

It is known that there are certain radiations coming from the stars and the space between the stars which bombard the earth constantly from all directions. The light and heat rays from the sun (itself a star) are an obvious example, but there are many others less easily recognized. The well-known cosmic rays have been identified for some years, but are still the subject of the most intensive study. Another type of ray is called "sidereal" (pertaining to the stars).

The Townsend Brown Foundation in Los Angeles, California, has made a study of sidereal radiation for the past twenty-five years, recording the impulses by an instrument developed some twenty years ago. Complete records, however, have only been kept since 1937, except for the war period when the equipment was taken over by the Naval Research Laboratory. The conclusion of the Brown Foundation is that the sidereal rays are not electromagnetic in nature, but are (1) tremendously penetrating and (2) are subject to decisive changes in intensity in an irregular wave-like pattern.

Purely as a hypothesis, physicists have suggested that these rays are electrically neutral particles of energy — perhaps a "sub-atomic dust," similar to the neutral constituents of atomic nuclei which are released during atomic fission. On that basis, it is highly probable that these tiny particles drifting in space are the residue of countless stellar atomic explosions (novae) which have been occurring in the depths of the universe since the beginning of time. The Earth, in its movement through space, presumably runs into — and through — invisible clouds of these sub-atomic ashes.

Such a hypothesis is easily accepted, but in connection with the stock market, it must also be assumed that the intensity of sidereal radiation affects man's emotional state or that precarious balance between optimism and pessimism. Physiologically, there is no definite answer. It has been suggested that the secretions of the endocrine glands may be subtly affected, but such "explanations" are necessarily conjecture.

Nevertheless, the studies of the Brown Foundation do indicate a correlation between the intensity of sidereal radiation and various records of human expression, including the trends of stock prices — not, of course, with absolute perfection, but to a degree suggesting that more than chance is involved.

A Solar Postulate

The "tie-in" between cyclical studies is highly interesting in its implications. Over 70 years ago, Benner recognized a cycle origin in the solar system without any understanding of it. Smith has come to the conclusion that his two weather indexes are the measure of some third force or condition — possibly "sidereal radiation," or some closely allied force. The link is but vaguely perceived, and is not susceptible to tangible proof, but at the same time, its existence appears quite possible.

In the book "Cycles," Dewey and Dakin offer a postulate as follows:

> "We know that our space is permeated by radiation from the sun — there are light waves, for instance, of a wide band of differing wave lengths. We know that here on earth some objects, such as a red pencil, respond to

waves of the 'red lengths'; that other objects, such as a blue pencil, respond to waves of the 'blue lengths'; and that a third object, such as a woman's dress, responds to both 'red and blue waves' and reflects a combination of these which we regard as purple. Light of all wave lengths, including yellow, is falling on these three objects; but they are 'blind' and unresponsive to any waves except those of a length which 'fit' their respective natures.

"We also know that there are, in the universe, waves longer than light waves, with a longer time interval from crest to crest, which are used for radio transmission. Here, similarly, certain waves may be affecting one radio, whereas another radio, in the next room, may be totally unaffected by them, but is being affected by other waves of different frequencies.

"Now, let us suppose that there are still longer waves in the universe — 'Y' waves we may call them. Imagine some of them with peaks which come 3½ years apart, others with peaks 9 years apart, 18⅓ years apart, 54 years apart, and perhaps much farther spaced. It is not inconceivable that these longer waves could directly or indirectly affect the sun, the weather, animals, and human beings, and that just as a red pencil may respond to light waves of only one length, so a particular kind of organism might respond only to Y waves of one particular length.

"Such a state of affairs is wholly imaginary. But the idea might serve to explain how so many different phenomena could oscillate with rhythms of identical length, and how one set of phenomena could fluctuate in waves with lengths entirely different from those of rhythms in adjacent phenomena. But such conjectures completely outrun the facts in hand.

"That we have discovered solar rhythms only in the past few years, and are only learning about human rhythms now, may be put down to the same sort of slow human development which kept us from knowledge of such vital matters as electromagnetic radiation until the nineteenth century of our era.

"There is, of course, an excuse. For these rhythms are extremely complex. How long, for instance, might it have taken men to discover the rhythm of the tides, if the earth — like Jupiter — had nine moons instead of one? Suppose, in addition, that our earth were so surrounded by fog we could not see the moons. How complex the tides would be, and how mysterious! We might even yet have failed to discover that the tidal sweeps of our ocean were gravitational rhythms united in a complex synthesis."

Market Forecasts

The "Y" waves postulated in "Cycles" could, for example, be sidereal radiation. It should be understood, however, that the studies of the Townsend Brown Foundation were — and are — primarily a matter of scientific research. The stock market angle arose by chance, because the degree of correlation between the price trend and the intensity of sidereal radiation happened to be noticed some ten years ago. The Lake States Securities Corp., which has published market forecasts since August, 1947, is completely owned by the Foundation (a non-profit organization), and any profits are, therefore, returned to the Foundation for further scientific research.

There appears to be a lag of several weeks between changes in sidereal radiation intensity and changes in stock prices. This could be explained on the basis that although variations in the radiation have a physiological effect on man, the psychological effect is delayed. Not every market projection on this basis has been completely correct by any means, but the "batting average" has been good for the brief period they have been available. The predicted pattern for early 1948, for example, showed the market declining from 183 to 170 (Dow-Jones Industrial Average) by mid-February (actually 181 to 166) and then rising to 208 by the end of May. This latter goal was too high, but the market was nevertheless in a rising trend from February on.

Although the approach is quite different from that of periodic cycles, the "Wave Principle" is nevertheless an allied conception, since it assumes that price fluctuations occur according to a definite pattern which has its basis in a law of Nature. It was first elucidated by the late R. N. Elliott. As a working theory, the Principle holds that all stock price trends, whether minor movements or major cycles, are composed of a fixed number of "waves" or fluctuations, which occur in an ordered sequence or rhythm, but are not of equal extent or duration. This applies to individual stocks, to groups, to commodities, and to "averages," since Elliott contended that it represents a natural law which dominates and controls price movements. Unexpected news, for example, does no more than affect the amplitude or time of any given wave.

According to Elliott, "Bull markets are composed of five Primaries (primary waves), three of which are upward and two downward . . . The upward or advancing waves are always composed of five intermediate waves. Each of the three intermediate advancing waves is composed of five Minors. . . . Bear markets and all other corrections between advancing waves, of whatever degree, are composed of three waves." For example, if we give numbers in sequence to the five waves composing an uptrend, 1, 3, and 5 are up, and each is composed of five smaller waves. The downward corrections 2 and 4, however, are composed of *three* waves instead of five.

Such sequences as those described above are claimed to

reflect the working of a natural law — a subsidiary manifestation, perhaps, of the cyclical rhythms. Support for such a "law," according to Elliott, is afforded by certain phenomena in mathematics and nature. (See description of dynamic symmetry and summation series on pages 294 and 295 of the Supplement.)

The practical difficulty lies in the confusion which is likely to attend identification of the correct waves as they develop. Just as in the case of cycles, mathematical precision is ordinarily lacking. Likewise, however, the indicated sequences of advances and declines seem to have worked out more frequently than can be accounted for by the laws of pure chance.

Pattern of the '40s

Perhaps the "Wave Principle" can better be grasped at present by fitting the market fluctuations of recent years to the framework of the principle and making the necessary future projections. Elliott's hypothesis — and that of his collaborator (Mr. John C. Sinclair of the New York Stock Exchange house of Francis I. duPont & Co.) — was that from the bottom in 1942, stock prices began an important five-wave upward movement which, in turn, represented the last part of an even larger rhythmic move. The first upward wave of the series thus ran from 1942 to December, 1945, which was considered the true, or "orthodox" top, despite its having been overrun by a few points in the Industrial Average a little later.

Elliott felt that the second downward wave then indicated would be of subnormal extent, and this was assumed to have culminated in May, 1947. The next important move (third wave of the whole series) was, therefore, expected to be up, and to go substantially higher than the first wave. Development of the component minor waves as time goes along will afford closer clues. After a fourth downward wave, the fifth and final wave, should — if the hypothesis is correct — exceed even the 1928 high point (regarded as the true top of that particular period), although it is obvious that any such development must lie considerably ahead in point of time.

LONG-TERM FORECASTING (MARECHAL)

As in the case of the "Wave Principle," Marechal's "Fifteen-Year Forecast" as shown in Figure 10 is not based upon the simple cyclical repetition described in the earlier part of this Section. Nevertheless, it is still pure "forecasting," and hence is included at this point.

The top line of price fluctuations in Figure 10 is an exact reproduction of a copyrighted market forecast as calculated and drawn in late 1933 by George Marechal, formerly of Montreal, Canada. One of the original copies has been in the author's possession since 1935. As each year was divided into six parts, the actual fluctuations of the Dow-Jones Industrial Average have been added below on the same basis by taking the high and low for two-month periods.

Clearly, the pattern of the forecast and the actual pattern of the market miss many times in detail and exact timing. Nevertheless, the broad picture of the trends from 1934 through 1947, at least, is remarkably similar. The basic downtrend from 1936-1937 to 1942 is plain, and likewise the uptrend from 1942 to 1946, although the latter shows up as a much more zigzag pattern in the forecast than was actually the case. Thus, the year 1944 by itself, for example, appears as a down period, whereas it was really an up year.

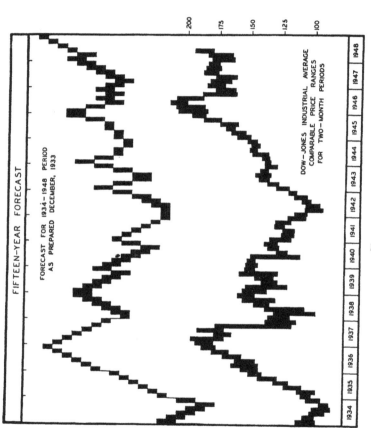

FIGURE 10

A Remarkable Projection

When the year 1947 ended, the Dow-Jones Industrial Average had spent sixteen months within a 16% price range — one of the narrowest and longest such movements on record. It is interesting, therefore, that the forecast also showed sixteen months of similar back and forth movement within — except for one quick dip — exactly the same price range.

The timing is somewhat different, that of the forecast running from May, 1946, to September, 1947, while in the market "as was," it extends from September, 1946, to May, 1948. This, however, is in keeping with the time discrepancy between the forecast and the actual market after 1945, since the 1946 top in the market did not come until five months after it was indicated in the forecast. At the same time, that is not bad "shooting" for a projection made so many years in advance.

As far as the situation at the time the comparison in Figure 10 (June, 1948) ends is concerned, it is evident that if the broad accuracy of the preceding 14 years is to be maintained, 1948 must — on the whole — witness a rising price level. A definite downtrend going substantially into new low territory by the year-end would produce a greater discrepancy between the forecast pattern and the actual course of prices than at any other time in the record. The fact remains to be seen at this writing, but in line with his original forecast made years before, Marechal always insisted that 1946-47 was not a "bear market," but an interruption in a long upward trend, comparable to the break and market hesitancy during 1926 in the long upswing from 1921 to 1929.

Complicated Study

The details of all the processes involved in Marechal's forecast cannot be given here, but it was originally described as a *"record of the conclusions reached from a painstaking study of trend and resistance lines projected into the future, and taking into consideration past causes and effects, all important cycles, and tendencies of certain patterns of market movements to repeat themselves in new ways and at varying intervals of time."*

As a matter of interest, some of the unique "trend and resistance lines" used by Marechal in his long-range projections are shown in Figure 11. The 1929 peak is regarded as an abnormality which would ordinarily not have exceeded the top upward slanting line extending the full width of the chart. Hence, the area above this line is dotted to distinguish it from the other cross-hatched areas above and below what Marechal regards as the dividing line between bull and bear markets.

However, since 1929 was obviously the important end of one long phase, it is taken as the starting point for the projection of new trends as shown by the other diagonals in Figure 11. It will also be noticed that the time element is considered important, and the number of trading days from the 1929 top, indicated on the upper edge of the chart, enters into the calculations. Although not based on cycles in the ordinary sense of the word, the "fan lines" from fixed points through subsequent highs and lows do form recurrent patterns which give the work a cyclical content.

CURRENT UNANIMITY

The "hard-headed" individual will not be inclined to place any faith in such esoteric approaches as have been

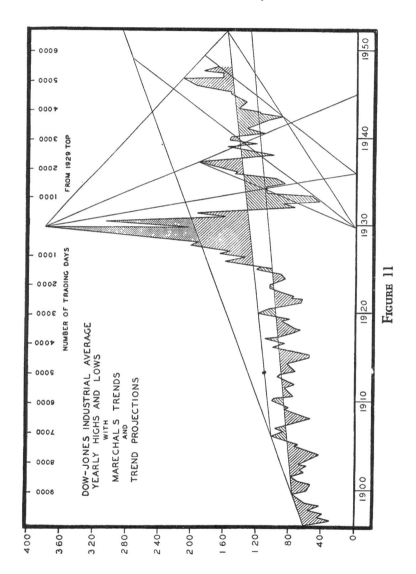

DOW-JONES INDUSTRIAL AVERAGE
YEARLY HIGHS AND LOWS
WITH
MARECHAL'S TRENDS
AND
TREND PROJECTIONS

FROM 1929 TOP

NUMBER OF TRADING DAYS

FIGURE 11

discussed in this Section. For the sake of the record, however, it may be pointed out that there is a common thread running through most of them as to the broad pattern of the next few years. This is being written in February, 1948, when the prevailing view is that the business boom is about to "bust" and that stock prices are therefore headed for substantially lower levels.

On the other hand, Edwards' Cycle studies, Smith's Decennial Pattern, Elliott's Wave Principle, and Marechal's Long Term Forecast (carried further) — all projections of the future from varying bases — suggest just the opposite, and imply instead a rising trend in stock prices which will probably not culminate until late 1949 at the earliest and more likely 1950. There seems to be an almost similar agreement thereafter as to a serious decline reaching a nadir about 1952.

How valid this may appear five years hence is obviously conjectural, but it may well either discredit cyclical forecasting, or prove with Hamlet to the skeptics that "There are more things in heaven and earth, Horatio, than are dreamt of in your philosophy."

MEASURES OF PSYCHOLOGY

THEORY OF CONTRARY OPINION

THE theory of "Contrary Opinion" was originally discussed in the 1941 edition of this book in connection with the "Letters of Contrary Opinion" written and circulated informally to a limited group by Humphrey B. Neill. Mr. Neill has subsequently retired from an active financial career. On rare occasions, he discusses the stock market in his avocational column "The Ruminator" in the *Bellows Falls* (Vt.) *Times,* but the market "Letters of Contrary Opinion" are no longer written.

Importance of Mass Psychology

The premise of these letters, however, is often a practical aid to judgment, and likewise forms the basis of a more specific method developed by the author which will be described later on. The original "Letters of Contrary Opinion" merely sought to point out what prevalent market opinion might be and then investigated the reasons for believing that it was likely to be wrong. Indeed, it was assumed that any very widely held opinion would inevitably prove wrong, and there is considerable truth in that assumption as anyone familiar with the market knows.

Since Neill has had many years of market experience and is the author of *Tape Reading and Market Tactics,* in which he stressed the study of human nature and market philosophy, his letters of "Contrary Opinion" represented the further evolution in his thinking to a point where he came to regard mass psychology as the element of primary importance in market determination — a view shared by all successful speculators and investors.

Price is determined by average human opinion. If something changes opinion, there will be changes in price, regardless of whether the cause of the change was rational, irrational, political, economic, military, or even entirely obscure. It is of little importance — over the near term, at least — whether the change of mind turns out to be well-founded or not.

The price level of stocks is never what they are "worth" but what people *think* they are worth. Lord Keynes once gave an extremely apt definition of speculation as the process of forecasting the psychology of the market. The psychology which leads investors to pay, say, thirty times earnings for a stock under one set of conditions, and makes them refuse to buy the same shares at ten times earnings under another set of conditions, has always been the most important single factor in shaping market trends.

Seldom, however, has this been more forcibly demonstrated than between 1946 and 1948. In May of 1946, the Dow-Jones Industrial Average stood at 22.8 times the average per share earnings of the companies represented by its 30 stocks. In the spring of 1948, the comparable ratio was 9.5 (measured against 1947 earnings). Earnings were higher, but stock prices were lower.

Prices Made by Human Beings

Even the composite curve of business activity is fundamentally a curve of mass psychology which goes to even greater extremes in the stock market. There was never any statistical justification, for example, for the record high prices of 1929 or the lows of 1932. After all, "The Market" is not a mysterious entity in itself, rising and falling alone. Its price fluctuations result from the actions of a great many human beings, motivated in buying and selling by their own personal knowledge, emotions, and opinions. If it was known just how the public would react to any given market situation, how professional traders would behave, what investment trusts would do, etc., "beating the market" would be comparatively easy.

As a matter of fact, all so-called technical study is really directed at discovering this very thing, only it is usually called "determining supply and demand". But just as financial commentators talk about "The Market" doing something or other, so does the technical field obscure the real issue with its jargon of resistance levels, triangles, oscillators, etc. Actually, it is just an attempt to analyze the changes that are taking place in the activities of the thousands of individuals whose collective action makes all the price movements of the market.

All other things being equal, a good psychologist should come out better than an economist, in trading activities at least, by applying his training to the determination of the probable reactions of other groups. That is undoubtedly the conscious or unconscious basis of all who have achieved outstanding success as individual market operators. Bernard Baruch has remarked that he frequently rereads Mackay's *Memoirs of Extraordinary Popular Delusions and the Madness of Crowds,* and Gustave LeBon's classic study of the popular mind, *The Crowd.*

Crossing the Crowd

Every successful speculator and every student of psychology knows that the mass of people are less intelligent than the few. It has been said that only 5% of the population think for themselves, 10% copy the 5%, and 85% believe what they read and hear, and do what they are told. The percentages may be inexact, but any politician of experience knows the truth of the general supposition.

Since there are many thousands interested in the stock market, it is reasonable to assume that they are a fairly representative cross-section of the public. Therefore, if the majority are less capable than the few in all things, this must hold true likewise with their market behavior. The implied idea of coppering the bets of the crowd is not a mere theory, because it is obviously just what successful investors or speculators do. As everyone knows, the public is most bullish around tops as in 1929, 1937, or 1946, and yet those are exactly the times when — to be successful — one must be selling.

In order that a few may be right, the many must be wrong.

Thomas F. Woodlock voiced this eternal truism some years ago when he said, "*The principles of successful stock speculation are based on the supposition that people will continue in the future to make the same mistakes that they have in the past*".

One individual, who both made and kept a large fortune, remarked that his success merely lay in doing what other people wanted him to do. When they clamored for buyers, he accommodated them by buying, and when they were anxious to buy stocks at high prices he agreeably permitted them to buy his.

Majority Lose in the End

It is, indeed, a law of the market place that the majority must be wrong and can make money (on paper) only while the trend of prices is upward. A moment's reflection will show that this must be so. Suppose everyone decided at once that it was time to sell stocks at the prevailing price level. In that case, there would be no one to buy. If one half should sell to the other half, then subsequent events must put more wealth into the hands of one group than the other. What actually happens is that more wealth gravitates into the hands of the few while the many have less.

Ask yourself how many people you know who have really made a net retained cash profit from original capital in the stock market over, say, the last twenty or even the last ten years. If you know of any, do you not know several times their number who have lost? Or, put the question to your broker who sees a good cross-section of accounts. Does it not follow that, if the majority lose, it is necessary to think and do the opposite of what your neighbors are thinking and doing over a period of time? Certainly, everyone seems to "make money" during a period of steadily rising prices, but, as far as the majority are concerned, the profits remain on paper and eventually turn into at least semipermanent losses.

The Profit Illusion

In fact, apparent profits are always necessarily an illusion for the great majority. When duPont, for example, sold at 227 in 1946, virtually all stockholders had a "profit", because that was the highest price in 17 years and had been barely exceeded (at 231) in 1929. The holder of 100 shares mentally figured the "worth" of duPont in his investment account at $22,700 on June 13, 1946, although to be realistic, the tax liability if sold should always be deducted from the apparent value in such appraisals. The investment trust holding 18,000 shares — as one of them both did and does — could figure the share of duPont in its "asset value" that day at over $4 million.

But such "value" was completely theoretical. Actually, only 100 shares changed hands at 227, and only 400 shares were traded during the whole day. The top price meant nothing more nor less than the fact that, at that particular moment, someone was willing to sell and someone else was willing to buy just 100 shares at a price of 227. In all, there are 11 million shares of duPont outstanding, and it is a rare day when the turnover reaches 1,000 shares. On some days, the stock is not traded at all. How many stockholders, then, could really cash in on their apparent profits? Purely as a practical matter, the trust holding 18,000 shares could not and cannot sell except, perhaps, in driblets over a long period of time and at widely varying prices. If it had tried to dump the holding regardless, when the price touched 227, it is a fair presumption that the market would have broken 50 points.

Or, let us suppose that a great number of people had recognized that 212.50 in the Dow-Jones Industrials was the top in 1946. How many could actually have sold their miscellaneous stocks at — or even anywhere near — that general level? The answer is only a tiny fraction — perhaps only 1 out of 1,000. If 10,000 people with 5,000 shares apiece wanted to sell, there would be 50 million shares offered for sale. If trading was 1 million shares a day, it would take two months to liquidate, assuming that enough buyers could be found who would be willing to take that much stock at the same price level.

The only money that investors can take out of the market at such a point is the same money that other investors are willing to put in at the same time and the same price. Or, look at amounts that are under unified control. Some of the largest investment trusts may be holding as much as 3 million shares of stock. The directors might decide that a certain price level represented the top of the market and that stocks should be sold. But, 3 million shares cannot be sold like 300 shares.

It is a mathematical impossibility for the majority to make *and keep* large profits in stocks. They may fondly watch their cake grow in bull markets, but they must not try to eat it too.

Price Changes and Total Values

This profit illusion may be illustrated another way. A stock selling at, say, 20 may decline to 17 with perhaps only 1,000 shares changing hands. And yet there may be 3 million shares outstanding "worth" — at 20 — $60 million, and at 17 only $51 million. In other words, $20,000 of cash (or selling) brought about a decrease in "value" of $9 million. The stockholders are poorer (on paper) by 450 times the amount of the actual cash dealings. In this way, ten stockholders out of 10,000 can make the other 9,990 suffer a "loss" of 15%.

To have "values" rise or fall on the Stock Exchange by, say, $10 billion, it is necessary to have only a diminutive fraction of that amount in dollars or in shares change hands. There is great naïvete in the newspaper headlines during panics which shriek "$5 Billion Lopped from Stock Values Yesterday". The "values" never existed, except on paper, for 99.9% of investors.

Of course, this works the other way around as well. In practice, a stock may sell at an unconscionably low figure, but this does not mean that any substantial amount could be bought at the apparent price.

Opinion Not Always Crystallized

Returning to the theory of "Contrary Opinion", however, it is clear that as a matter of practical application it cannot be consistently used at all times, which has always been the difficulty in trying to go opposite to the crowd. The "Crowd" may seem to be right for a time as, for example, in the late stages of a bull market. Secondly, it is necessary to be sure what the "Crowd" is really doing. Day in and day out, there is not likely to be any general opinion sufficiently crystallized to feel justified in taking the apparently opposite view. One large investment trust attempts to sound out sentiment scientifically by sending questionnaires to brokerage houses. Although this may give them a good composite of "Street" feeling, it is probably not a good cross-section of prevailing market opinion as a whole. (Perhaps a "Gallup Poll" would be the best solution.)

On the other hand, there are unquestionably junctures when a certain view of the probabilities is so universal that it can safely be crossed. It will probably be difficult for the reader to recall the investment moods which existed just before various examples of this sort in recent years, but it is instructive to trace their development.

The Unexplained Rise of 1938

One of the most remarkable advances occurred in June of 1938. In the late spring, "everyone" was convinced that prices would be lower during the summer. As always, this looked completely logical. According to the then very popular Dow Theory, the market was in a major bear trend which was only one year old, business was at a low ebb with no pickup likely before fall, and stocks were not particularly "cheap" on a statistical basis. It was impossible to make out anything like a convincing bullish argument. The market was dragging along on a succession of 300,000 share days, and the average person interested in stocks had given up all hope of a rise.

But suddenly on June 20, stocks were bid up sharply on more than three times the average trading volume of the preceding weeks and, in six days, had risen about 20 points in the Dow-Jones Industrial Average with volume rising to over 2,000,000 shares daily. Now, if there had been some news which could have been construed favorably to act as a stimulus to investors and speculators, the rise would be easy to understand. However, there was absolutely no such news at the time in question. Neither could the rise be subsequently explained on the theory of inside buying by those who knew of some forthcoming "favorable" event. Farther on, an explanation will be offered, but for now, it is desired only to emphasize the way in which the general and apparently logical expectation of lower prices proved to be entirely wrong.

Reactions to War

The reactions to war — prospective and actual — were an extremely marked example of "Contrary Opinion". Prior to the declaration of actual conflict in September, 1939, the market had habitually declined on "war scares" each time that Hitler moved into another country. But, when war came, the result was a sensational rise which germinated a belief in the public mind that intensification of the conflict later would stimulate a rise in stock prices. Had not American business reaped a bonanza from European war orders in 1914-1917? And, of course, the United States would never send an army to Europe again!

Then followed the months of "phony war", but it was still confidently expected that when the fronts became active, it would mean more war orders from abroad, and hence that the market would rise as soon as one side or the other made a move. When Hitler invaded Norway, however, it marked the last gasp of a very minor advance in stock prices.

The Fall of France

The news of the invasion of Holland came the next month early on the morning of May 10. At ten o'clock, the stock market opened higher with active trading as if about to fulfill the theory that real war meant more profits to American business. It was hardly a matter of minutes, however, before a plunge began that carried the Industrial Average down from 149 to 128 in four days. At the end of ten trading sessions, it had reached 111. Some may be inclined to argue that the success of Hitler's "blitzkrieg" against France at this time, took the market by surprise. That is partly true, perhaps, but the impact of the news nevertheless came upon a market that had been internally weakening for some time. It was weakening because the buying was weak — that is, the public was purchasing and, moreover, was purchasing on the basis of an unjustified assumption.

An Example from Elections

By the fall of that year, the war was temporarily at a stalemate. The "Battle of Britain" in the air had been won, the threat of invasion was over, and to a considerable extent, investment attention had turned to domestic affairs. In October (1940) the belief was widespread that if Willkie were elected, the market would have a substantial advance, while the re-election of President Roosevelt was assumed to have the opposite effect. Neill wrote one of his "Letters of Contrary Opinion" on this subject, naturally calling for just the contrary behavior.

No one can prove what might have happened if Willkie had won, although the chances are that Neill would have been right, because if Wall Street had expected a Republican victory (which it did *not*, the Street's betting odds remaining consistently on Roosevelt), stocks would have been bid up *before* the election and sold after "the news was out". The fact that the market advanced briefly but sharply after Roosevelt's re-election, when the reverse had been expected, is merely an informative example of contrary minor-swing fluctuations.

Discouragement of 1941-42

The year 1941 was devoid of crystallized sentiments and definite market expectations. The mood was more one of dull discouragement[1] than active pessimism, and even the blow of Pearl Harbor had little immediate effect on the market as compared with the fall of France a year and a half before. The chief consideration from a market standpoint in early 1942 was the extent to which wartime taxes would restrict corporate profits. The Dow-Jones Industrial Average, which had been 106 shortly after Pearl Harbor in December, 1941, continued to sag, reaching the famous low close of 92.92 on April 28, 1942, from which a bull market lasting over four years and rising nearly 120 points was to start.

The mood of most investors at this time can best be illustrated by quoting from a letter received by the author two days after that low point was reached:

---

[1] This was the period when the first edition of this book was published, and the author was asked why he should publish a book on profits "when there were no profits".

"As things are shaping up with the stock market, I have reached the conclusion that there is going to be no money made in war stocks, either as to dividends or increases in value. I feel the market is due for a further decline; all the war news is bad and I think the worst is yet to come as the summer progresses. With labor getting in the driver's seat and big business being kicked around and having little to say about the running of their business, it makes one think how much of individual business and private enterprise is going to survive the war in this country and whether common stocks are any good as investments."

Such a point of view was typical. Moreover, it seemed logical enough on the surface. What the writer of this letter — and thousands of others — overlooked was the fact that all their "bearish" arguments were well known to everyone and hence were already appraised or discounted by the existing price level of stocks. After all, if the majority had not entertained similar sentiments, the bottom at 92.92 would never have been reached. "Contrary Opinion" again. Few could visualize one of the most important uptrends of years getting under way at that point.

Prospective Peace

A year later, great skepticism still ruled (normally) despite the upward trend. Military victory was taken for granted, but prevailing thought was that the end of the war would be bearish on stock prices. The theory was that "reconversion" from war production back to peace production would produce so many strains and dislocations that industry would be in for a long period of chaos. Consequently, anything that seemed to herald a possible end to the conflict was the signal for a temporary decline.

One well-known financial analyst made several speeches

at the time to the effect that the stock market was all wrong in looking across to the "green hills of peace" and ignoring the valley of "reconversion" that lay in between. That prevalent opinion is likely to be wrong does not apply only to outside public sentiment. The popular ideas on Wall Street are likely to prove just as much mistaken.

Expert Opinion

For example, in connection with its painstaking study of the drastic price decline on September 3, 1946 — to jump ahead a little in time — the Securities and Exchange Commission examined the literature disseminated by 130 broker-dealers and 36 investment advisers during the week of August 26 to September 3. This period preceded the sharp drop of 26 points in the Dow-Jones Industrial Average from a level which was not touched again for nearly two years.

Following is part of the Commission's findings:

General Market — Attitude on Long-Term Outlook
Number of Letters and Wires

Bullish without qualification	260
Bullish, but uncertain on day to day market action	97
Cautious	74
Definitely bearish and/or advised selling at least part of holdings	20
Inconclusive	38
	489

In other words, only 4.1% of the professional comment and advice at this juncture was correctly bearish which may be regarded as a normal expectation rather than otherwise.

Invasion of Europe

Although getting ahead of the chronological story again, there was a curious similarity in the reactions to war and peace — both prospective and actual. In 1938 and early 1939, "war scares" drove prices down; actual war drove them up. In 1943-1944, "peace scares" put prices down; the final peace in 1945 sent them up.

In any event, although many expected an end to the rise when Italy dropped out of the war in 1943, the uptrend was soon resumed. In the first half of 1944, it was obvious that the invasion of Europe from Britain might come at any time. This news was to be bearish on stock prices, according to general opinion. Again, to quote from a letter received in April, 1944, will most forcefully recapture the prevailing sentiment of the period:

> "I contemplate investing ——— dollars in common stocks at the right time, but my idea is to sit on the side lines for the present. I feel that by being patient I can buy stocks at lower prices between now and the reconversion period — or between now and the end of the reconversion period. I am reasoning on the basis that if we have a cross-channel invasion at any time, it will be a success, and therefore the end of the war."

At the time this letter was written, the Dow-Jones Industrial Average stood at about 135. Despite the apparent public trepidations about the outlook, stock prices continued to rise. Obviously, then, there must have been less articulate, but stronger (in terms of buying power), elements who were willing to buy even at the additional cost of bidding up prices. When it was officially announced that the U. S. and British armies had hit the Normandy beaches on June 6, stock prices immediately rose further, reaching above 150 for a new bull market high. The "bearish" news had again boomeranged.

V-J Day and the Eight Million Unemployed

The final collapse of Germany had little effect since it had obviously been in the air for some time, and the country was still at war. It looked like another year, at least, before the Japs could be subdued in their own homeland. Hence, Japanese overtures for "conditional surrender" and the first atomic bomb on Hiroshima were greeted with some selling of stocks. The dreaded "reconversion period" was approaching, and investors in general would have agreed with the wildly erroneous forecast shortly to be made by Government economists that there would be eight million unemployed within six months.

Retail trade and the machine tool industry were believed to be particularly vulnerable. Notice how logical such a view appeared. The pressure for production at any cost would be over; therefore, the high wages and the overtime pay of war plants would disappear; hence, public purchasing power would diminish — or, if it did not actually diminish, the urge to spend would be curbed with a "return to normalcy" in the offing. It was difficult, if not impossible, to argue against this view at the time, but — reverting to "Contrary Opinion" — retail sales began to soar after V-J Day, and continued to do so for well over a year, thus astonishing the "logical" thinkers.

Likewise, the machine tool industry confounded the prophets who had previously said that it had "dug its own grave" for ten years by the outpouring of tools for war purposes. Instead, there was a tremendous influx of new orders from regular industry which regarded the war-born machines as obsolete and felt it was not worth waiting to hunt up the latter and go through the red tape of purchasing from the Government.

Almost regardless of industry classification, stock prices soared following the actual surrender of Japan. Forgotten or ignored were the problems of "reconversion", the postwar strikes, and the shortages of materials. The only thing that mattered was how much could industry earn with excess profits taxes out of the way, and when it really got squared away on filling the "pent-up demand" for the things people had so long gone without. In the midst of the company's worst strike in history with not a car rolling off the lines, the stock of General Motors reached its highest price in seventeen years. The postwar boom was on — good for two, three, four, or perhaps five years. How could stocks go down? Logically, it did not seem that they could, but "Contrary Opinion" had its day again.

Prosperity Falls Flat

Stock prices started down just as industry did really get going on the anticipated boom which was to result in record profits a year later. But the investor who bought U. S. Steel at 97 during the steel strike because of what he expected it would earn afterward, saw his holding sell at 62 in 1947 when the company was actually earning at the rate of over $15 per share.

Just as the Presidential election of 1940 mentioned earlier provided an informative minor example of "Contrary Opinion", so did the Congressional elections of November, 1946. It was a foregone conclusion, as anyone could discover from newspaper editorials and popular magazines, that there would be a substantial gain for the Republicans — a development which Wall Street and most investors regarded as essentially bullish. A considerable amount of stock, therefore, was purchased on the assumption that prices would rise afterward. It may merely be noted in passing that the Industrial Average dropped nearly six points on the day after the elections.

In the spring of 1947, gloom was rampant for no discernible or tangible reason. Business, earnings, and dividends were still on the upgrade, but it was widely assumed that the stock market break of 1946 — actually representing nothing more than payment for previous speculative excesses — had "forecast" a business recession which was merely delayed in its arrival.

Dire Forecasts Prove Unfounded

Stocks seemed to be undergoing persistent liquidation, and although the Dow-Jones Industrial Average hung by a hair above the low point touched the preceding fall, the majority of stocks went even lower than they had then. One widely-read market commentator concluded on May 21 — almost exactly the day of the lowest prices in 1947:

> "A world-wide economic crisis is slowly becoming worse, and economic distress leads to political upheaval. . . . It is not an accident that the attempt of the stock market to stage a recovery failed in April when it became apparent that the Moscow conference had failed. A greater downward movement will be required to discount the future outlook."

This is not quoted to disparage an individual opinion — which, indeed, seemed the only logical one under the circumstances — but to illustrate the apparent illogic of stock market behavior in doing the opposite of the generally expected. It is not, perhaps, too much to say that the adoption of a "Contrary Opinion" was the only thing that could have made one feel that the worst might be over at this particular point, as it actually proved to be. Two months later the Industrial Average had risen sharply to a new high for the year.

The following market comment, however, had appeared in Neill's newspaper column (mentioned at the beginning of this Section) on May 8, just a few days before the market low was established:

> "During this period of some two-and-a-half months (since February, 1947,) stock market sentiment has become blacker and far more bearish. The opinion has been widely held among 'forecasters' that stock prices were on the way down into new lows, far below those registered in the brief panic of last October.
>
> "That is to say, as stock prices have grudgingly given way, opinions have increased rapidly on the 'bear' side, until today there is no question in the Ruminator's mind but that the general opinion about the near-term future of the stock market is decidedly of one mind: Down.
>
> "Inasmuch as this writer never recalls a time when the opinions of both professional forecasters and the public have been right when they have been in agreement, this would appear to be another instance where it would be unwise to join mass opinion and expect immediate lower prices and a continuation of the bear market.
>
> "A good friend [1] of the Ruminator's has made it also a practice to check contrary opinions and we exchange 'findings' every now and then. A letter from him came to hand as this column was started and he confirms the comments written above. Indeed, he has had an opportunity to check a large number of 'advisory services' and reports that 'at least half' of the financial services are outright bearish, with a good many others at least 'bearishly inclined', and only one or two real 'bulls'.
>
> "Moreover, this analyst-friend of mine checks the actions

---

[1] The author.

of the public in the market by keeping track of 'odd lot transactions' which frequently reflect what 'the little fellow' is doing. In April, according to this analyst, the amount of 'odd lot short selling' was the highest for any point in the history of these figures except before the outbreak of war in 1939.

"Perhaps nothing is more indicative of 'weak selling' than when the public indulges in short selling. In consequence, the foregoing is significant from a contrary-opinion standpoint."

The result of this particular set of circumstances was that inside of two months the Dow-Jones Industrial Average had risen from its lowest point of 1947 to what proved to be its highest level for that year.

History Repeats Itself

By early 1948, however, prices had again receded to the low levels of May, 1947, and gloom was once more rampant — not only for business reasons, but also because of the "Russian jitters". Many people felt convinced that the country would be at war within a matter of months. Farm commodities were slumping, and one newspaper headline said in large letters — "Truman Fears Crash". Nevertheless, from the middle of February to the middle of March, the Dow-Jones Industrial Average hung around its lowest ebb of 1946-47, scarcely moving in more than a three-point range. On March 17, however, a sharp advance began which carried from about 165 to nearly 195 in about thirteen weeks. This not only represented the highest level seen in nearly two years, but also confirmed a "bull market" according to the Dow Theory.

In view of the case histories already cited, it will be evident that this development must have been quite unexpected by the majority. Following are some different advisory service comments appearing just before the advance, typical of those who depend primarily upon rationalization of the apparent surface facts, either as to events or market action. These are not exceptions to the rule, but accurately reflect general opinion at the time. The remaining few who changed to a correct position belonged for the most part to the school more deeply analyzing the character of the market as described in Section III. These comments — taken from different sources — were published during the ten days preceding the start of the advance.

"We suspect that the weight on the market . . . is composed of several depressants that do not allow much room for rally. The international situation is one. The inflation at home, which sucks funds out of the market, is another. The indications of a nearby period of business and commodity price deflation is a third. Over coming weeks, we expect these will combine to put stock prices down to lower levels."

"From the news standpoint, the market faces a critical period over the month or two ahead, based upon anticipated Russian pressure in various European areas as a countermove to the Marshall Plan. There is also evidence of a hesitant tone in general business."

"The rise of one average and the decline or lag of the other, is an indication of market weakness. . . . When business, earnings, and dividend payments are presumed to be good, the plotting of a line on low volume, such as is occurring now, instead of a slow zig-zag advance on expanding volume, is an indication of the absence of demand, and therefore is an unfavorable omen."

"We can see no bullish signs at the moment, nor have our formulae given any bullish hints. . . . No rally of any possible consequence seems imminent, and we are entitled to expect immediately lower prices."

It may be reiterated here that junctures like this one and the others described from 1938 on are not occurring every month. These represent the high lights of a ten-year period which means that the average occurrence was about once a year. During the greater part of the time, it is impossible to apply the theory of "Contrary Opinion", because the necessary circumstances do not exist. When they do, however, the validity of the theory has always been proved.

Professionals and the Public

Now, if it is true that stock prices are likely to move in the direction not generally expected at important junctures, the question arises — why? Only the buying and selling of human beings make price trends. When "everyone" seems to expect, let us say, a decline from the X level, but an advance occurs instead, it is obvious that not "everyone" acted upon that particular belief. Some others did just the opposite by buying all the stock offered — not only at the X level, but also on a rising scale.

Basically, all the individuals and groups who buy and sell in the market place may be thought of as divided into two broad opposing groups — "Professionals" and "The Public" — although that statement is greatly oversimplified and conjures up a picture of the "wolves of Wall Street" robbing the widows and orphans by running the market up and down. That, of course, is ridiculous. The major movements of the market are the result of economic conditions and cannot be manipulated. Neither is there any mysterious "They" — those invisible sages who the very simple-minded sometimes think consciously operate the market to suit themselves.

But there is such a thing as a professional element that — given the circumstances — does influence the market and generally does it by going contrary to the public. It is very seldom that the public is a dominant element in shaping the trend of stock prices.

An Explanation of 1938

On page 174, the sequence of developments in June of 1938 was outlined as an extremely marked example of the theory of "Contrary Opinion". To follow this through a little further, *who* did the buying which produced that remarkable advance? There was no "news" — then or later — to account for it. Certainly, it seems rather inconceivable that the public at large decides all at once that stocks should be bought on some particular day unless it has a definite stimulus in the form of some unexpected development which may be construed as "favorable".

The real explanation rather appears something like this. The "professional" element — or some nucleus of it — which necessarily has a tremendously keen sense of the market, realized that people in general had resigned themselves to "stagnation" of business and the market during the summer months. Therefore, the public was assumed to have sold all the stock it was going to, and to be prepared to await the lower prices considered probable — or at least a time nearer to fall — before doing any buying. Faced with that situation, the professionals could not sell because there would be nobody to buy from them in any appreciable volume.

What was more obvious and simple, then, than to cross the public by purchasing stocks which at first this skeptical group would willingly sell to them, but might later buy back at higher prices when convinced by the advance that things were not as bad as they had believed? After that? Well, the professionals would see. What they saw in June was simply a chance to make a profit — which is their business —

by buying a sold-out market. This explanation is not a pure hypothesis. It will be shown later in this Section that supporting evidence exists in the data now available on the trading of different groups.

Classes of Buyers and Sellers

It will naturally be asked — who are the professionals? The word should not be regarded as implying any unchanging and tightly knit group. There are many groups and individuals not known to each other. In fact, anyone whose market operations are profitable with reasonable consistency belongs to this element. Conversely, a New York Stock Exchange member is not necessarily a professional.

But unquestionably, there are certain groups whose judgment and influence are such that their operations are successful with reasonable consistency. Security trading is their business, and they *must* make a profit from it, or go out of business. It is not to be inferred that these groups work closely together or always in harmony. All may be intent upon making money, but if opportunity offers, any one group may profit at the expense of another. It is obvious, then, that "the public" — as the term is used here — merely means those whose poorer judgment causes them to lose more often than they profit in their market operations.

Those who account for the millions of shares turned over every week may be broken down as follows:

Group I — Investors, Institutions, Trusts, etc.

Group II — The "Public".

    1. Board-room sitters.

    2. Businessmen speculators, etc.; in fact, all amateurs trying to "beat the game".

    3. Uninformed self-styled "investors".

Group III — The "Professionals".

1. "Insiders" — important bankers, large corporation executives, etc.

2. Stock Exchange members, professional operators and, in fact, all intelligent and successful speculators.

3. Semi-professionals — astute men, more of the investor type who deal correctly with the major trends. (Much less active than the professionals of No. 2.)

Group I is not important because they act so seldom that they account for only a very small part of the stocks exchanged in one day's trading. The issue lies primarily between the professionals of Group III (largely the second sub-division) and the amateurs of Group II. The latter are merely the customers to whom the professional hopes to sell his merchandise. Every transaction represents a purchase *and* a sale, and as both sides can seldom be "right", the majority of transactions must be between the public on one hand and the professionals on the other. Thus, the total number of shares bought and sold by the public during any given time must about equal the amount dealt in by the professionals. Since the latter are greatly outnumbered by the public, this means that the average professional customarily deals in a much larger number of shares.

Facts Behind Contrary Opinion

The public pays the profits of the professionals, because in stock speculation nobody can make money in the end except at someone else's expense, whether that expense is direct or indirect. If A buys a stock at 40 and sells it to B at 20, only to buy it back from B at 40 again, B has obviously profited directly at A's expense. But, suppose A has bought at 10 and sells to B at 20 who then sells to C at 40 and C later sells the stock back to A at 10. In that case, A and B have profited at the expense of C. But, in addition, B has also profited at the expense of A, because A could have sold directly to C at 40. A sold wrongly and C bought wrongly. Only B was "right", although A made money.

Although the public does outnumber the professionals, the latter can usually exert more influence on the market because all their funds and energies are devoted to that purpose. Moreover, they possess ample working capital and so can stand taking losses as must occasionally happen. Or, in "testing" the market, they can afford to buy large blocks of stock to find out whether purchase is difficult or easy, thereby learning how the public feels in order that they may do the opposite.

That is the basic principle of professional operations — going contrary to the majority. From this it follows that the market will seldom do the obvious or take the course generally expected. In other words, this the reason that the theory of "Contrary Opinion" is usually found to work in practice. The point is that the professionals cannot make money by buying or selling at the same time as the public. It is not always the case, but ordinarily, they must anticipate public desire and meet it when it appears by taking the opposite side.

Characteristics of Public Reaction

The whole thing is based upon a few elementary observations in crowd psychology, boiling down to the fact that the public is usually "wrong". Thus, the public (1) is almost always bullish, (2) is little interested when markets are low and dull but becomes more so as they advance, (3) is attracted by market activity, (4) is more easily "shaken out" by inactivity than by reactions, (5) will buy on good news and sell on bad news, and (6) will absorb an amazing amount of stock on the decline following the culmination of an important advance.

It is commonly supposed that the public becomes more bullish as prices rise, which is only true in a very broad sense. "Interested" would be a better word than "bullish". Actually, the public reasons this way. If a stock rises from 30 to 50, the price is "too high" because it was 30 just a short time ago. But if it reacts to 40, then it is "cheap" because only recently it was selling at 50. And, the lower it goes, the "cheaper" it will be regarded, because the high point of 50 will persist as the standard of comparison for a long time. This basic behavior pattern has always been the foundation of the deliberate "manipulations" designed to "distribute" any particular stock. There is the classic reply of one early manipulator who was approached by a group owning a large quantity of some railroad stock and asked if he could get rid of their holdings at the market price (then around 80). "No, gentlemen," he said, "I cannot sell your stock now at 80, but — I can put the price up to 120, and then sell it for you at 100."

Psychology in Speculation

It is evident that if the professionals win, the public loses, and the reason the former win is not that they are cheating, but simply that they are playing a game they know. It should not be supposed that the public is *always* wrong and the professionals *always* right, although "right" and "wrong" are very elastic terms in the stock market since, as pointed out earlier, making a profit is not necessarily synonymous with being "right".

It has been remarked that a good psychologist might well

be a better speculator than an economist. He would, for instance, try to analyze the stimuli professionals receive and decide how they would act, either in response to certain prospective conditions or to the public's action. Public reaction is more simply analyzed in that, broadly speaking, the public will buy on good news and sell on bad news. And, as has been shown, the professional element, which is strong enough to exert more influence, will probably do just the opposite.

ODD LOT INDEXES

This method really belongs with the group determining the character of the market, but the Section is placed here because it should be read in conjunction with the immediately preceding discussion. The difficulty has been mentioned in connection with being "contrary" of ascertaining true public feeling merely by reading, listening, and generally sounding out opinion.

It is the author's contention, however, that changes in the market sentiment of the public — and also that of the professional traders — can often be measured with reasonable accuracy through the figures released by the Securities and Exchange Commission on odd lot trading and the operations of New York Stock Exchange members. These data are a fairly recent innovation and, for the first time in Stock Exchange history, have afforded definite information on the question of who is doing what.

Data Available Only for Recent Years

Odd lots are the less than 100 share units of stock traded which do not customarily appear on the tape. The data on each day's odd lot purchases and sales are consecutively available since March, 1936. Since June, 1937, information on the number of odd lot orders to buy and to sell has been given out. In June, 1939, odd lot short sales (both shares and orders) became available. At the same time, data were made public on all short sales and the short sales of New York Exchange members, in addition to the regular sales and purchases of the latter which had been published since the latter part of 1936.

It may be remarked here, however, that the data on the "member" transactions comes too late to be of much practical use, but, as will be shown, it is not as necessary as it might seem. Until September, 1940, the "member" figures were three weeks late, and there is still a lag although it is somewhat shorter. The time of the odd lot transaction releases has been cut down until the figures for one day are usually released through the Securities and Exchange Commission before the market close of the succeeding day.

Samples of Trading

There is every reason to believe that odd lot trading is ordinarily a fair sample of what the public is doing. In the first place, the odd lot transactions (less than 100 share units) consistently average about one-eighth or more of the total trading volume. This is slightly less than in the '30s and perhaps is one result of the many stock splits during the past five years. Thus, they represent nearly one-fourth of the public's dealings as that term is used here, since the latter obviously account for about one-half of total trading.

Similarly, New York Stock Exchange members account for a slightly larger proportion of the other half of professional operations. Quite naturally, the public and the professionals are ordinarily on opposite sides of the market, a fact rather easily proved by close analysis of odd lot trading as compared with that of members. That is why the time lag in the member figures is not particularly important. One can be reasonably certain that member trading will show just the opposite tendencies from those revealed by the odd lot data.

Rapidity of Turnover in Odd Lot Trades

Except under special circumstances, odd lot dealings largely represent speculative trading (or perhaps it should be called gambling). This is definitely indicated by the finding of the Brookings Institution that 80% to 95% of all odd lot trades were turned over within one month during the period of its study (1920-1938). Possibly, the subsequent provisions regarding taxes on capital gains have lowered the percentage, but it is doubtless still true that a large proportion of odd lot trading is for the "quick turn". A very heavy proportion of such trading is concentrated in 50 share units, such units being over 40% of the total.

It is also clear that , to a considerable extent, odd lot transactions represent the buying and selling of those with insufficient capital to deal habitually in 100 share units, since odd lot trading is more expensive because of the odd lot dealer's extra commission. If, in the course of a week, there is a marked preponderance of the number of shares purchased in odd lots over those sold, it is a reasonable inference that the public thinks stocks are cheap and vice versa. They may, incidentally, prove to be quite "right" in this respect, but there are other considerations that may make them "wrong".

Many Misapprehensions

Many have noted the obvious buying or selling by the odd lot public, but no great weight has been given to the odd lot balances because excellent buying points have developed when odd lot purchases exceeded sales, and there have been other times that the market was a sale when odd lot trading showed a selling balance. Therefore, the conclusion was reached that the public had been shown to be less wrong than this study contends it is and, hence, that the odd lot figures had little value as a forecast of market trends. In fact, some rather wild and, in some cases, totally erroneous statements have appeared in various financial publications.

There seems to be no subject concerning which there are so many general misapprehensions. For instance, a well-known financial columnist in New York remarked in connection with the State stock transfer tax, "The present rate bears most heavily on the trader in odd lots, those of less than 100 shares, mostly investment commitments, as distinct from speculative." Now, if there is one thing obvious about odd lot trading, it is that just the opposite is true as the Brookings Institution study clearly showed.

Here is part of a typical comment which was headed "Odd Lotters Not Always Wrong":

> "It may be that the average odd lot trader guesses wrong more often than right, but that he is wrong most of the time is far from true. In several of the wide swings of the last three years, in fact, odd lotters as a group seem to have an edge on those who trade in round lots. The odd lot faction bought 47,588 shares on balance in the week of August 16, 1939, the week in which the lows were set immediately before the rally that marked the start of the war. . . . The record is, thus, neither good nor bad. The only point that it seems to establish is that to copper the odd lotters is to invite trouble."

Or, the exhaustive study of odd lot trading (for a purpose other than forecasting) by the Brookings Institution which was based on monthly data over an 18-year period taken directly from the dealer's books, says in part:

> "Public net sales are generally followed by price advances and public net purchases by price declines. This phenomenon has been observed frequently enough to give rise to a tradition that the public is always wrong, or is wrong so often that the movements of the odd lot balance furnish a serviceable forecaster of stock prices. In the writer's judgment, however, the correlations have little or no real forecasting value because a forecast based on the behavior of the odd lot public would be substantially the same as one based on the movements of the market itself. Thus, the tendency of the odd lot public to be wrong, if its trading results are tested by the price movements of the next few months, is largely accounted for by the tendency of prices to change in the same direction for several consecutive months, coupled with the propensity of the public to buy on breaks and sell on advances."

Overlooked Factors

Both of the foregoing comments are perfectly correct as far as they go, but they minimize one factor and entirely overlook two more important ones. The first point is that there is a normal buying excess representing the purchases by real "investors" of perhaps a few shares of American Telephone or duPont which they buy whenever they have the money — regardless of where the market is — to put away in strong boxes and with no intention of ever selling. The Institution has calculated that about 6% of all odd lot purchases are in this category. Therefore, it is obvious that a moderate excess of odd lot purchases over sales may actually represent some excess of selling as far as the public trading element is concerned.

And this element is by far the greater part of the whole.

The trading public is ordinarily most interested in this day, this week, and this month. It is far more concerned with market movements than with intrinsic values. Business prospects, earnings, and dividends mean little in comparison with a ten-point rally or decline, and it is in its largely futile attempts to "catch" these moves perfectly that the public is "wrong".

To go back, a second and more important factor usually missed on odd lot trading is that — because it is essentially a speculative "quick-turn" affair — its volume is always directly proportional to the total volume of trading. Therefore, it is not the number of shares bought or sold on balance that is important, but the proportions of buying or selling to each other.

Side of Market Not Important

Most important, however, is the fact that *the trend of sentiment as indicated by the odd lot balance of trading is more important than the side on which the balance lies.* Both of the comments quoted above drew their conclusions from whether a buying or selling balance actually existed prior to any given market movement, and disregarded entirely the significance of changes in the size of either balance. To illustrate, odd lot trading will be well on the buying side at the bottom of a drastic decline, but it will be proportionately less so than it was on the way down. The weekly balances never show a preponderance of selling around important bottoms, although on a few individual days there may be such a balance. Primarily, it is always just a matter of less buying. The converse is true with respect to odd lot selling on a top, although here there will be more times when an actual buying balance exists.

These conclusions were derived from a statistical usage

of the daily odd lot purchases and sales (available continuously since March, 1936) which will be described later. However, they are also borne out by the monthly data employed by the Brookings Institution which found that on the more important trends the odd lot public invariably bought on declines. Its action on advances was about equally divided between buying and selling.

Changes of Sentiment Almost Always Wrong

Thus, although the public is never "wrong" in the sense that it buys around every bottom, it is almost invariably wrong in that it buys proportionately less at the bottom than it did on the way down. Similarly, as an advance progresses toward its peak, selling may either become less or change to actual buying. A change of sentiment on the part of the public after any market trend has become well established is almost always just the opposite of what it should be.

Such changes are graphically shown by the line marked Balance Index in Figure 12 which is a ten-day moving average of the daily ratios (or percentages) of odd lot purchases to sales (shares sold divided by shares bought). Figure 12 is the original illustration of the "Odd Lot Indexes" from the 1941 edition, and shows their basic habits and tendencies just as well as would some more recent period. Indications have, however, tended to be less frequent in more recent years. Some of the special charts later on will indicate the specific application of the Indexes to market junctures which are fresher in mind.

Index Interpretation Not Simple

The reader may be warned at this point that the going for the next few pages will be heavy. This can hardly be

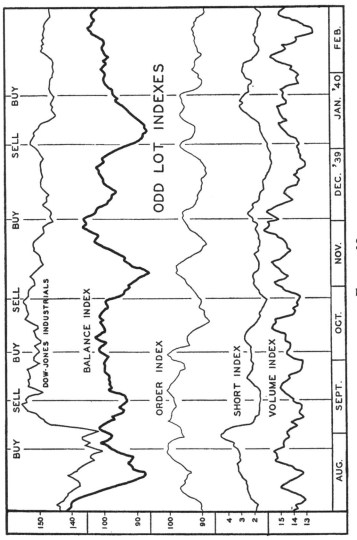

FIGURE 12

avoided, because the analysis of the trends in odd lot trading cannot — by its nature — be a simple matter. Once the underlying principle is grasped, however, it will be found simpler than it appears at first glance.

Source of Data

The data on odd lot trading for the preceding day first appear as a news release by the Securities and Exchange Commission on the Dow-Jones news-ticker (found in most brokers' offices) between about one and four in the afternoon. Figures for Friday and Saturday come out on the following Monday. They are reprinted in the *Wall Street Journal* and some New York newspapers of the succeeding day, usually in the following form:

Odd Lot Trading on N. Y. S. E.

		Customers' Orders to Buy		Customers' Orders to Sell		Short Sales	
		No. of Orders	Shares	No. of Orders	Shares	No. of Orders	Shares
Oct.	1*	1,928	50,136	2,670	56,853	24	780
Sept.	30*	2,082	37,187	2,635	65,589	39	1,299

* Preliminary figure.

This is followed by a summary of weekly figures, including the dollar values and odd lot dealers' daily transactions. These are not necessary for the purpose being described here. Other interesting ratios and indexes can be developed from them, but the point is that they do not add anything to the indications that may be derived earlier from the figures in the preceding table. Of course, in this routine table, data for two days are given in accordance with the customary procedure, but once the records are set up, only the figures for the latest day are necessary to keep up to date. It will be noticed that these are "preliminary" figures, but there is such a small variation between them and the "final" data which appear a week later that they are entirely satisfactory for showing the important trends.

Major Balance Index

The Balance Index in Figure 12 represents a moving average of the daily ratios of odd lot buying to selling. For example, using the data in the preceding tabular form, the ratio for October 1 is 1.134 (56,853 divided by 50,136) or, expressing sales as a percentage of purchases, 113.4. The Balance Index itself is a ten-day moving average of the ratios (see page 42 for construction of moving averages). Mathematically speaking, this procedure is not strictly accurate, but it is easier and shows the trends just as well as the more tedious method of deriving the Balance Index from ten-day totals of sales and purchases.

The number of orders could be used for the Balance Index just as logically as the number of shares, but the latter seem to show a clearer picture. This Index rises when odd lot trading either tends toward the selling side or the amount of selling increases. Purchases divided by sales would give just as useful an index, but the other relationship is used, because a tendency on the part of the odd lot public to become more bearish ordinarily means that the market should go up, and it is easier to think of a rising line as having bullish connotations.

The resultant figures, of course, fluctuate around 100, which represents perfect balance between buying and selling. They are plotted on the vertical line of the day representing the last item in the moving average. The daily central price (average of high and low) of the Dow-

Jones Industrial Average is shown on the chart for convenient comparison with the Balance Index, which is necessarily read in conjunction with the market's movements.

If the actual buying and selling balances were used instead of the ratio, the line would be too erratic to be of much use, but that ratio has a very logical basis in fact. As previously pointed out, there exists a very close relationship between the volume of odd lot trading and total round lot trading. This shows that — as is known from other investigations — a large proportion of odd lot trading is speculative in character and controlled by the same factors that determine the volume of round lot speculation.

Subsidiary Volume Index

There is a strong tendency for the volume of purchases and of sales in odd lots to go up and down together, the net balances of stock bought or sold by the odd lot public always being a small percentage of the total amount turned over during any period of time.

This tendency in itself yields another series of figures, or index, which is useful in confirming — or determining the relative importance of — trends in the Balance Index described above. The volume of odd lot trading *averages* about 12% and 13% of the total round lot volume, but naturally varies somewhat above and below that figure. On a monthly basis, the high has been about 21% and the low around 8%. It is ordinarily high around market bottoms and low near tops, whether applied to long-term trends or to short-term fluctuations.

Offhand, one would assume that it would be just the opposite on the presumption that the odd lot public's interest would be highest around tops and lowest around bottoms, but this is not the case. The explanation, however, is apparently a combination of two factors. First is the fact that the greater — and often mistaken — confidence which may be engendered by an advance leads the person who ordinarily trades in odd lots to go in for round lots of low-priced stocks, thus reducing the usual proportion of odd lot trading.

The second is that in market breaks, the ranks of the odd lot traders are temporarily swelled by the addition of the bargain-hunter class. This last would also explain why there is usually a preponderance of odd lot buying around bottoms. In any event, experience shows that a decline in the ratio of odd lot trading to total trading during a market advance is a bearish indication, and vice versa.

This ratio is obtained by adding together the odd lot purchases and sales for each day and dividing the result by twice the total reported daily volume of trading. The latter is doubled because it represents sales only and for every sale there must be an equal purchase, whereas the odd lot figures, of course, represent both. Doubling the volume is not absolutely necessary because the ratio would still be proportional, but it makes the resultant figures closer to the actual percentage of total trading constituted by the trading in odd lots.

To be entirely accurate on this percentage, the odd lot trading would be added to twice the total reported volume of sales before taking the percentage, but this would be largely of academic interest, and would only add an unnecessary operation in calculating the Indexes. Fluctuations in this ratio are represented by the line marked Volume Index in Figure 12, which is a five-day moving average of the daily ratios. Since the series of figures is less erratic than those used in the Balance Index, a shorter time element for the moving average can be used.

Short-Sales Index

A third useful index compiled from the data on odd lot trading shows the proportion of short selling in odd lots. (The figures on odd lot short sales did not become available until June, 1939.) If the odd lot public is likely to be wrong, then obviously the proportion of short sales made in relation to total sales should have valuable implications.

This ratio is obtained by dividing the number of shares sold short in odd lots each day by all odd lot sales. During the period in which these figures have been available, this has varied between nearly 8% and less than 1%. Placed on a five-day moving average, it is represented by the line marked Short Index in Figure 12. It is readily seen that the proportion of odd lot short sales very consistently tends to increase on declines and decrease on rallies.

Characteristics of Odd Lot Short Selling

The odd lot short seller is apparently a different breed of cat than the average member of the odd lot public, which is not surprising, since comparatively few members of the public understand short selling and even fewer are willing to put it into practice. However, he is even less "right" than the average odd lot trader, and the reactions of those willing to employ the short side more nearly conform to the supposed habits of the public than is indicated by the buying and selling share balances themselves.

It will be readily seen from Figure 12, for example, that odd lot short selling tends to reach its maximum around low points, and vice versa. This chart covers the first period after the short sale data became available which happens to include the outbreak of war in 1939. It will be seen that just before the sharp market uprush that marked the actual beginning of hostilities, odd lot short sellers were very confident of lower prices, and their sales were averaging around 5% of all odd lot sales. Conversely, just before the top of January, 1940, as shown in Figure 12, and when short sales would have proved profitable, virtually no short selling in odd lots was going on. The Index, in fact, showed that only about one-half of one percent of all odd lot sales were short transactions.

Figure 13 is even more striking in this respect. It shows the Short Index on a monthly basis from the date when the figures first became available through the end of 1947. Every time, for example, that odd lot short selling rose to an amount indicated by the 3 level (meaning that a three-month moving average of the ratios showed odd lot short selling to be running at 3% or more of all odd lot sales), the market rose sharply in defiance of the obvious expectations of the short sellers.

Contrariwise, it will be seen that when odd lot short sales receded to a negligible amount, the market was likely to decline. Notice how the Index steadily declined during the market advance of 1944 and 1945 until —when the top area was formed during the first half of 1946 — odd lot short sales were running at less than one-half of one percent of the total. The great majority of those who had been willing to sell short at lower levels had finally become convinced that the market could not go down — just at the point when it was due to do so.

Minor Order Index

Still a fourth (and last) useful index is obtained by using the figures for the number of orders placed to buy and sell odd lots. These (available since June, 1937) correspond roughly in proportion to the number of shares

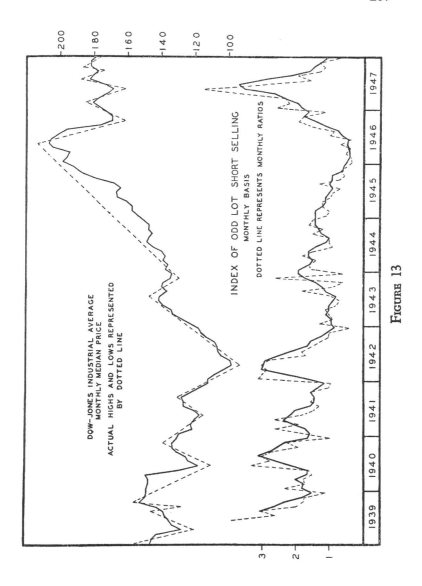

FIGURE 13

bought and sold in odd lots, but there is a consistent variation in the proportion.

The index of this variation is obtained by dividing the number of shares sold in odd lots by the number of orders to sell which, of course, gives the size of the average selling order. The size of the average buying order is similarly obtained. Then the ratio is taken by dividing the average sell order by the average buy order, and the Order Index shown in Figure 12 is a five-day moving average of this figure. As in the case of the Volume and Short Indexes, it will be seen that this Order Index also tends to rise on declines and fall on rallies. This simply means that around bottoms the number of shares in the average sell order tends to exceed the number of shares in the average buy order, and vice versa.

The explanation for this phenomenon is perfectly logical. A decline in stock prices brings about a certain amount of fear and caution among the odd lot public. Consequently, they are likely to be selling the lower priced speculative stocks (bought when they had greater confidence) and buying only in the higher priced and less volatile brackets. Since they will naturally have had more shares of the lower priced stocks, the average odd lot selling order is, therefore, likely to be for more shares than the average buy order, the latter reflecting the acquisition of fewer shares of higher priced stocks. Just the reverse, of course, is true on advances when public sentiment becomes emboldened.

Principles of Interpretation

The last three Indexes are ordinarily used in confirming the implications of the Balance Index. Use of moving averages for each line, or Index, smooths out the otherwise erratic fluctuations, thus making the actual trend easier to discern. At the same time, it eliminates the effect of any one day's possible misleading abnormality. Thus, if all four lines — the relation of all odd lot selling to buying (Balance Index); the relation of odd lot short sales to all odd lot sales (Short Index); the relation of the average sell order to the average buy order (Order Index); and the relation of the amount of odd lot trading to all trading (Volume Index) — show a rising trend *against any market decline,* it has bullish implications for the market, and vice versa. It is in this order that their importance should — as a rule — be rated.

When the Balance Index line, for instance, goes down while prices are rising, it means that the odd lot public is becoming more bullish on the advance than it has been previously. It makes no difference whether the Index declines because purchases are exceeding sales by a widening margin or whether sales are exceeding purchases by a narrowing margin. *It is the fact of the trend, and not the level at which it appears, that is important.* Such a picture is bearish on the market, since the change of sentiment thus portrayed is probably mistaken. Similarly, if the Short Index rises while the market is going down, it is a bullish indication because it means that the more prices fall, the more bearish odd lot short sellers are becoming, and they are also likely to be wrong.

It is important to recognize that uptrends and downtrends in the Indexes are significant *only* when they appear as diverging from the trend of stock prices. When they move parallel to the trend, it means that the odd lot public is exhibiting its normal reactions — that is, a tendency to sell on advances and buy on declines. Hence, there is no particular significance to the picture. When, however, this group becomes "abnormal" in its behavior (growing bullish after having been increasingly skeptical during the course of a market advance, or turning less confident after first following a decline with increasing purchases), the Indexes diverge from the market trend, indicating a change of sentiment which will almost invariably prove wrong.

Comparison with Member Trading

Now, if the whole hypothesis is correct, it is evident that the trends shown by the Balance Index should represent in reverse an index of the rise and fall of professional sentiment, since it is assumed that the professionals habitually copper the public. In fact, it is possible to see that this is the case, because the Securities and Exchange Commission also releases the buying and selling of N. Y. Stock Exchange members. In the same way that the odd lot traders are a fair sample of the public, so may the Stock Exchange members — who very consistently do between 15% and 20% of the total trading volume — be regarded as a fair sample of the professionals.

When a weekly "Balance Index" of member purchases and sales is constructed, it is found that with rare exceptions the trends are exactly opposite to those in a comparable "Balance Index" of odd lot trading. (In these Indexes, the weekly ratios are placed on a four-week moving average.) Such a study shows that members seem to have a natural predilection for the selling side of the market, but that is quite normal, since the public has a natural predilection for the buying side.

For the same reason, it is found that New York Stock Exchange members account for something like 70% of all short sales made, while the odd lot public does not average more than 5% or 6%. The proportion of buying to selling by the odd lot public has also reached far higher levels for given periods than have ever been attained by members. Likewise, members have reached much higher ratios of selling than can be found anywhere in the odd lot figures.

Apparently, some inkling of all this emerged from the Brookings' study of odd lot trading, because the parenthetical remark was made that "the odd lot public tends to be on the opposite side of the market from that element in the round lot market which dominates the price movement."

When it was remarked that the trends of member trading were opposite to those of odd lot trading, there was no implication that one side was necessarily buying and the other selling. It is exactly the same as described in connection with the trends of odd lot trading alone. For example, in the period of November-December, 1946, weekly odd lot trading changed from heavy buying at the beginning to almost an even balance between buying and selling by the year-end. During the same period, member trading changed from substantial selling to moderate buying. The trends were thus exactly opposite, despite the fact that odd lot trading remained consistently on one side of the market, while member trading happened to change sides.

Buying and Selling at Important Turns

As a rule, the side of the market is not important, although it does appear to have some confirming significance at certain junctures. Thus, in the bull market culminating in 1937, odd lot traders did not climb consistently on to the buying side until November, 1946, while at the same time, members apparently switched to selling and stayed there.

In the case of the 1946 top, the normal opposite tendencies appeared, but as far as the side of the market was concerned, members stayed in the selling zone where they had been all during 1945, while the odd lot public remained with its purchases exceeding sales. The diverse *trends*, however, were "according to Hoyle". For example, during the uncertain trend of July-August, 1945, centering around V-J Day, odd lot trading changed from heavy buying to an almost even balance between purchases and sales (weekly basis) while, at the same time, member trading went from substantial selling to a buying balance during the second week of August (which included V-J Day).

While prices rose sharply during the remainder of the year, odd lot buying and selling stayed in about the same proportions. In early 1946, however, when the Dow-Jones Industrial Average broke through its last major peak of nearly ten years before, odd lot buying began to increase, and shortly thereafter reached the highest proportion in several years. Member selling increased moderately at the same time.

After decreasing somewhat following the sharp reaction of February, 1946, odd lot buying grew consistently greater from April to the middle of July. At the same time, the proportion of member selling increased sharply, reaching a high-water mark of over 30 shares sold to 20 purchased in the week ended July 6. During this period, the Industrial Average was fluctuating between 200 and 212.50 — clearly shown since to have been a "distributive" area.

Public Habits

Of course, members and the odd lot public are merely samples of two larger groups, but it may nevertheless be said that no major bull market ever does end until the public is willing to buy a considerable amount of stock from the professional "merchants".

The spring of 1946 was the period when the public was responding eagerly to glowing estimates of potential corporate earnings. Thus, as usual, the bull market peak was reached on anticipations of the future. The anomaly in this case, however — and which made the top different from all its predecessors — was that the anticipations of business facts proved quite correct and did not represent the usual false hopes at such junctures. (See discussion on page 242 of Section VII.)

Study of the trends of odd lot trading shows that the public's habits are not just what they are usually supposed to be. The general belief is that the public becomes progressively more bullish as prices rise and does most of its buying at the top, only to end up so discouraged by the ensuing decline as to sell out at the bottom. There have always been two schools of thought in Wall Street about the perspicacity of the public. One, which might be called that of the "lamb and wolf", holds that the small investor or speculator is always wrong, and that if he is buying, it is a danger signal. The other school is represented by those who have observed that in panics many small investors are buying stocks being dumped on the market.

Skepticism of New Trends

Actually, both are right, or at least partly right. It is a danger sign when the "little fellow" gets around to buying after a long rise, but not when "he" — or at least some of his confreres — also buys at the later bottom. Broadly speaking, what happens is that the public is skeptical of any major bull market rise for a long time and is inclined to sell or to buy less as it progresses. As the end of the move approaches, however, the public finally becomes convinced of its lasting qualities, and begins to buy confidently and in greater proportion. Then, when prices soon after embark upon the downgrade, the buying increases for some time, although when the final bottom is reached, the purchasing is proportionately *less* than it was on the way down.

In other words, people are slow to believe that any important trend — once started — will continue for long and expect it to change, buying or selling accordingly. Their minds have been conditioned by what has gone before. Once the duration of the new trend has convinced them differently, however, they are just as slow to change back after the trend has really reversed itself. This is why they do not buy heavily until near the end of a bull market and then proceed to buy even more in the earlier phase of a bear market. However, this does not work exactly in reverse, because they never actually swing over to the selling side at the end of a bear market. It is then simply a matter of less buying.

This is confirmed, incidentally, by the stockholder lists of large corporations. There is a definite tendency for the number of stockholders to increase in a falling market, and decrease in the next rising phase. Thus, the small investor buys too soon and sells too soon, even though his inclination is to buy on weakness and sell on strength. Although right in this general principle, its ill-timed application makes him wrong in practice.

Monthly Data Since 1920

The monthly odd lot data since 1920 show the tendencies described above very clearly. These are obtained for the period since 1936 by adding the daily figures. Prior to that year, the only information is contained in the Brookings Institution study which has monthly totals from 1920 on, and thus makes it possible to see the Balance Index on a monthly basis back that far. Because of space limitations, it is shown in Figure 14 covering only the 1937-1947 period.

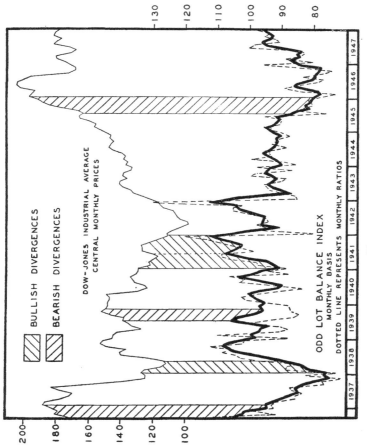

FIGURE 14

The Index is constructed in just the same way as that in Figure 12, except that the monthly totals of odd lot purchases and sales are used, and the ratios placed on a three-month moving average. The actual ratios are also indicated. It is always useful to plot such base figures as well as the moving averages, since they show why the latter move as they do, and any unusual distortion can readily be noted if primarily due to the figure dropped off rather than the current ratio.

Prior to the period shown in Figure 14, the same uniform behaviorism was shown in the data on odd lot trading. In the bear market of 1919-21, the odd lot public bought more and more heavily through February, 1921, until in that month the ratio of buying to selling was 3 to 2. By that time, the Dow-Jones Industrial Average had dropped to 70 from around 105 where it had been a year before when the odd lot buying was only slightly in excess of the selling. However, as prices continued to trend downward until the ultimate bottom in August, 1921, the odd lot buying diminished until its ratio to the selling was about 8 to 7. When the market then started its eight-year advance, the public began to sell, reaching a maximum of liquidation around the end of 1924, and continuing more or less in the same fashion until 1927.

The 1929 Top

It was not until early 1929 that real bullishness is apparent in the odd lot buying. This period, incidentally, was the "true" top, even though most averages show the peak in September of that year. The majority of stocks hit their highest prices between November, 1928, and April, 1929. During this period of "distribution" and up to September, there was no large general advance, although there was some spectacular isolated group or individual stock strength, covering the steady liquidation in the majority of issues.

The interesting point is the huge increase in odd lot buying when the collapse finally arrived. By November of 1929 — after prices had crashed 200 points — this buying was again in a 3 to 2 ratio to the selling. Recalling the tales of wiped-out margin accounts, etc., in those days, one wonders where the "little fellow" got the money. The answer probably lies in mortgages taken out on homes and similar loans in the conviction that stocks were on the bargain counter and that only thus could losses be recouped. It is also probable that not "everybody" had been in the market, and that many — even of the public — had been waiting for just such an "opportunity".

From 1931 to 1937

The odd lot public went along on this basis for some time, buying stocks heavily until the latter part of 1931. At this point the Balance Index began a steady rise, showing that the public had finally become somewhat frightened by the continued market decline and, even though prices were going lower, was only willing to buy less all the time. This is a prerequisite for the end of a bear market. It was thus evident somewhere along in the spring of 1932 that the long decline in prices was at, or near, its end. Such divergent action, with stock prices declining and the Balance Index rising, is obviously a bullish phase which indicates that stocks should be bought.

As would be expected, the 1933 advance was regarded as a chance to sell, and this trend continued for two years, odd lot liquidation reaching its maximum in mid-1935 when the public obviously could not imagine that the trend would be up for another two years. Figure 14 begins at the end of 1935, and it will be seen from this that, in the early part of 1937, the public was becoming more bullish on the final phase of price advance; i.e., the Balance Index was declining against a rising market. This is the first area marked "Bearish Divergence" in Figure 14. Although the declining Index was the fact of major importance, it was also significant that odd lot trading had actually swung over to the buying side below 100 on the Index scale, for the first time since the bull market had begun. In other words, the public was finally convinced that the market must continue to rise simply because "it had been doing so" for nearly two years.

Following what will now be recognized as the normal sequence, the public buying increased on the collapse of 1937, reaching the familiar 3 to 2 ratio by November of that year. In the first part of 1938, buying diminished as prices declined, and the divergent action of the Index and the market indicated a bullish phase, or probable end of the bear market.

Final Market Phases Indicated

It will be noticed that, for the most part, the monthly Balance Index tended to follow the trend of the market; i.e., the odd lot public was responding normally. The periods of marked divergence are relatively infrequent, and it should not be assumed that they provided "signals" as of particular dates. What they ordinarily do is to indicate when the final phase of bull markets and bear markets have arrived. Such phases ordinarily last for a matter of months. Consequently, a bearish or bullish picture in the Balance Index is usually premature in so far as the actual initiation of the new trend is concerned. It provides an important background, however, for the shorter term indications. If, for instance, the monthly Index has shown that stock prices are in the last phase of a bull market, much more weight will naturally be attached to a short-term selling indication in the daily Indexes. Under such circumstances, any possible short-term buying signal would be looked upon purely from a trading standpoint.

The bearish divergence in the latter part of 1939 may be plainly seen in Figure 14. For some time thereafter, no important divergent trends appeared because of the erratic character of the market. The odd lot public apparently just jumped back and forth from buying to selling in quick response to the news of the moment. But, at the end of May, 1941 — when the Average had declined from about 138 in the preceding November to around 115 — a definite bullish background was apparent, since increasing bearishness was evident rather than the normal disposition to regard a decline in prices as a "buying opportunity". (See "Supplement" as quoted from the 1941 edition.)

The 1941-42 Bottom

In other words, the first indication that the final phase of the long liquidating movement since 1936 was at hand appeared in May, 1941. By the year-end after Pearl Harbor, the picture was even more bullish. The price level at this time was only about five points lower in the Average (around 110) than it had been in May.

Purchases made on this assumption looked quite premature, since the actual low was not reached until April, 1942, at around 93. The Industrial Average, however, was just as deceptive as it usually is around the *major* tops and bottoms. Many important groups and individual stocks had already made their lows sometime in 1941. (See introduction to Supplement.)

Uptrend to 1946

In any event, even the Averages got under way in April, 1942, for a rise which was to continue for about four years. The first eight months of this 1942-1946 bull market were marked by normal increasing bearishness on the part of the odd lot public who could not believe that the rise would last. However, the extreme peak of selling reached in December of 1942 was undoubtedly the result of tax sales rather than representing a high-water mark in pessimistic psychology. Almost everyone had losses to take at that time, and the new wartime heavy income taxes made it unusually desirable to take advantage of them.

It might be asked whether the subsequent sharp decline in the Index during the first quarter of 1943 against a rising market would have been a bearish indication. The answer is "No", because the decline was both short in time and was distorted by the abnormal amount of tax selling in December and evident replacement purchases in January. The sharp fall in the Index for March clearly resulted from the dropping off of the high December figure in the moving average. It will be noticed that the actual monthly ratios in Figure 14 do not show a declining trend during the same period. As pointed out previously, this is the reason that the "why" of moving-average behavior should be considered — whether or not due to the figure dropped off.

Then, for over two years, until mid-1945, it will be seen that the Balance Index fluctuated within the same narrow range, thus affording no useful indications. The first decisive divergence between the Balance Index and the Industrial Average did not occur until the last part of 1945 when the Index dropped sharply against a rising price trend. This showed clearly that the final phase of the bull market had arrived. By November, 1945, the picture called for the realization that any short-term selling indication might well prove to be the last long-term chance to sell.

By January, 1946, the relationship of the Index to the trend of stock prices was even more bearish with a new low in the former and a new high in the Industrial Average. The last phase of the bull market thus indicated continued for several months, with the Average reaching a new high by a small margin in May. Nevertheless, the whole period did, indeed, prove to be the "final phase" as most clearly indicated earlier by the monthly Balance Index.

Index Behavior at Selling Climaxes

Exactly the same tendencies of the public that appear in the monthly odd lot figures with respect to the major market trends also show up in the shorter term moves. The timing here, however, can be much more exact. For example, just as a bear market bottom is marked by progressively smaller buying for several months while prices are still going down, so is an intermediate "selling climax" identified by the same tendency in terms of days instead of months. A "selling climax" is the bottom of a sharp decline which occurs with greatly accelerated volume of trading and wide breaks in prices, ordinarily followed by an equally sharp recovery. In general pattern, it may be called a "V" bottom as opposed to a rounded "U" base.

Figure 15 shows the typical behavior of the Odd Lot Balance Index during sharp declines ending with volume selling. From this, it will be observed that during the early and middle phases of such market reactions, the odd lot public regards the drop as a Heaven-sent opportunity to buy stock "cheaply" and increases its proportional purchasing as indicated by the decisive declines in the Index parallel with the market trend. This, of course, represents normal be-

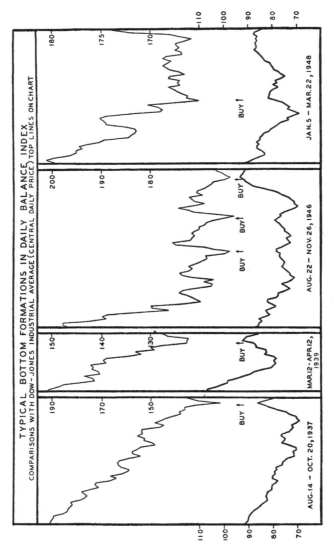

FIGURE 15

havior. Finally, however, the Index turns up as continued price weakness shakes this confidence, and proportionately less stock is purchased.

The Collapse of 1937

It is the pattern of divergence which indicates that the decline has about run its course. Notice also that the Balance Index has provided an excellent safeguard against buying too soon in such declines. This was true in the great collapse of 1937, as shown in the first panel of Figure 15. The complete extent of the drop was far beyond any reasonable expectations, but no divergence appeared until the final bottom.

The only semblance of an upturn in the Index (prior to the final bottom) occurred near the end of September, but it will be seen that this accompanied a temporary market rally. The odd lot public — following its normal procedure — had a tendency to sell this rally, but turned to heavy buying as soon as prices weakened again. Eventually, of course, they were sufficiently frightened to sell even on weakness (or rather, buy considerably less), thus producing a rise in the Index and a consequent buying indication. In this particular instance, it was primarily a matter of less buying, and there was only one day — the very bottom — when odd lot sales exceeded purchases.

A Textbook Illustration

The second panel in Figure 15, which shows the climactic bottom in the spring of 1939, is a perfect textbook illustration. Another reason for its inclusion, however, is to show that it is the trends of the Index which count, and not the buying or selling level at which they appear. It is just chance that the upturns in the first, third, and fourth panels all begin at about 70 for the Index.

In the 1939 instance, the upturn begins around 80, but it will be noticed that the preceding decline starts from a higher level (nearly 110) than in the other cases. Thus, during the brief period shown, odd lot trading went from the selling side to the buying side, while in the three other illustrations, it was on the buying side all the time (below 100). What these show is moderate buying at the market tops; then increasing buying during the greater part of the ensuing declines; and finally, a lessening of buying as the ultimate price bottoms are approached.

Recent Instances

The last two panels in Figure 15 are taken from more recent market history. Although quite typical cases, they nevertheless have some unusual aspects resulting from rather unusual market action. In the market drop of September-August, 1946, the Balance Index performed its usual function of avoiding premature buying indications, its upturn not coming until the first of the three almost identically placed bottoms was reached. When the second one arrived, the market looked almost surely headed for a further substantial decline, but the previous rise in the Index had correctly indicated that it was another stopping point. This picture was repeated a third time, although it may be noted that the more extensive upturn in the Index was not construed as being a stronger indication than the first two. The year-end was approaching, and there is little doubt that the beginning of the tax-selling period exaggerated the trend.

The "Buy" clearly indicated in February, 1948 (see fourth panel of Figure 15) after the preceding sharp decline was unusual, because the market rise indicated was delayed for about five weeks while prices moved sidewise in a very narrow range. Ordinarily, the market rebound after such patterns as this one is immediate. It may be recalled that there was a great deal of general uncertainty during this sidewise period with not a few convinced near its end that another market drop at hand. However, the Balance Index afforded some further confirmation of its previous "Buy" position by rising further during the latter part of the narrow market trading range; i.e., the odd lot public was growing skeptical and decreasing its buying.

Duration of Divergences

The question may properly be asked how long a divergence between the Balance Index and the market should last in order to provide a valid buying indication. The answer seems to be six to twelve days, depending upon the speed and decisiveness of the trends in both the market and the Index. For example, in the first, second, and fourth illustrations in Figure 15, it will be seen that prices were dropping sharply and the Index was rising steeply. Hence, six days of Index upturn were considered sufficient — a period of time which has been borne out in other similar climactic instances as April, 1936; March, 1938; June, 1940; and February, 1946. On the other hand, prior to the first bottom in the fall of 1946 (third panel in Figure 15), the Index was trending up only gradually, and a full twelve days was allowed. This would also be the case with more gradual market declines than those shown here for purposes of illustration.

Top Formations

A top is, of course, indicated by exactly opposite action, i.e., a downturn in the Index while the market is rising. Since even so-called buying climaxes are never as swift and sharp as selling climaxes, there are rarely as sharp reversals in the Index at such a time. The divergent trends are thus likely to last longer. Figure 16 shows some typical tops that have occurred.

The first — in November, 1936 — is quite unmistakable, the decline in the Index against a rise in the market being unusually sharp. It will be seen that, during the first part of the period shown, the odd lot public was normally selling the advance, but finally — and rather suddenly — became willing actually to buy (Index declining below 100), which was apparently the first time they had bought an advance during the whole bull market then approaching its end. Incidentally, the majority of issues made their tops around this time, despite the fact that the Dow-Jones Industrial Average did go a little higher the following March.

Two Sides of a Move

The March, 1939, top is such a perfect pattern of divergence in its later stages that little comment is needed. Notice that the formation shown happens to precede the second panel in Figure 15 of a typical bottom formation. Thus, in that total move, the Balance Index did a virtually perfect job on the top and bottom of a decline generally assumed to have been caused by Hitler's occupation of Czechoslovakia. No doubt that played an important part, but the point is that the impact of the news came upon a price structure weakened internally. It required a decline of about thirty points to restore technical strength as indicated by the Balance Index in Figure 15.

In the case of the preceding top shown in the second panel of Figure 16, it is interesting to notice that the decline in the Index was caused not by a swing to actual buying but by a tendency to sell less. In fact, this top period is

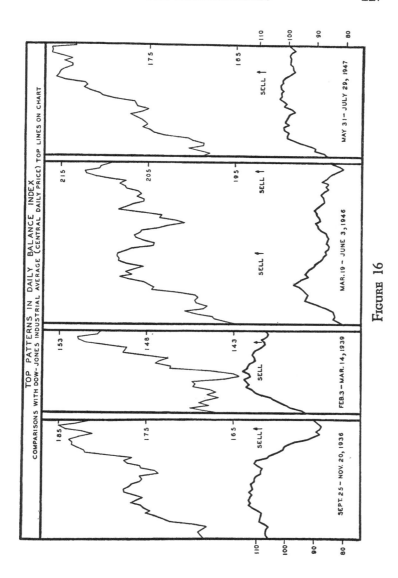

FIGURE 16

another excellent illustration of what has been emphasized earlier — that whether the odd lot public is buying or selling is far less important than its tendency to buy proportionately more (or less), or similarly to sell more (or less), as the case may be.

Repetition of Indications

As with the illustrations of bottom formations, the last two top patterns shown in Figure 16 are taken from more recent history. The third panel shows the final topping out of the Dow-Jones Industrial Average in May, 1946. The first "sell" occurred in April when the price level advanced to about 208, at which point the Balance Index had been declining steadily for twelve days. On the final advance to 212, another distinct divergence appeared. Although the level of the Balance Index is ordinarily of no importance, it did have a little significance in this particular case. Notice that the second decline or divergence from the market, occurred at a lower level than the first (from about 91 to 81 as against the earlier drop from around 97 to 86).

This phenomenon of two "Sell" signals in succession with the second at a slightly higher level than the first had occurred before in connection with major tops. The same sequence appeared in January-March, 1937, and again in July-August of the same year just before the final collapse, as described in more detail in the first edition of this book.

Characteristic Divergences

The fourth top shown in Figure 16 for July, 1947, is a little different, since the Index is simply flattened out rather than actually declining on the last part of the market advance. Translated, the odd lot public did not become more bullish to the extent of increasing its buying, but did not pursue its normal tendency to buy less.

Thus, the divergence is not as strongly marked as in the case of the other three tops shown. This has likewise happened on some other occasions, and is one reason for the use of the three subsidiary Indexes (Short, Order, and Volume), shown in Figure 12. Although the divergence between the Balance Index and the market in July, 1947, was not as decisive as it might have been, the simultaneous declining tendencies in the other three Indexes — particularly that of the odd lot short sales — left little doubt as to the proper course of action.

It was stated in the discussion of bottom formations that a divergence should last six to twelve days — depending on the speed of the movements involved — in order to afford a basis for action. The same time element, however, does not apply to tops for the reason that the speeds seldom reach comparable proportions. Ordinarily, the time element is never as short as six days, and the period of divergence should run ten to fifteen days with twelve the normal in the majority of instances.

There has been just one exception to this at the outbreak of war in September, 1939 (see Figure 12). The market advance was extraordinarily sharp and accompanied by almost an equally steep decline in the Balance Index, so that an eight-day divergence was taken as a sufficient duration. Also, notice in Figure 12 the typical bottom formation shown just prior to the advance with the Balance Index finally turning decisively up against a still falling market. This was another perfect job on both top and bottom as in March of that same war-year, shown in Figures 15 and 16.

Variable Factors

The principles of interpretation have been made clear in the foregoing discussion, but they are exactly that —

principles — and it is seldom that two cases are exactly alike. Use of the Odd Lot Indexes cannot — wisely, at least — be reduced to a formula for calculating signals mathematically. There are certain variables which must often be weighed in evaluating the picture.

For example, the influence of tax-selling is apparent in the amount of odd lot sales reported toward some year-ends, but this is not a constant from year to year. Figure 14 shows how important it was in 1941 and 1942, for example, but it is likewise clear that it was a negligible factor in 1945. The reason is obvious. Almost everyone had losses which could be taken at the low levels of 1941-1942, while at the high prices of December, 1945, the great majority of investors had paper profits. There is another seasonal tendency for the percentage of odd lot short sales to decrease during the last few weeks of the year — partly, perhaps, because total odd lot sales are somewhat swollen by tax selling.

Those are the most important variable factors, although one or two minor ones may also be mentioned. The Volume Index can be distorted when there is an unusual amount of activity in some very low-priced stock, or stocks. There have been times when nearly one-fourth of the total reported volume of sales for some one day has been accounted for by thousands of shares of some stock selling at a small fraction, but representing no more turnover of value than 200 shares of Allied Chemical or American Telephone. As also mentioned in connection with the monthly Balance Index, it may be important on occasion not to accept a moving-average Index on its face appearance, if a marked change which appears to have significance is caused by the figure dropped off rather than that added. Even in the daily Indexes, therefore, it is worth while to plot the daily ratios themselves as well as the moving average.

Limitations

If the Odd Lot Indexes showed every intermediate top and bottom as clearly as in the illustrations of Figures 15 and 16, and on many other occasions, they would be a practically perfect device for the identification of turning points. But, they are not perfect, and it is important to understand where the imperfection lies. Knowledge of the limitations is what makes it possible to avoid trouble on occasion. The imperfection lies in the fact that not *every* intermediate top or bottom is preceded by a divergence between the market trend and the Balance Index. The parallel course may continue throughout, thus producing not a wrong signal, but simply no signal at all. It can be said, however, that when such decisive divergences as those in Figures 15 and 16 have appeared, they have never been wrong in the sense that the market failed to reverse its trend in the indicated direction. In other words, the imperfection of the Indexes lies in occasional errors of omission rather than positive errors of commission.

It must also be realized that they are not going to show a definite picture each day, each week or each month. In order to have the decisive divergences which afford a valid basis for action, it is evident that the market as well as the Balance Index must move in definite intermediate trends. Between 1937 and 1942, it was customary for moves of 25 to 40 points (Dow-Jones Industrial Average) to occur in a matter of weeks.

On the other hand, during almost all of 1943 and 1944, the total price range hardly exceeded 20 points, and intermediate trends were of such a lackadaisical character and so ill-defined that comparisons with the likewise mildly changing Index were virtually valueless. There was simply nothing in the picture, and it was a period far more suited to the technical analysis of individual stocks than to the market as a whole. It can be seen from Figure 14 of the monthly Balance Index that, during this time, it remained within a relatively narrow range, and tended to follow such minor market fluctuations as did occur.

Prior Indications

Parallel trends between the Balance Index and the market may continue for long periods, in which case the last decisive indication of divergence remains in force unless definitely disproved. Suppose, for example, that prices decline as anticipated after sales have been made at an intermediate top. Later on, a recovery sets in which carries prices back to, or above, the point where sales had been — up to that point — correctly made. It would be evident then that the Indexes had failed to show a buying divergence where they should have done so, and a long position would have to be reinstated on that assumption.

Such instances are quite infrequent, but if the policy outlined is not followed, they could make trouble if the move following the missed point turned out to be substantial. One — and perhaps the only — case like this occurred in 1946. It will be noticed from Figure 16 that there was a second short-term sell divergence at almost exactly the final top around 212 in July. The price level then dropped as it should have to around 195, at which point a short-term buy was indicated by a rise in the Balance Index. This was likewise correct in the sense that prices rose for the next month to the 205 level.

Since this was the point from which the drop to 165 began, a selling divergence should have occurred to maintain a perfect record. The Index, however, just moved parallel to the market, so protection had to lie in abandoning the purchases made at 195 when prices returned to that level. The investor should have been doubly quick to take such action in view of the fact that the Monthly Balance Index had indicated several months before that the 1942-1946 bull market had reached its final phase.

Conclusions

As a rule, the Indexes have been more decisive in their indications of bottoms than they have been at tops. In fact, every important low point of a climactic nature since the beginning of 1936 has been correctly indicated by the type of formation shown in Figure 15, with the one exception of May, 1947. The daily Balance Index at that time continued to parallel the decline all the way to the bottom, which meant that in this case the odd lot public correctly did its heaviest buying at or close to the low point.

However, even though the orthodox pattern did not appear in this particular Index, the Indexes as a whole showed a very strong picture. The three subsidiary Indexes were rising, particularly that derived from odd lot short sales. Moreover, as shown in Figure 13, the monthly Short Index had reached a height touched on only three previous occasions (all followed by substantial advances) and was clearly going to be even higher for the current month. Here again is an illustration of the fact that interpretation in the light of the current circumstances is necessary, and that no rigid formula can be applied to every situation.

Although there are a few instances such as those previously described to mar the record, it can be set down as a truism that no perfect approach ever will be developed. And the Odd Lot Indexes do have some very definite values. On the record, one is that during the course of violent and straightway declines (such as 1937), they have always prevented premature buying, and have come very close later to indicating the exact bottom. It is a virtue of any method if it characteristically can buy on weakness and sell on strength, rather than after the new trend has started.

The monthly Balance Index has been excellent in showing when the market was entering upon final bull or bear market phases. No decisive divergence has ever proved wrong as far as a temporary reversal of trend was concerned. Stress has been laid throughout on the word "decisive", because it may be a temptation at times to read into the picture something that may not be there, either as a result of "wishful thinking" or the desire to "do something". It will pay to wait until a clear picture develops when there can be little doubt as to the action indicated.

Heretofore, there has been no regularly published interpretation of the "Odd Lot Indexes", but it is presently planned to make such information available within the near future. (See page 300 under *References.*)

SOME CONCLUSIONS

MARKET TIMING VS. STOCK SELECTION

THE trail of forecasting price trends has been well blazed since the early crude attempts, and it is safe to say that no possible avenue of approach has been neglected. Unless the result of new information becoming available as in the case of the author's "Odd Lot Indexes", no really original methods are likely to appear. Most of those, which appear at first glance to be new, turn out to be merely variants of some method described here. The ideas that are actually new somehow do not seem to meet the application of tests for practicality.

In fact, the forecasting "cycle" is apparently just about complete. From having nothing to speak of fifty years ago, there is now almost everything. Yet, although there never will be a perfect method, the cycle is also complete in another sense. There are schools of investment thought today which hold that it is impossible to forecast market movements with even a reasonable degree of accuracy.

Three alternative solutions are, therefore, offered. One — and the most extreme in its abnegation of any sort of forecasting — is the use of a formula plan (see Section IV) which is nevertheless still within the broad "technical field". The other two stem from the "fundamentalists" who feel that the ultimate answer must be in the study of "values" —

235

in the prospects of industries and of companies, trusting that always there must be a good investment somewhere. This point of view appeals more to the layman than does the timing approach. The average investor likes to keep his money "working" for as large a return as possible, and ordinarily abhors what he feels is the futility of holding cash or the equivalent (such as high-grade, short-term bonds). What he fails to realize is that, in a period of declining stock prices, cash which is allocated to common stocks is actually an appreciating asset. If an investor sells a stock at 100, holds the proceeds of the sale until the price reaches 50, and then reinvests in the same issue, his money has doubled in terms of that stock since he can buy with the same amount of dollars twice as many shares as he sold.

The Right Industries

It has been pointed out that if the right industries could be selected, it would be possible always to be invested in common stocks which were in a rising price trend. Even in the devastating bear market of 1929-1932, gold stocks were an exception to the rule of declining prices. All other things being equal, a business depression benefits gold producers because the full production can be sold at a fixed price, while costs go down. Thus, the investor would have enjoyed a constantly increasing value who had bought steels in 1915, switched into merchandising stocks in 1918, oils in 1919, rails in 1920, utilities in 1922, electrical equipments in 1926, gold shares in 1929, liquor shares in 1932, silver shares in 1933, automobiles in 1935, aircrafts in 1938-1939, railroads in 1941, amusements in 1945, oils in 1946, and no doubt *something* in 1948.

Using hindsight, it is easy to see what could have been done in this respect. In practice, it obviously involves putting all investment eggs in one basket. Few would dare to go to this extreme. Secondly, it involves a tremendous amount of one sort of "forecast" — in fact, a far more difficult type of forecast than is ordinarily the case with "timing". To buy gold stocks in 1929, for example, the investor would have had to foresee a long business depression of considerable severity. At the other extreme, he might have sold on the basis of the Dow Theory or some other trend method, content merely to wait until the trend itself proved to have changed and without any attempt to foresee exactly what might happen.

Growth Stocks

The third approach which eliminates timing attempts to solve the problem by confining all purchases to "growth stocks" on the comfortable theory that, whatever happens to them temporarily in declining markets, they will always go ahead to new highs afterward. Growth stocks are the equities of companies whose earnings have demonstrated underlying long-term growth and give indications of continued secular growth in the future.

As a group, chemicals have been the most outstanding example of "growth stocks" within the last two decades. The 1929 investor in Monsanto Chemical at its high (equivalent for the present stock) of 13½, for example, suffered during the next three years when the price dropped to 2¼, but he saw it recover to his cost in 1933, reach new highs at 36 and 40 in 1937 and 1940, drop again to 22 in 1942, and hit a new all-time high at 64 in 1946-1947. Basically, this reflected a long-term expansion in sales and earnings, due to the exploitation of new discoveries and products by an exceptionally able management. Conversely, the stocks of older and more mature companies like U. S.

Steel, American Telephone, and General Electric have never since come anywhere near their 1929 highs.

There are obvious advantages in the theory of growth stock investment, but there are still many risks in that some unforeseen element may change the growth factor, or so great a premium may be paid for it that the anticipated new highs do not materialize, to say nothing of the fact that a severe business depression and bear market would — temporarily at least — make the picture look extremely sick.

Like Monsanto, the outstanding "growth stocks" of the last twenty years sold at higher prices in 1937 than in 1929 and at higher prices in 1946 than in 1937, but how many could have been initially selected? Few investors had ever heard of Monsanto in 1929, and if they believed in the long-term future of the chemical industry would have been much more likely to have selected duPont which — although it has been a much better than average holding — has never quite recovered to its 1929 high. As an individual organization, it was simply farther along the road to maturity at that time.

The point is that "growth stocks" are seldom outstandingly attractive by the time their growth qualities are widely recognized. This may conceivably be true of the chemicals today. The potentialities of the industry have been so widely touted for several years that the investor at present price levels for the stocks of the leading companies is already paying a considerable premium for those potentialities. Stocks of even the most promising companies frequently sell at levels which only the remote future can justify, and at times discount even the future beyond the point of ultimate realization. Price-to-earnings ratios of 20 or 25 for some chemical stocks are, in effect, already discounting a doubling of earnings at the potential peak that may or may not materialize. Even if it does, the stocks would not necessarily be worth then more than they are selling for now, since the attainment of earnings maturity would not justify the same high price-to-earnings ratios that now exist. Hence, to invest most successfully in growth companies, one must recognize them for what they are — or will be — well ahead of the crowd and thus buy only at a reasonable price.

None of the foregoing comments is intended to disparage the "growth stock" approach. It is a more practical solution than the attempt always to be in the exceptional industry group. On the other hand, as a long-term program, it is a difficult one for the individual investor or even the professional analyst because it is likely to require the most intimate and continuous knowledge of companies and managements as well as industry prospects. The individual probably has a better chance with "timing", because the assumption is not justified that growth stock investment is the best answer on the ground that "forecasting" is impossible. Granting that mistakes will inevitably be made in dealing with the price swings, it is certainly questionable whether there is not just as much room for error in attempting to pick growth stocks at the right time and price.

Limitations of Forecasting

However, the school of thought which assumes that there is no dependable way to forecast the stock market is quite right if "forecast" is taken to mean the ability to predict the beginning, the duration, and the extent of price swings — either major or intermediate — with anything like close accuracy. Even cyclical forecasting does not attempt to go quite that far. Nor, for that matter, do "forecasts" in far more tangible fields. A mining engineer called in to examine a given property usually classifies his findings as proved ore (in sight) probable ore and possible ore. Doctors are constantly pressed by their patients to be definite about things that cannot be definitely predicted — the duration of a disease or expectancy of life. If the doctor is honest, he must say that he does not know — that there are conditions, psychological and physical, which cannot be foretold. Yet, even though he cannot be completely definite, neither the engineer nor the doctor completely eschews "forecasting". Indeed, anyone of either profession who disclaimed any ability whatsoever to make forecasts would be viewed with some suspicion himself.

Moreover, it should be remembered that most of the methods described in this book are *dealing with* stock market fluctuations rather than forecasting them. To sell because the trend is down according to the tenets of some particular trend method is not "forecasting" that prices will go lower for some specific reason. It merely assumes that they will do so until proven otherwise in the full knowledge that the assumption may be proven wrong. Similarly, a character-of-the-market method will indicate that prices are at a turning point or in an area of trend change without in any way suggesting what the extent and duration of the new trend may be.

Advantage of a Method

Regardless of actual "forecasting" ability, the logic and record of some of the methods described definitely show that it is not impossible to deal with price fluctuations so as to have even more than a reasonable assurance of profits just so long as the market does not go completely dead for years on end. The real difficulty is that human nature being what it is, investors are inclined to expect the impossible from "forecasting" (and forecasters) and lack the patience required to follow consistently any of the surer methods outlined here.

Or, they always feel that *this time* something new and unexpected has happened, and hence that they are justified in ignoring the rules and doing what their own or someone else's "judgment" (in reality, usually emotion) tells them to do. One of the greatest single causes of loss is the proneness to take important action on the basis of transient news of the day or trivial market indications.

The average person is his own worst enemy in the stock market because he is too easily swayed by hope, fear, or greed based on insecure grounds. Perhaps the strongest argument for almost any logical system is that once the decision is made to stick to it, 90% of the worry and strain to which most people subject themselves is eliminated. Long worrying declines occurring without apparent reason until near the bottom are avoided, and one is not driven to wonder what effect this or that piece of news will have on the market. There are many other advantages. And, if the system is not perfect, the chances are a hundred to one that its timing of purchases and sales will be infinitely superior in the long run to those chosen because "the Republicans have a good chance", "taxes are going to be raised", "the market looked strong last week", et cetera, et cetera.

As a matter of fact, it is possible at almost any given time to make up a list of fifteen or twenty apparently cogent bullish factors and equally as many bearish points. Either list alone will look like a good case for the side taken. Unconsciously, the average investor concentrates upon the few that come within his own sphere of experience, and rationalizes his position from them. Often, they conflict and the result is confusion. That is where use of some definite technical method eliminates indecision and all the brain-addling that goes on in attempting to determine the side on which the balance lies.

Technical Approach Often the Only Answer

Even the fundamentalists who decry "technical market timing" say that purchases should only be made when the general price level is low and then sold when the level is high "as judged by objective standards" — something that is likely to result in very poor timing indeed. How high is high? Stocks seemed irrationally "high" in 1927 to experienced investors, but during the next two years they went much higher. Similarly, they seemed "low" in 1931, but they soon after sold at one-third their average price of that year.

There have been frequent occasions when technical analysis was the *only* thing that could possibly have given the correct answer to the future trend of the market. This was true, for example, in the spring of 1946. If any investor had then possessed a crystal ball which would have shown him what corporate earnings were to be a year later, he could only have concluded that stock prices would be considerably higher. Instead, they were substantially lower in the face of record earnings and dividends.

There was nothing in the "fundamentals" — either in 1946 or 1947 — to explain why prices had collapsed in the meantime. But, there was considerable evidence of a weak *technical* situation in the market beforehand as described in Sections III and VI. It did not seem to make sense, but it was there. The investor who acted on technical grounds did not need to concern himself with *why* the market should seem to be acting irrationally, whereas the analyst of business facts and probabilities — unable to find a "reason" —

was forced to conclude that the market could not do what it actually did.

An Example in Railroads

In early May, 1946, a well-known financial editor asked five specialists in railroad securities to tell him where they thought the Dow-Jones Railroad Average — then around 63 — would be in three months, six months, and twelve months. The independent answers of all five were surprisingly close for each period of time, but the average level predicted compared as follows with the facts.

	Average Predicted Level	Actual Level
After three months	65.4	62
After six months	83.4	50
After twelve months	106.0	43

Thus, for the prediction covering one year, there was actually a decline of nearly 32% as against an anticipated gain of more than 68%. Now, the point is that the analysts polled were not amateurs carried away by bullish enthusiasm. Their forecasts were based on sober, expert appraisal of what railroad earning power would be, and in this respect, they were entirely correct.

But, to predict a market level involves another type of forecast. It is necessary not only to estimate future earnings correctly, but in addition to form an opinion as to how those earnings will be appraised by future buyers and sellers. In other words, will investment psychology be pessimistic or optimistic? The particular group involved here not un-naturally assumed that railroad stocks would continue to sell in the same relationship to earnings that prevailed at the time they were making their calculations. For that reason only, their forecast of market prices proved to be entirely wrong.

Price-to-Earnings Ratios and Psychology

In a broad sense, the experience of the past ten years has very clearly demonstrated that the price-to-earnings ratio is a much more important factor than the actual level and/or trend of earnings themselves. Since the ratio is determined by investment psychology, the study of technical market action has, on the whole, been more fruitful than fundamental analysis. As in the case of the railroad analysts, it was quite possible to be perfectly correct in estimating future earnings, but entirely wrong on the level of stock prices at the same time.

From 1938 to 1948, earnings and stock prices pursued different courses. The reasons for the diverse trends are quite understandable, but it should nevertheless have been an illuminating experience for the businessman investor accustomed to an orthodox relationship.

Corporate profits were at their lowest ebb in 1938 when the Dow-Jones Industrial Average rose to nearly 160 — a level not seen again until 1945. Profits more than doubled, however, from 1938 through 1941 in reflection of war and "defense" orders, but because of the war background, stock prices pursued a downward course. Excess profits taxes and — later — strikes and material shortages brought about a generally declining trend in earnings during the 1942-46 period, but stock prices rose in anticipation of the high postwar profits which actually materialized by 1947. Again conforming to contrary and apparently illogical behavior, however, the stock market dropped in 1946-47 as corporate earnings rose sharply. Investor psychology swung to the view that such earnings were just too good to last.

Hopes in "Uncle Joe"

There is one "security" which is the example *par excellence* of the fact that the waxing and waning of optimism and pessimism may be the most powerful force acting on security prices — a statement which in no way denies or belittles the long-term importance of value. With most securities, however, some reasonable excuse for assigning value or a potential value can be found. But, it does not appear reasonable to assume that the U.S.S.R. will ever make a settlement giving some actual value to the old Imperial Russian Government dollar bonds originally sold to investors in this country during 1916.

The Soviet Government years ago flatly washed its hands of all contracts made by the liquidated Czarist regime — and certainly with complete logic, considering its road to power and its anti-capitalistic principles. Neither has the Stalinist group ever given the slightest reason to assume that its original denial of such obligations might be modified.

The fact remains, however, that for many years, the price of the old Imperial Russian Government bonds has undergone tremendous (percentagewise) advances at times. Following are some extreme highs and lows of recent years as registered on the New York Curb Exchange where the bonds have unlisted trading privileges.

1929	19¼
1932	¾
1933	8½
1940	¼
1945	22
1947	2

In late 1945, investors talked wistfully of the 700% or 800% profits they might have made by purchasing Pepsi-Cola, Warner Brothers, etc., in 1940 at $4 or $5 per share, but would have found it difficult to believe anyone who told them they could have made far more (about 8,700%) in Imperial Russian Government bonds. It is not surprising that the latter may command a fractional market, since hope always springs eternal. Nevertheless, it is a cause for wonder that anyone has recently paid a price of 22, which means $220 cash for a theoretical face value of $1,000 printed on the certificate — worth only its area in wallpaper to the best of any reasonable belief.

If anything is calculated to inculcate faith in the hypothesis that some cosmic force affects man's emotional state, this seems to be it. Seriously, however, it is a striking example of the part which investor psychology — whatever its motivation — plays in determining the price level.

Reasoning and Technical Analysis

In the 1946 situation, the cleavage between the analysts and some technicians was unusually distinct, because the reasoning on both sides was apparent. As pointed out before, one group must always profit in the end at the expense of another. For someone to sell Schenley Distillers — to use that as an example — at the price of 100 in August, 1946, someone else had to be willing to pay what proved to be that inflated price. As Lord Keynes once put it, stock market dealings in practice are like the old game of musical chairs in which someone is certain to lose in the end, but meanwhile everyone has a good time. The art of "timing" is, therefore, an entirely selfish affair since the "right time" to have sold for one individual means that it was the wrong time for someone else to have bought.

The successful speculator using judgment alone obviously must outthink the other fellow, and the reasoning involved may be extraordinarily complex. Lord Keynes had another metaphor, in which he compared speculation to a contest in which the competitors had to pick the six prettiest faces from a hundred photographs, the prizewinner being the one whose choices corresponded most closely to the average preferences of all the competitors. He called this the "third degree" of reasoning where intelligence had to be applied to anticipating what average opinion expected average opinion to be, and added that in speculation, it might be necessary to carry such reasoning to the fourth, fifth, or even higher degrees.

The many who are motivated by such reasoning, by the impulses of the moment, or by the study of values, make the price fluctuations and trends, of which the follower of a technical method attempts to take advantage in one way or another. As the various sections of this book have made clear, his approach may be from any of several angles.

Qualifications of Various Methods

It would be difficult to say that one method is necessarily better than another. The "best" in one period may be relatively poor under a different set of circumstances, for the character of the price movement never remains the same indefinitely. Advances and declines are sometimes explosive, and then again, it will take months to accomplish the same change in the price level that occurred in days or weeks only a short time before.

Theoretically, "cyclical forecasting" would be the ideal method, but it lacks complete trustworthiness and anything like complete accuracy. Moreover, it would defeat itself if it were so accurate as to be universally accepted. Although there is evidence of some substance to the shadow, only the most rabid devotee of cycles would be willing to pin his market position 100% on the indicated cyclical pattern at any given time.

Next to such an impossible ideal, "character-of-the-market methods" (Sections III and VI) are certainly the most soul-satisfying. There is no pleasanter feeling for the individual — whether he calls himself an investor or a speculator — than to buy or sell and then see prices immediately move a substantial distance in the desired direction. That will happen occasionally, but no method in this category is so good as to have that always the case, nor is the market so obliging as always to move decisively. There is simply no such animal as the method that will infallibly pick all the tops and all the bottoms. Errors will occur, trends will reverse themselves quickly, and a good "batting average" still remains the only reasonable goal over a period of time, even though some approaches will often "click" almost perfectly in certain periods. The line formation of mid-February to mid-March, 1948, has been used as one example of the working of some character-of-the-market methods in earlier sections of this book. Despite the apparent uncertainty of the picture at that time, it will be recalled that the Lowry and the Mills price-volume measurements, Hood's Group Action, and the Odd Lot Indexes all clearly showed that the direction of the move out of the line should be up.

"Timing" according to such methods is best adapted to the individual because of the flexibility of policy ordinarily required. The large investment trusts, for example, do relatively little in this direction for several reasons. One is that the large blocks of stock necessarily used make it difficult or impossible to act quickly on the basis of a prevailing price, whereas that can be done when holdings range from perhaps only one hundred to several hundred shares. Moreover, stockholders of a trust are likely to look askance at a liquid position with little or no income, and the publicity attendant upon substantial selling might be harmful. Indeed, it is not difficult to imagine a Congressional Committee attempting to show after a break that some trust had "undermined" the market by selling all its holdings.

The general management investment trusts with the most successful long-term records seem to have accomplished it not by "timing", but either through their astuteness in picking "growth stocks", or by using a general "formula plan" policy. None — except one recently organized fund — have said specifically that they were using one particular such plan, but an analysis of their operations suggests that the principle, at least, has been applied. Even the best of the trusts, however, have fallen short of perfectly attainable marks which the individual could easily have reached in more ways than one.

PROBABILITIES AND PROGRAMS

The goal of each individual is not necessarily the same. The person who is trying primarily to build up capital will be interested in methods which have no appeal to anyone looking only for safety and a fair return on his money.

Choosing an Approach

It is not only a matter of the potentialities of the method or methods adopted, but also of what the individual is willing to put forth in the way of close attention, work, and a certain nervous strain. Obviously, to conduct operations on the basis of character-of-the-market methods offers the best profit potentialities, but the fact that there is room for error and that the "timing" will seldom be perfect, means that no relaxation is possible.

At the other extreme, if the investor feels that he will be satisfied with the modest results of a formula plan and makes up his mind that he will stick to it — which is, indeed, the primary requisite — he can sit back, knowing exactly what he will do under all circumstances that may arise. Because their *modus operandi* is slanted more, perhaps, towards the private investor than the institution, the individual stock plans described in Section IV seem to have considerable appeal for the average person, although adaptation of any good basic formula will doubtless afford satisfactory results.

Others will prefer a trend method (Section II) so that they may be sure of not being "caught" in any catastrophic decline of the 1929-1932 variety. Here again, however, as in the case of formula plans, the decision must be made initially to stick to the rules, or the whole purpose of the approach will be defeated. Simplicity of operation is one virtue of the trend methods to an even greater extent than with formula plans. It is important, however, that the user of trend methods understands what they will and will not do; that he elects to follow just one procedure; and that, if the market runs into a protracted sidewise period, he realizes that he will be "whipsawed" with only the consolation of knowing his position will be right when an important trend does develop. The "whipsawing" is the price which must be paid for such assurance.

To be completely logical, selling signals should be acted upon with short sales as well as liquidation of the previous long position. This is because an indication to sell has just as much chance of being right as one to buy, and losses are limited by the method itself if the price trend does reverse its anticipated direction. Also, only one trend approach should be used. It would not gain anything, for example, to employ both the Ten Percent Rule and Moment's Dow Theory Rules for the major trend on the assumption that if both have the same indication, its validity would be enhanced. The actual "forecasting" quality of such methods is nil, and two times nothing is nothing.

Because the character of the market for several years now has been poorly adapted to methods working on the basis of secondary trends (such as the "Semaphore" or "Technometer"), it seems best to apply trend methods only to the major direction of prices. The future may very well witness the type of fluctuations which made the secondary trend devices so profitable prior to 1938, although as explained on page 38, there are some grounds for believing that the change may be more or less permanent. Moment's rules on the major trend — essentially the Dow Theory (page 33 of Section II) — have a simplicity and definiteness which avoid one of the adverse criticisms usually leveled at the better-known Dow Theory expositions; i.e., conflicting interpretation. Moreover, they have stood up well over a period of time, and — in the class of methods determining and acting upon the major trend — deserve a high rating, despite the fact that they lack publicity.

Character-of-the-Market Methods Most Popular

There is doubtless more appeal to the majority of those interested in the stock market, however, in the character-of-the-market methods. Most people want to keep more of a finger on the market's pulse than the formula plans or major trend methods allow. In using such methods, the element of interpretation bulks much larger. In fact, whereas success under the other approaches depends upon following fixed rules implicitly, there can be a distinct danger in trying to reduce character-of-the-market methods to rigid formulas giving buying and selling "signals".

For example, it was shown in Section III that the indexes of daily advance and decline ratios tend to oscillate above and below the 40 mark, and that getting 20 points away on either side often indicates an intermediate top or bottom. This particular technical analysis could, therefore, be reduced to a "system" under which action would be indicated whenever both indexes moved more than 20 points away from 40. As a practical matter, this would sometimes be right and sometimes wrong. Certainly, a turning point should be *looked for* at any time that the natural limit areas are approached by the indexes, but there should be confirmatory evidence in other comparable character-of-the-market methods.

This illustrates another important difference between character-of-the-market methods and other broad classes. The fact that two trend methods both say to sell does not add to the validity of the indication. On the other hand, if two character-of-the-market methods both show a weak market position (or vice-versa), there would be a very definitely increased probability that the indication would be right. The reason is that both are inherently capable of showing the same picture at the same time, even though in practice they will not always coincide. However, suppose there has been a sharp fall in the market with heavily increased volume of trading. In other words, a possible "selling climax" is at hand.

If, in such a case, the Odd Lot Balance Index had turned up sharply for five or six days, the Advance and Decline Indexes were down twenty points or more from the center line, and the Lowry or the Mills Short-Term Indexes had reached their usual extremes of below 60 and over 100, respectively, it is not going too far to say that the chances for a substantial recovery would be 100 to 1.

Odds in Favor of Majority Indications

Purely on a mathematical basis, the odds in such a case — or even one that is less unanimous — are much greater than they appear on the surface. It is assumed that the character-of-the-market methods, on which the principal reliance may be placed, are of equal weight. That is, each is capable of showing the same picture at the same time, has a logical *raison d'être*, and has been found to be right the greater part of the time. If three such methods are simultaneously bullish and a fourth one bearish, it might appear that the odds were 3 to 1 in favor of buying. The actual odds are much greater, because each of the bullish indicators reinforces the other two, and each two reinforce the other one, etc. There is a theorem in mathematics by which the true odds in such instances may be worked out precisely. For the case just cited, they are 16 to 1 (not 3 to 1) if an 80% accuracy for each method is assumed. Similarly, if five methods of equal weight can be employed, and four of them give the same indication at the same time, then the odds are 66 to 1 in favor of that indication being right.

The illustration of three character-of-the-market methods all fulfilling certain requirements to indicate a selling climax after a sharp decline, is one of the rare instances when the facts might logically be reduced to a specific "formula". As a rule, however, each method should be used more on an interpretive basis, because of the variables involved. For example, in a year when prices have been declining, there will be more December tax-selling than in a period when prices have been rising. Such sales obviously can cause some distortions in price-volume data or odd lot trading, and hence must be weighed in evaluating the situation.

Neither should it ever be inferred that a picture in an index identical with some previous juncture means that the same market result will necessarily follow. The monthly Index of Odd Lot Short Selling reached as high a level in May of 1947 as it had five years before, but this could not be construed as meaning that the subsequent advance thus indicated would be of an extent and duration equal to that which occurred after 1942. It merely meant that the picture was equally strong from that particular technical standpoint and at that particular time. The strength indicated would be dissipated after the advance had run for a month or two, and from that point on, other forces would take over.

Combination of Methods

Although the three basic types of methods (trend, formula, and character-of-the-market) cannot be "mixed" in order to arrive at a forecast, it would be perfectly logical to use them all by segregating parts of a total investment fund. For example, a fund might be divided into thirds, one-third to be managed on the basis of Moment's major trend rules, one-third to be managed under an individual formula such as the New England Plan, and the other third according to the indications of the Odd Lot Indexes and/or any other character-of-the-market methods.

At times, this could very well mean buying a stock in one part of the total account and selling it in another at the same time. That is, a partial buying level for the formula plan might represent a selling level for the trend method. The orders thus placed would sound insane to the broker, and yet they would be perfectly logical as steps in soundly conceived plans aimed at successful long-term results, but pursuing different paths in arriving at the same goal.

Importance of a Program

Whether such a combination is used or whether just one approach is elected, the important thing is to have a program and then stick to it. It is doubtful whether one investor in a thousand really knows what he is doing or where he is going. All, in a vague sort of way, want "safety"; also, they want "income" and, in varying degrees, "appreciation" of their capital. But, they have no definite plan for achieving these ends. In practice, most acquire a miscellaneous list of securities, each bought because at the time it appeared attractive for one reason or another.

These securities are switched around frequently or infrequently. Sometimes a good many may be sold because something disturbs the owner's confidence. More often, they are held indefinitely, long after the original reason for purchase has been forgotten. Their "investments" become just that, and are not viewed as pawns in a game which — in order to win — must be played according to the rules. This may sound "speculative", yet a formula plan — really one of the most conservative approaches — is a clear instance of how securities serve merely as mediums for a program.

Time, Patience, and Perspective

The second step after adopting a specific program is to school oneself — not only to stick to it, but to see it in perspective and realize the patience required. Time, patience, and perspective are all-important, and it has been truly said that in the market place, patience is a rarer jewel than judgment. It is all very easy to look at the excellent and indisputable ten or twenty-year results of many methods described in this book, and realize that they are, indeed, infinitely superior to the results of judgment for, perhaps, 999 investors out of a thousand. But, the compression of a decade of time into ten minutes of reading is deceptive unless this point is fully comprehended.

It can be well illustrated now (mid-1948) with the position of a soundly conceived formula such as the duPont Institutional Plan (see Section IV) which has been only 32.8% invested in common stocks since July 1, 1946, and will not buy more at the present time unless the Dow-Jones Industrial Average gets down under 150. Assume for the sake of argument that the "cycle forecasts" are correct, and that the market will advance to a new high over 1946 from the 1947 and early 1948 lows.

Since the duPont Plan would not be buying any more stocks in such an event and, in fact, would begin to reduce present holdings still further at somewhere around the 225 level, the tendency might be to feel quite displeased with its performance at that point. But, that would have nothing to do with its long-range merits in its class. It would simply be performing within its known limitations, and one could be sure that the day would come when the Plan would be buying stocks again at what would prove even later to have been a low average cost.

Ten years, however, is a long time when living through the day-by-day fluctuations of prices — particularly if one is close to the scene — and the temptations to diverge from a program are many. The heat of bull market enthusiasm, the gloom in periods of depression, and the arising of apparently "new" circumstances all combine to make the investor forget, or depart from, the sound program with which he so bravely started out.

Or, perhaps he has a mental reservation in the beginning

that he is going to "try this thing out" for a year. But a year may not be enough. The market may be such during that particular period that its fluctuations simply do not fit well the particular approach or approaches adopted. The tendency then is to blame the method rather than the true culprit — the market itself — and toss the plan overboard just when, perhaps, a type of price fluctuation is developing in which the method would function ideally. Or, it may work the other way around. The initial period may be the ideal one, and so much therefore comes to be expected of the method, that a perfectly normal degree of failure at some point along the way is regarded as evidence that it has lost all its usefulness.

Know the Limitations

It is important to know and realize the limitations as well as the advantages of any method to be used, under the varying sets of circumstances that are sure to be encountered. A trend method will not get tops and bottoms, and may be whipsawed on occasion, but will always be right on a big move. A formula plan will appear to be bucking a trend that seems to have no ending, but will inevitably come out ahead over the course of a complete cycle (from top to top or bottom to bottom). A good character-of-the-market method will make mistakes, but be right considerably oftener than it is wrong.

The Lowry or the Mills measurements, for example, are subject to whipsaws in erratic markets, while the Odd Lot Indexes may fail to give a signal at some points of reversal in the market, and hence require a different sort of protection. Nevertheless, the records show that such untoward junctures are in the minority. But, whatever the method in question, it is only the average result over a period of time that is the true criterion.

The primary concern of this book is with "timing", but timing can only be implemented by the purchase (and sale) of individual stocks. Since the latter may be chosen on technical grounds as well as by what is ordinarily called security analysis, a brief discussion of the subject is pertinent at this point.

A conservative individual might reason that, since he is working on a study of trends in the Dow-Jones Industrial Average, he would evenly divide his timing purchases among the 30 well-known stocks making up that Average. Thus, he could be certain that his holdings would follow the general trend, even on relatively short swings. He would know at the same time, however, that his profits would be relatively small as compared to what he could make by selecting issues that would outperform the Average as so many do.

In the 1942-1946 major upswing, the Industrial Average appreciated from 92.92 to 212.50, or a percentage gain of about 128%. During the same period, however, countless stocks rose anywhere from 200% to 700%. There were not a few spectacular instances such as the 2100% rise of Schenley Distillers or the 2650% gain in Gimbel Brothers. Without getting off into isolated examples picked by hindsight, however, such performances as the following were typical among issues entirely familiar to investors — American Airlines, 700% — American Radiator, 530% — Armour, 640% — Celanese, 460% — Crane, 380% — Flintkote, 405% — International Paper, 610% — Nash Kelvinator, 660% — Paramount Pictures, 620% — U. S. Plywood, 690% — Zenith Radio, 450%, etc.

Leverage and Better-Than-Average Performance

To take the most highly leveraged security available, there were the Tri-Continental Corp. warrants which rose from $\frac{1}{32}$ to 5⅜ between 1942 and 1946, or an appreciation of 17,100%. These warrants can be relied upon always to follow major swings in the Average, but multiplying the amplitude of such swings many times over, despite the fact that they have never had any tangible value. Each simply represents a perpetual option to buy 1.22 shares of the common stock of Tri-Continental Corp. (a highly leveraged investment trust issue itself) at $18.46 per share.

The common has never sold higher than 12⅝ since 1930, but because it is always conceivable that some day it will be worth more than $18.46, the warrants always command a market — fractional when Tri-Continental may be down to $3 or $4 per share, but surprisingly high with any gains in this common stock, even though the latter may come nowhere near the option price. When Tri-Continental sold at 12⅝ in 1946, the warrants touched 5⅜, ridiculous as that price may seem from the standpoint of value. In a period of very low stock prices, the purchase of Tri-Continental Corp. warrants is one of the surest means of being in a position to benefit to an extraordinary extent from a subsequent major upswing.

They are, of course, an extreme medium, since their price movement will be many times greater than the Average, the exact ratio depending on the price level. The lower the price, the greater the relative volatility. This unusual volatility results from a double leverage. Tri-Continental Corp. common stock itself is highly leveraged by senior securities, and hence the per share asset value fluctuates much more widely than the total value of the assets held themselves. Then additional leverage is supplied by the nature of the warrants. The farther below $18.46 the price of the common may be, the greater this is. A gain of 8% in the Industrial Average has produced a 100% rise in the warrants from a price of 1. At 2, however, the Average has had to rise about 16% to bring about another 100% gain, and so on up the line. In fact, the higher a leverage issue may be, the more is the amount of leverage cut, so that a point may be reached where the risks on the downside outweigh the upside possibilities.

Leverage is a double-edged sword. Purchased at the right time, Tri-Continental Corp. warrants offer the chance of extraordinary profits, but also — at the wrong time — of substantial loss. They declined from 3 to $\frac{1}{32}$, or nearly 100% during the 1937-1942 downtrend which was reflected in a 52% decline in the Industrial Average. On the relatively minor Average drop of 22% in 1946-47, the Tri-Continental warrants fell 67% from 5⅝ to 1¾.

It will be noticed, however, that the mathematical odds on potentialities favor the purchaser. A loss cannot possibly exceed 100%, while the potential gain on occasion may be several 100% to several 1000%. Success in using a medium of this sort is completely one of timing.

Use of Investment Trust Shares

Without getting into such a highly leveraged situation as Tri-Continental Corp. warrants, however, investment trust stocks as a class do offer one logical medium for "timing purchases". Although some trusts have concentrated holdings in particular groups, the majority are well diversified in their common stockholdings, and hence the purchaser of the trust stock itself may be sure that the price will follow the general market trend. The extent to which the movement may exceed the Average depends largely upon the starting level, and the leverage involved through the existence of senior securities. A trust with no leverage may, however, still move more than the Average if its holdings are largely in low-priced and volatile stocks.

The table below will illustrate where three actively traded trusts on the New York Stock Exchange with similar diversified holdings, but with different degrees of leverage, might be expected to sell at different levels in the Dow-Jones Industrial Average. This is based on the present character of holdings and cannot take into consideration possible long-term changes in the relation of asset value to the average price level, brought about by the degree of management success in meeting conditions of the future. Moreover, some guesswork is involved, since the premium or discount of the price in relation to asset value depends upon the psychology of investors at any given time. Ordinarily, a discount narrows with a rising price level, but investors are becoming more sophisticated about leverage trust shares, and might be sufficiently cognizant of the decreased leverage and increased risk at higher levels to keep the price at a substantial discount.

Although not to be taken too literally, the following table nevertheless shows the approximate expectancies.

With Dow-Jones Industrial Average At	High Leverage Tri-Continental Company	Medium Leverage U. S. & Foreign Securities	Low Leverage General American Investors
240	20	48	25
215	14	40	21
190	10	32	18
165	5	17	12
140	3	12	9

Naturally, the high leveraged Tri-Continental Corp. shows wider percentage moves than the low leveraged General American Investors. On an advance from 165 to 190 in the Average, or about 15%, as actually happened to occur in the spring of 1948, Tri-Continental rose nearly 100% and General American Investors about 45%. Either of these gains could have been forecast with fair accuracy on the assumption of an Average rise to 190, although Tri-Continental really exceeded the normal expectancy — another indication, perhaps, of the growing sophistication of investors with respect to this particular field.

Other Reasons For Better-Than-Average Performance

It would be impossible, however, to pick out individual industrial company stocks and say just where they might sell at given levels in the Average, since too many variable and imponderable factors would be involved. In general, however, there are several reasons why some stocks will move over a wide range as compared to the Average. These are as follows:

1. Leverage on per share earnings
2. Low price
3. Small floating supply
4. Market sponsorship
5. Long-term romance possibilities in the business.

Only one or two of these factors may be present in any given instance, or conceivably all five might be combined. The leverage on per share earnings ordinarily is derived from the existence of fixed charges on senior securities, so that earnings per common share fluctuate much more widely than total income. The stock of a company with only common shares outstanding may be the safer *investment,* but the stock of a company with a large debt and/or a large issue of preferred stock is likely to go up much faster in a rising trend, and vice versa.

Low-Priced Stocks

A starting low price at the inception of an upward trend unquestionably means a greater-than-average rise. A study covering 35 years showed that, on the average, stocks selling at less than 5 increased over six and one-half times as fast in bull markets as did stocks selling at 100 or over.

A very rough rule of thumb is that stock prices move equal increments on their square roots. If a $100 stock in a bull market moves to 144 (square of 10 to square of 12), a $25 stock will move at the same time to 49 (square of 5 to square of 7) — a gain of 96% vs. 44%, although each stock moves only two points on its square root.

To put it the other way around, assume an anticipated move in the Industrial Average from 100 to 169. In that event, where will a $9 stock go? The square root of 169 is 13 and that of 100 is 10. The difference is 3. The square root of 9 is 3, so the difference of 3 is added to it, making 6. The square of 6 is 36, so it is assumed that the $9 stock should go to that figure.

The "rule" should not be taken literally for any individual case, because there will be any number of individual divergences. It is derived merely from the averaged experience of a large number of stocks, but does illustrate the springboard effect of low price *at the right time.* The stock which is still "low-priced" at the top of a bull market can hurt the investor just as much as it would have helped him when it was even lower around the beginning of the upward trend.

Volatile and Romance Stocks

The other three factors making for high volatility in some stocks need little explanation. "Floating supply" refers to the number of shares changing hands fairly frequently. Very often, a large amount of stock in some company will be held by the founders and/or officers, and will never come on the market, regardless of the circumstances. The greater the amount of such closely held stock, the smaller the floating supply and, therefore, the more volatile the price is likely to be.

Sometimes, certain investment quarters will be closely identified with some particular company, and in these cases, they may be quite active in buying and selling the issue. If the circumstances warrant, it is hence not likely to be found "behind the market".

"Romance possibilities" in a business attract attention to its stock in bull markets, and this alone often results in much greater price advances than are justified by actual earnings. Radio Corporation in the '20s was an outstanding example. The imagined postwar growth in air travel as a result of the war brought about some ridiculous prices for airline stocks by the end of 1945. A "romance business" is sought more eagerly by investors than a prosaic one, spurred on as they are by memories of the development of automobiles, radios, airplanes, the wonders of chemistry, etc.

Relative Group Performance Approach

A logical approach to the problem of what stocks to buy when timing indicates that purchases are in order, lies in group analysis. It is assumed that, under such circumstances, the investor will want issues which promise to outstrip the prospective Average rise. To a limited extent, he may solve the problem with leveraged investment trusts, but too much concentrated purchasing there would defeat its own purpose. Moreover, as mentioned before, there is a point on the upside where the leverage factor will drop so low as to have the risks outweigh the possibilities of gain.

Studies of industry group price performance are made in order to discover those which are likely to outperform the Average and conversely, of course, to avoid those which are likely to be relative laggards. For example, around the inception of the 1942-46 major upswing, an investor might well have concluded on the basis of fundamental logic that steel and copper stocks — particularly with a war background — should prove better-than-average mediums for investment. If they had been viewed on the basis of relative price performance, however, it would have been found that these two groups were tending to lag behind the general market, and hence they would have been avoided in favor of rails, liquor stocks, and many other groups which were in the forefront of the advance. The character of any individual group's action can always change for better or for worse, but relative trends nevertheless usually persist for fairly long periods of time. In the example mentioned above, the better-than-average groups continued in that category until early 1946, while the poorer-than-average steels and coppers continued to lag for over two years.

Group Studies Available

Adequate study of relative group action is no simple matter, to say nothing of its time-consuming aspects. There are, however, three available services at present giving technical analyses of group action. These are *R. W. Mansfield Co., Ray*Signals*, and *Hood's Group Action*, the last having been discussed in a different connection in Section III.

(See References on page 299 for more complete information.)

Hood uses his own group compositions and so does Mansfield. On the other hand, Ray employs Standard & Poor's 60 group indexes. Mansfield's breakdown is extraordinarily complete with 120 groups in all, getting into such minor classifications as fountain pen and clock manufacturing, while railroads, for example, are logically broken down into four classifications — Eastern, Coal, Transcontinental, and Midwestern.

Ray∗*Signals* is concerned with group action alone. The general market trend is not covered, and hence the comments are concerned only with the relative desirability of the respective groups and are not given as a prediction of an absolute advance or decline in price. The basic comparison of each group is made with Standard & Poor's 402-stock index, using a monthly ratio combined with an average ratio for a ten-month period. It is pointed out that the studies show four useful, recurring patterns of price performance, which indicate a reversal of — or change in — relative group action. At any given time, the groups where superior performance is indicated do not average much more than 20. This alone is a long step toward solving the problem of "what", since there are 60 groups in all.

Hood uses 38 groups, but goes beyond the selection of the best performers by employing the character of group action as an indication of the general market trend (see discussion in Section III).

Mansfield covers a very wide front in his "Book of Indices" with a great many "forecasting barometers", and statistical information. Also, the company presents its own interpretation of the factual data, making specific recommendations both as to general policy and individual issues.

However, the primary concern here is with the Mansfield group analysis. Based on relative price performance, the 120 groups are rated at any given time as Buy, Hold, Dubious, and Sell. Passing from Buy or Hold to Dubious (or Sell) indicates that a switch should be made, while passing from Sell or Dubious to Hold (or Buy) indicates that new purchases should be made in the group.

Technical group analysis of the sort under discussion is unquestionably a logical first step in the approach to the problem of "what". It results in occasional whipsaws when the character of some individual group's action may be subject to change with undesirable frequency. Nevertheless, it does have the positive virtue of assuring the investor of having some representation in the groups which prove to be the most spectacular leaders in a bull market, and the negative virtue of getting or keeping him out of persistent laggards or those which may almost literally fall to pieces; i.e., the airline stocks after the end of 1945.

Question of Individual Issues

After the group analysis, there still remains the question of the individual issues to be purchased in each favorably situated group. Here again, the criterion of relative performance can be applied. In its simplest application, this may take the form of relative volatility tables. This is a computation of the degree to which a given individual stock has moved more than some Average selected as a standard of comparison during the last three or four intermediate swings of that Average. If it is found that some particular issue has ordinarily had an amplitude of movement twice that of the Average, it is a reasonable presumption that it will continue to approximate the same figure on the next move. Obviously, further refinements may be applied to this type of study, but the very broad field of individual stock technical analysis lies outside the scope of this book.

There are, however, several services which classify individual stocks on the basis of relative performance as a foundation for future expectancies. Such lists are provided by Lowry's Investment Reports and the Mansfield Mills Co. (see Section III).

Although subject to the same limitations as group analysis because of changes in characteristics, this type of individual stock study also has similar advantages. If the basic timing method employed is correct in indicating a general market advance at any time, the approach of group performance in relation to an Average, and individual stock performance in relation to a group and/or an Average, can surely result in a selection of stocks which — in the aggregate — will outstrip the Average advance to a very considerable degree.

Relationship of Technical and Fundamental Studies

The criticism has sometimes been made of the relative performance approach that a group or stock moving higher than the market may become overvalued at some point, and — contrariwise — that a worse-than-average downside performance may continue to a point of undervaluation. True enough, but that is simply one disadvantage to be weighed against several distinct advantages. Moreover, better-than-average performance is not confined to an uptrend. It may be indicated by relative resistance in a downtrend which is a reasonably good indication that upside action is likely to be outstanding after the trend has changed — conversely, for a laggard performance during an uptrend.

There is nothing in this sort of approach to stock selection *after* a timing approach has indicated a long position, which denies the role of orthodox security analysis. Indeed, it might be said that it is dependent upon the latter. If an investment trust, for example, has studied with positive results the prospects for an industry and a company within that industry, it must buy the stock in question in order to implement its conclusion. Since it is such buying that may result in the better-than-average performance shown by the analysis of relative trends, everything goes back to the same root. Or, the buying which makes the price performance may stem from company officers, directors, or other sources very close to the situation who are presumably in a better position to appraise the company prospects than any outsider. Whatever the sources or reasons, however, a better price performance than would normally be expected in the light of all the known facts, means that there must exist a strong demand factor which may be right or wrong, but is usually right — at least in a relative sense. The reverse applies to the presence of supply as evidenced by a performance poorer than the known facts and circumstances suggest as normal.

AND A PREDICTION

Venturing a comment today on the probable future scene is a quite different problem than it was seven years ago. The apathy toward the stock market evident in 1941 does not exist now. The keynote of 1948 is rather bewilderment — and not without good reason.

Uncertainty of 1948

Everyone knew — or thought he knew — in 1941 that various eroding influences at work implied an indefinitely prolonged long-term downtrend in the price level. Today, no similar widespread conviction exists. Except on the part of a few positive individuals — some of whom are categorically bearish, while others are equally bullish — a plainly uncertain mood exists.

Has inflation still further to run? If so, will the lush earnings and dividends of the inflationary period since 1946 ultimately be reflected in stock prices? Or is deflation just around the corner, with its implied rapid slide into the red by companies now riding high, but with break-even points far above prewar levels? In an equally uncertain realm, will there be war with Russia? In that case, will stocks be worth less, or will they be worth more on the grounds that another major war must assuredly cheapen the dollar much further? These and similar questions churn endlessly through the investor's head as he tries to reconcile the seeming cheapness of stocks from the standpoint of earnings and

270

dividends with a price level that appears "high" in relation to the past.

And he has good reason for his bewilderment. There is nothing which really seems to be crystallized anywhere. Popular opinion may have been wrong in 1941, but at the same time, the view itself was evidence of a situation that was coming to a head. Moreover, a downtrend had persisted for a long time, and there were several straws in the wind which suggested that a logical reversal was quite certainly in the making.

Market Betwixt and Between

Today, however, the position of the market is neither fish, flesh, nor fowl. Measured against median price levels of the past, it is high. By the time-honored yardsticks of price-to-earnings ratios and yields from dividends, it is low. If the academic and already once-reversed Dow Theory definitions are excluded, no trend has been in evidence for two years. August of 1948 found the market just where it was in September of 1946 with the interim tops and bottoms not much higher or lower.

To put in perspective the whole picture of the near-term future as well as the past, the problem might be stated this way: Will new highs (substantially above the 210-215 area in the Dow-Jones Industrial Average) be seen in 1949, thus making the 1946-48 decline and sidewise drift appear merely as a temporary interruption in one long uptrend from 1942? Or, will a decline well below 165 definitely show that an important downtrend began in May of 1946, comparable to the 1937-42 period of liquidation?

One Element of Similarity

Dissimilar though the picture is as compared with 1941, there is nevertheless one striking resemblance. The two things preying on investors' minds seven years ago were Hitler and the New Deal — one bogey abroad and another one at home.

Substitute Stalin for Hitler and Inflation for the New Deal, and again there are two dominant factors resulting in a basic lack of investment confidence, which — except for fleeting periods — has characterized the past 17 years.

The Russian Possibilities

It is unquestionably true that much in the outlook for the next few years depends upon whether there is a full-scale war with Russia, as many now fear. Remembering the incredibly uninformed assumptions upon which the Japanese leaders proceeded, one is certainly led to feel that anything is possible. The men in the Kremlin may — in desperation or ignorance — be willing to provoke a conflict with the U. S. and the latter's allied powers, but the logic of the known facts is entirely against it.

Major wars occur when the aggressor side wants war, is prepared for war, and feels sure of winning. That was true of Germany in 1939, but it is difficult to believe that it can be true of Russia in 1948. Although atomic bombs are probably not decisive weapons of warfare, it hardly seems sensible to start a war when your enemy has such an edge. And surely, Stalin can have no illusions as to America's productive capacity as compared with that of Russia.

War Unlikely

It is possible to theorize endlessly about the relative vulnerability of targets, the problems of transport, et cetera, but the basic fact is simply this: Russia is too weak industrially vis-à-vis the United States to fight an aggressive war.

Oil, for example, is vital in modern warfare. It was not

long ago that Stalin set a goal of 60 million tons by 1951. U. S. production in 1947 was 270 million tons. Similarly, U. S. steel production has long been more than half again as much as Russia hopes for several years hence. Internal transportation is an outstanding Russian weakness — huge territory, few roads of importance, and about one-fourth the rail mileage of this country.

Russia's strength is in her almost impregnable geographical location, the size and character of the terrain, and her numerical manpower. Fighting a defensive war on her own grounds, Russia could be very strong as Hitler discovered, but to carry war to the enemy is a different story

Rather than being ready and willing to start World War III, it seems far more likely that Stalin envisions Russian gains by provoking the U. S. into making so many foolish and costly moves that economic and financial chaos will ultimately result. A capitalistic depression, such as Russia both looked for and hoped for after V-J Day, would be the best thing in the world to promote the cause of Communism, and no one knows this better than "Uncle Joe". Let a business slump give this country a few million unemployed, and watch the membership of Henry Wallace's party grow.

One Clue to Russian Policy

Although the tiny struggle in Greece has been obscured by more dramatic developments elsewhere, it nevertheless provides a clue as to how far Russia is really willing — or unwilling — to go.

Greece is important strategically and politically to Russia, and yet the Communist rebels have been allowed to be defeated when very little Russian assistance would have been necessary to keep them going. The only answer seems to be that Russia was unwilling to risk a clash with British troops for political and not military reasons, or to conflict openly with the Americans who are official military advisors to the unsatisfactory — but at least anti-Communist — Greek government.

War and Stock Prices

For the near future, World War III is highly improbable. But should the contingency develop, it could not be considered other than as a bearish influence on stock prices. The excess profits tax would probably be 100% and Government controls over everything even more stringent.

The actual market effect could be before or after the event, depending on how war came about. When England declared war in 1939, for example, British stock prices went down only a few points, because there had been an anticipatory downtrend for some time. In fact, a recovery during the first few months of the war period more than regained the ground initially lost, and it took the unexpected disaster of Dunkirk to produce a final wave of liquidation, from which a seven-year bull market was to start.

It is often remarked today, however, that even if war would be temporarily bearish on stock prices, stocks should still be preferable to cash in the long run, because another war would mean a tremendous inflation. The Federal Government spent over $330 billion on World War II, and the national debt was raised to over $250 billion. After another war, it might be $500 billion. Either one is a far cry, incidentally, from the days in the '30s when it was argued solemnly that the New Deal expenditures were increasing the national debt to the breaking point and that the country could not "stand" a debt of more than $100 million.

Inflation and Stock Prices

All other things being equal, the contention that a long-term and more violent inflation would mean higher stock prices is true, but other things are not always equal. As many investors learned between 1946 and 1948, inflation *per se* does not necessarily mean higher stock prices, despite the textbook teachings.

In the first place — unless there is a sheer flight from the currency as such, so that almost anything else is regarded as more desirable — it is necessary that inflation works in such a way as to result in higher corporate earnings.

The experience in France during the inflation after the first World War was illustrative of the process. Theoretically, utility stocks are a poor investment under inflationary conditions, because earnings are squeezed between relatively rigid service rates and mounting costs. Steel stocks, however, are theoretically good, since prices can more easily be raised to offset the greater production costs.

In practice, however, it worked out exactly the opposite in France. The utilities were permitted to raise rates freely, so that earnings increased. But, the steel industry found itself with too much capacity, and surpluses kept steel prices down at a level where high production costs allowed no profits. The stocks of steel companies declined, while those of utilities rose.

Secondly, if the inflation does produce higher earnings, there must be a willingness on the part of investors to evaluate those earnings in terms of higher stock prices. The reason that the inflation since 1946 has not resulted in higher stock prices in the U. S. has been the complete and universal lack of assurance as to the continuance of those earnings. All this comes back to one fundamental truism — namely, that the psychology which determines price-to-earnings ratios for common stocks is just as important as the trend or level of the earnings themselves.

Long-term Trends Against Stockholders

Regardless of what the inflationary aspects of the situation following another war might be, however, there would still be a question mark as to corporate profits. The role of private enterprise would undoubtedly have been further weakened and the Government would be even more omnipotent. Taxes would, of necessity, be even heavier. The investor cannot, therefore, conclude that he will necessarily be better off with common stocks in the long run.

In fact, leaving out entirely the possibility of another war, but conceding the continuance of long-term inflationary trends, the assumption of gradually higher stock prices is not easily justified. Because there has been a tendency in that direction for the past 50 years does not mean that it will continue. On the contrary, there are various influences at work which lead to just the opposite conclusion.

Various social forces are operating against the long-term position of stockholders. Ownership and management are no longer closely linked in the majority of cases. Only too often, a business functions primarily by virtue of an agreement between the Government and labor unions, with management supplying little more than the technical know-how of production.

When the choice is between saving money by laying off workers or cutting the stockholder's dividends, public opinion favors the worker rather than the stockholder. Pension funds are socially most desirable, and yet from the stockholder's standpoint, they add another fixed expense before his share in any earnings can be figured.

Examples can be multiplied of the ever-increasing costs

of doing business, but the point is that they all take precedence over the owners' (stockholders') return. And, more important, they must be recognized as permanent changes in the economy. There can be no reversion to the institutional arrangements of the past. The trend toward socialism, or a greater power of the State for the (presumed) good of the many is an inexorable fact of the Twentieth Century. It has been under way for years, and did not suddenly spring into being under the Roosevelt Administrations, although the latter doubtless helped to accelerate the process. Can anyone think that labor will give up its gains of the past fifteen years, that corporate taxes will be reduced, or that the Government will play a smaller role in the regulation of private business?

The extent to which progress has already been made in this direction is evident in comparing the income statements of twenty years ago with those of today. In 1929, for example, General Electric's sales were $415 million, of which $67 million was carried through to net income. In 1947, sales were $1,831 million, but net was only $95 million. To express it another way, if General Electric could operate with the same profit margin and under the same tax rates as in 1929, it would have earned about $10.00 per share in 1947 instead of the $3.30 actually reported as the final net.

This is not to imply that common stocks should be avoided. There will continue to be bull markets and bear markets, and just as many opportunities for profit as in the past. The foregoing comments were intended only as a caution against the assumption that a secular growth of the country and industry will necessarily find reflection in a long-term rising trend of stock prices. The growth of corporate *earnings* is something else again, and profits are the lifeblood of common stock prices.

Postwar Inflation Over

No one subject — with the possible exception of Russia — is so much talked about in 1948 as "inflation". This means the type of inflation of which everyone is conscious, because it has resulted in a higher cost of living. It was an inevitable result of conditions apparent long ago (see page 297 in the Supplement) but as usual, all the hue and cry is after the event. The ridiculous statements from Washington about the causes, who is to blame, and what should be done, are not worth discussing.

The important point is that this particular postwar inflation has, in all probability, passed its peak. It is evident that supply has already caught up with demand in certain fields — primarily non-essential consumers' goods. However, even more essential products such as glass containers and automobile tires are instances where sales have declined following satisfaction of deferred demand.

The developing 1948 avalanche of wheat and corn is prima facie evidence that the major cereals have seen their highest levels. Indeed, the farmer is already looking to the Government to keep him in the style to which he has become accustomed. In time, this means lower meat prices. Indirectly, the pressure for wage increases is thus diminished, since the price of food has been the ringleader of the whole inflationary trend. Because of rising food prices, workers have demanded higher wages which in turn raised the costs (and prices) of manufactured products. But the spiral is in its dying phase.

It does not follow, however, that an equally violent deflation will follow — yet. There are many fields where the need or demand is still tremendous in relation to supply, particularly in the capital goods industries. Hence, it is more likely that the economy will remain in a state of balance for some time to come.

Someday, however, the piper must be paid. If one were to consider only the full employment of the last three years, the high national income, and the average standard of living, it might be concluded that the war — leaving out the humanitarian aspects — was a very good thing. It seems to have left the country better off than ever before, but only because the Government (or "we") went into debt in a big way to mortgage the future and thus spread around a lot of new money. Actually, the U. S. is poorer than before the war in every sort of real wealth, and ultimately, this realization must strike home. It is not pleasant to contemplate, but depressions are part and parcel of a capitalistic economy.

Curiously, however, a depression or deflation will probably contribute to a long-term inflation. Whether the administration is Republican or Democratic, the role of Government is such that willy-nilly, the party in power must accept the responsibility of attempting, at least, to control the course of economic affairs. If the state of business is such as to breed unemployment, then it is to Washington that people will turn to provide — directly or indirectly — a substitute. The farmer will demand a higher price for his products than a free market will give him. And Washington cannot turn a deaf ear. The implication, then, is for much higher Government expenditures at a time when revenues are declining, and hence large deficit financing, which will contribute to an ultimate further cheapening of the dollar.

Pattern of the Market

It is evident that if the foregoing very broad outline of future probabilities has any substance, wide swings in stock prices can be expected over the next few years. A calm plateau might be highly desirable for the investor, but it seems more likely that it is the speculator who will be offered the opportunities. The chances are that it will be an ideal period for the use of such timing methods as have been the subject of this book.

Timing methods, however, cannot be of much assistance at the moment in determining what the exact pattern of the future trends will be. As emphasized earlier, such methods "deal with" price fluctuations rather than "forecast" them.

It would not be logical, for example, to be optimistic on stock prices for 1949 on the ground that the Dow Theory defined the existence of a major bull market in the spring of 1948. The investor on this basis should be mentally neutral, realizing that the uptrend might continue, but also that it might not, and that a reversal of his position — perhaps at a loss — could be called for. Similarly, the weakened market situation shown by some character-of-the-market methods in June of 1948 would not justify indefinite bearishness. An equally strong situation might develop at any time. The formula plan investor, of course, does not care particularly what happens, since he is not even "dealing with" fluctuations, but is rather just taking advantage of them in a very modest way.

The only clue to the possible pattern of the future which can be found in these timing methods would lie in the cyclical projections. However, since the solidity of their foundation is very much open to question, no prediction is ventured on this basis.

At the same time, what does seem to be a logical pattern — on other grounds — might coincide roughly with the indicated cyclical course. It was mentioned earlier in this Section that, ultimately, there will be a day of reckoning. Business booms cannot last forever, and when the inevitable subsequent reversal takes place, it must be accompanied by a bear market in stock prices. The question is only one of timing — in the near future, or not for several years? The reversal does not, however, appear imminent. Although the period of violent inflation is over, it is not likely to be replaced by serious deflation, but rather a balance between the two, accompanied not by the hectic and obviously unreal profits of 1947, but by reasonable business prosperity.

New Highs Probable

Despite the fact that this implies a level of earnings lower than that in the period from the middle of 1946 to the middle of 1948, it would — psychologically speaking — be bullish on stock prices. That may sound paradoxical, but it is not illogical if the background is analyzed. For two years, a tremendous boom in business, earnings, and dividends has been witnessed without a corresponding rise in stock prices. The reasons were (1) a partial discount of the boom by stock prices in mid-1946, and (2) fear that it was too good to last and that the bubble might blow up any day. Confidence was simply lacking. On many occasions during the previous decade, the mere threat of an assumed inflation was enough to shoot stock prices up, but confronted with the real thing, investors found a more potent and offsetting factor in a bust "just around the corner". If earnings had been much less than they were, but a reasonable assurance of their continuance had been felt, stock prices would undoubtedly have been higher.

It may well be, therefore, that a removal of the obvious froth and a shakedown in earnings to a level which has a reasonable chance of being maintained for a while, will make stocks appear much more attractive. Possibly, a long-awaited Republican administration will also contribute to a revival of confidence, although this appears to be already too much of a *fait accompli* to have much significance. In any event, of the two alternatives in the market pattern outlined on page 271, the first appears more likely; i.e., that new highs will be seen, making May, 1946, to February, 1948, appear as a temporary interruption in one long uptrend from 1942.

There are necessarily some "ifs" in this prediction. It is a probability and not a certainty. For that reason, it points up the necessity for flexibility in investment policy — for meeting conditions as they arise — in short, for *timing*. Perfection in this respect there will never be, but as long as the market fluctuates, there will be opportunities for those who can understand the problem, know their elected method of operation, and exercise the patience to stick to it.

SUPPLEMENT

The concluding section of the original edition of this book is quoted in full on the following pages. Both the description of the investment mood of 1941 and the extent to which the "contrary" prediction was fulfilled are interesting at this later date.

In substance, the position taken was that despite Hitler and the New Deal — those "two *bêtes noire* of the average investor", the market would not continue to pursue the anticipated "monotonous trend toward lower levels"; that there would be "dynamic and advancing markets"; and that in May, 1941, the over-all picture implied that stocks were already "turning from a bear to a bull trend".

The scope and duration of the 1942-1946 bull market amply confirmed the first two contentions, although to have said the market was "turning" in May, 1941, when the Dow-Jones Industrial Average was around 115, looks rather premature. At least, this is true in terms of that Average which did not hit its ultimate low until eleven months later (April, 1942, at about 93).

Actually, the statement was closer to the mark than it appears on the surface. For example, the bear market lows were reached in 1941 and not 1942, by such groups as farm machinery, amusement, auto, auto accessory, building, container, coal, cotton textile, rayon, liquor, shoes and sugar. Many others barely dipped below their 1941 bottoms in April, 1942. Rails were much stronger than the Dow-Jones

283

Rail Average looks, the weakness being confined to the eastern and coal carriers. The stock of the midwestern and transcontinental roads remained within their well-defined uptrend which had begun as far back as 1940.

The final drop in the Dow-Jones Industrial Average to around 93 was caused by the acute weakness in the blue-chip growth stocks to be hit hardest by the new wartime taxes; Allied Chemical, American Telephone, American Tobacco, duPont, Eastman Kodak, General Electric, General Foods, Sears Roebuck, Union Carbide, United Aircraft and Westinghouse Electric. It is interesting, on the other hand, that the following stocks in the Average had 1941 rather than 1942 lows — American Smelting, Standard Oil of California, Chrysler, General Motors, Corn Products, Loew's, Johns-Manville and National Steel. As this suggests, it is always better to be early than late in terms of the Dow-Jones Industrial Average, either in buying or selling for the major trends. Regardless of the timing of exact bottoms, the period from the spring of 1941 to the fall of 1942 may be characterized as the buying area for the ensuing bull market.

The complete text follows.

PREDICTION OF THE 1941 EDITION

"During the past year,[1] the author has been asked by many well-meaning friends why he should publish a book on stock market profits at a time when 'there are no profits'; when the financial business is supposed to be just waiting for the knockout punch; when the public is apathetic even to good stocks yielding 7 or 8%; when there is visualized

---

[1] This was the gloomy period following the fall of France in May, 1940, and prior to the entry of the U. S. into active war.

nothing ahead but a long vista of more tightly controlled economy that will choke off all free enterprise, and with it the Stock Exchange which is the nerve center of the whole system.

Certainly, fewer people will be interested in anything pertaining to the market than would be at a time when prices had been rising for a year or more and the volume of trading was high. The tape is its own best advertisement. But it is too much to hope—or, indeed, to expect—that things can ever be any different from this viewpoint. It is simply normal crowd psychology to reflect conditions as they are and to believe that because they have been, they must continue to be. Once an idea becomes firmly fixed in the mass mind, it persists for a long time, and is not eradicated until the new conditions—at first regarded with complete skepticism — have lasted for so long that they cannot be denied.

The deliberate stock manipulations of the past, for example, were predicated upon this simple fact, the technique being to put the price up and then sell on the way down. If a stock has been around 20 for a long time and is then bid up to 35, many holders are willing to sell and few new investors are willing to buy because the price looks high in relation to that which they have been accustomed to seeing. The same feeling persists on a further advance to, let us say, 50, although they are now looking for reactions on which to buy. The fact that it had been 20 is beginning to be forgotten, and, when the price is 40, they only wish it would come back to 30 so that they could get in on this splendid advance. Finally, after reaching the peak, the stock becomes a bargain at 45 and even more of an opportunity at 35 on the way down again. For was it not selling at 50 just a little while ago? The same price of

35 *that looked high on the way up in relation to the original level, now looks low in relation to the top. Note how this behaviorism is borne out by the odd lot buying and selling as discussed in Section IV.*[2]

Now, the same principles apply with equal force to less concrete situations. It is unquestionably true that, at the present time, the speculative interest of capital is at its lowest ebb for the entire period since World War I, although the heavy downtrend has been since 1929 relieved only temporarily between 1935 and 1937. Physical production is at a record peak, but stocks are selling at one-third of their 1929 high prices. A seat on the New York Stock Exchange can be bought for about one-twentieth of what it cost during the climax of what was once fondly referred to as the 'New Era', and at the lowest price since 1898 when only one-third as many issues were listed. The volume of trading in stocks in 1940 was less than one-fifth of that in 1929. And the capital issue market, which maintains the flow of money into business enterprise, is just as dead as the stock market. New issues in 1940 were less than 10% of the 1929 figure. Main Street may be having a good time with the 'defense boom', but Wall Street, State Street, and other centers that represent finance and the speculative mood of capital, look like deserted villages.

These are facts of record, but that does not justify the widely-held assumption that the financial depression will continue indefinitely. When the revival does begin — and the author believes that there will be a revival—it is equally certain that it will be regarded with complete skepticism for a long time.

Now the mere fact that a downtrend has persisted for

---

[2] This refers to Section IV of the 1941 edition.

a long time is not in itself a guarantee that it is about to reverse, but precedent—plus certain straws in the wind— does suggest that this is the case. After all, there is nothing basically new in the situation. Social and economic revolutions linked with wars have occurred before, but the spirit of enterprise has always lived. The rules of the game may be somewhat different, but it is quite impossible to visualize —borrowing a loosely used phrase—the 'end of capitalism'. And, assuming survival of the latter, capital activity cannot remain indefinitely dormant, since capitalism—which, if it means anything, means the active expression of the speculative instinct—simply cannot live forever in what amounts to a denial of its own nature.

The tendency today, of course, is to ask how can there be anything ahead but depression and misery when the world is bankrupting itself in an insensate conflict of nations which must end with all weak and exhausted. Tragic as the whole picture may be, compared with a peaceful world developing its knowledge as it might for the benefit of all, that is not a reason for pessimism as far as future speculative opportunities are concerned. Quite the opposite, in fact, for as the historian James Truslow Adams remarks in Building the British Empire *about one part of the eighteenth century: 'The period of peace, following the great wars, had, as usual, inaugurated a great speculation. . . . It was much like America in 1929.'*

Wall Street has had its own depressions before. In both 1911 and 1912, the range of the Dow-Jones Industrial and Rail Averages (the Rails then being higher than the Industrials) was confined to 14 points with a correspondingly low volume of trading. Money-making opportunities were almost entirely lacking from 1908 to 1915—a period midway between two great speculative eras. That which occurred *during the latter part of the 'Roaring 'Twenties' is fairly fresh in memory, but most people do not realize the extent of public stock market participation around the turn of the century. It was much less informed, but nonetheless extensive. The financial pages of New York and Boston newspapers in those days are entertaining reading for such advertisements as those offering to send (upon a $10 a month subscription) 'Guaranteed Special No. 29. . . . The more you carry, the more money you will make.' As pointed out in connection with Moment's 'secondary trend rules' in Section II, the opportunities for profit were as great between 1897 and 1906 as from 1927 to 1933, since price changes were just about as sweeping in both periods.*

Those who think that today's conditions are entirely new, and compare them only with the periods that they may have known as 'normal', are neglecting the lessons of history. It is granted that a gradually evolving social consciousness has outlawed the ruthless exploitation and the potential acquisition of tremendous wealth overnight that characterized some other periods, but that is not the same thing as a complete wiping out of the opportunities for enterprise and profit. This country cannot afford to neglect the driving force of private capital indefinitely, and some of the plans being studied in Washington with the idea of offsetting what would be the normal letdown from intense productive activity are interesting in this respect. Thus, it has been proposed to tax in such a manner as to force capital to take its chances in new enterprise. A tremendous amount of capital has been held in liquid form because of the belief that the risks in its employment outweighed the potential profits, limited as the latter are by existing taxes. But if other taxes involved a greater penalty in remaining liquid, capital would be forced to venture out.

The attitude of the New Deal toward Wall Street has become less punitive and more understanding than it was in 1933. At that time, it was answering a popular demand. Investors had suffered severely in the immediately preceding years, less through undisputed financial abuses than through uncontrollable economic forces, but attention naturally centered upon the former. And so the era of reform began. Like all such movements, it went perhaps to extremes, but the pendulum is swinging back to normal. Quite rightly, there will be no return to the 1929 sky-is-the-limit days of pool operation. The Securities and Exchange Commission will see to that. Through the same agency, more information will be available on securities and on what is going on in the market, but these things are highly desirable and should have come long before.

However, the tendency is disappearing on the part of Governmental representatives to regard all 'speculation' as harmful PER SE. Many of the New Dealers had had no practical experience with Wall Street, and thought of the Stock Exchange purely as a gambling institution. One day you played for a rise—on the next for a fall, the fluctuations occurring without rhyme or reason. They did not realize that beneath the froth of surface price movements a vital service in financing industry is performed. Emil Schram, ex-Government representative and President of the New York Stock Exchange since June, 1941, actually defended stock speculation upon assumption of his new post as 'a market aid to the more conservative investor and an essential economic function if risk capital is to go into new industry.' But, regardless of what the Government attitude may be, those who think that dictatorship or a totalitarian regime destroys stock values should ponder the fact that in 1941 the German stock market was above its 1929 high with *representative issues selling at prices to yield an average of only 3.7%.*

For that matter, even the twice-burned public of today does not desire that stock market speculation should be eliminated, for—given the slightest excuse—the eagerness for profits is quite evident, as in the flocking to buy 'war babies' in the latter part of 1939. Human nature reacts about the same as it did when it was tulip-mania time in Holland. The French public, under German domination, has turned to wild speculation in postage stamps, and of French stocks in the early part of 1941, the LONDON ECONOMIST *said: 'In Vichy-France, the boom is a boom in industrial equities. The rise has been so great that the authorities have issued constant warnings against excessive bidding up of quotations.' 'Inflation', yes, but that merely happens to be the motivating influence this time.*

The future probabilities for the stock market are important to the subject of this book, because no method is of any use unless the opportunity exists to use it, and that implies reasonably wide fluctuations in stock prices. Theoretically, it makes no difference what the direction of the trend may happen to be, although—human nature being constituted as it is—all but a few realists prefer to make their money through rising prices rather than by selling short in falling markets. But the money made (on paper) in a rising market is converted into cash and kept by very few, which is merely inherent in the nature of things. It can never be any different, and outstanding speculative success for any one individual implies failure on the part of others. Thus, it is quite a selfish affair and it would be hypocritical to pretend otherwise. Whether they admit it or not, most people who have anything to do with stocks are seeking profits in the end. Unfortunately, most of them confuse the issue with various extraneous factors to the detriment of ultimate results.

Application of such methods as those outlined in this book can lead anyone to profits in contrast with previous failure, but the great majority will continue to delude themselves with surface thinking. Indeed, any method universally followed would defeat its own purpose, but no method will ever be evolved sufficiently perfect to attract anything like a universal following. If everyone believed implicitly in the Dow Theory, for instance, no one would be willing to sell at certain junctures, and there would be only buyers for non-existent offerings of stock. Or, if all the smaller traders began to follow the implications of the 'Odd Lot Indexes', the trends of which they now largely create, the same index trends would not appear, but would be reversed before what would otherwise be their normal completion. They might still remain valid, however, since it is possible that a market pattern would result different from that which would otherwise have occurred, and in relation to which the public would still be wrong. Or, it might be said that, if successful, the present odd lot traders would make enough to graduate into the hundred share lot class, their place being taken by a formerly more wealthy group at whose expense they had profited. The exact processes in such a case are difficult to visualize precisely, but it is possible to be sure that the majority will never profit in the end simply because it is mathematically impossible for them to do so. Everyone may seem to make money— and does, ON PAPER — during a cyclical upward trend, because the 'value' of their holdings is increasing as quotations for the relatively small amount traded rise. But, nowhere near the amount of those holdings could be sold at the higher prices, for there would simply not be enough new money to buy.

In taking the stand that the future will see dynamic and advancing markets with, of course, corrective declines as well, the argument has so far relied on precedent and opinion. Nevertheless, as remarked earlier, there are some definite 'straws in the wind'. On the whole, the methods discussed in this book are of little assistance with respect to future long-term trends, because they deal primarily with the immediate picture. Hood's 'Group Action', for example, has been holding the purchases made at the low in June, 1940, for over a year as this is written, but could conceivably change within any four-week period. There are, however, some interesting aspects of the 'Odd Lot Indexes' (on a monthly basis) and the 'Natural Rhythm' methods.

In May, 1941, the long-term odd lot figures showed that a condition had come about which had previously been observed only at the major bear market bottoms of 1921, 1932, and 1938. That is, the public was showing a tendency to become more bearish as prices declined instead of the normal disposition to regard a lower price level as an opportunity to buy cheaply. And, as would be expected, the data on the personal trading of New York Stock Exchange members showed this group becoming more bullish. The implication was that the market was turning from a bear to a bull trend, although the duration of the latter could not be foretold. However, based on previous experience, it would be expected to be good for at least a year.

While on this matter of 'who is doing what', it is worthwhile to know that the Securities and Exchange Commission reports (about five weeks after the end of the month) the monthly purchases and sales in individual stocks

by the officers, directors, and large shareholders of the corporations represented. This information has been available
since the end of 1935, and, on the whole, it has shown persistent and fairly steady liquidation—a fact that has been
seized upon by some as indicating that 'wise money'—visualizing gradual attrition of corporate earning power—was selling out to the public. In the author's opinion, a more potent
reason has been the tax laws forcing liquidity in large estates,
even though 'New Deal pessimism' has doubtless induced
a certain amount of selling. Moreover, this selling has not
been particularly astute on its timing. The pace of liquidation was about the same in late 1937 and early 1938, when
the price level was low, as when the best selling opportunity
of a decade had existed a year before at much higher levels.
In fact, some 'insider' stock was sold that would have better
been held. However, corporate officials are usually recognized as notoriously poor judges of the MARKET PRICE
for their own stocks. As a rule, they are likely to become
bearish too early in rising trends and bullish too soon in
declining markets. In other words, they know the normal
'value' of their own stocks, but fail to recognize that market
prices often bear little relationship to theoretical worth.

But, whatever the reasons may have been for 'insider'
selling during the last few years, the point is that the spring
of 1941 looked as if it might mark a reversal of the liquidating process. As this is written, the extent of the reversal
is not yet sufficient to prove the case, but, since every important change of trend must have a beginning somewhere,
it is the fact of the change rather than its size which is of
real importance.

The 'Natural Rhythm' methods do, of course, afford a
long-term picture, the question being the extent to which
credence can be placed in their forecast. However, to re-

peat what has been said before, their indicated pattern in recent years has been far more correct than just chance seems to account for, and R. N. Elliott's record, for example, is carefully documented with unimpeachable outside sources. For that reason, the rising trend of stock prices definitely indicated for the coming years is at least interesting. Edson Beers, who also works on the principles of what is known as 'dynamic symmetry', wrote in BAR-RON's *for May 19, 1941, 'This is not a new bear market. Rather have we been seeing the winding up of the period of preparation prior to a new bull market. The Dow-Jones industrial-share level called for on the initial rise (not far off) is 165. After a sizable reaction, the market should then begin its real climb up to the 300 level.'*

Incredible? Certainly, 300 seems so in the light of the 116 prevailing when this statement appeared, but the 1935-1937 bull market seemed just as incredible when forecast in the former year by Beers, who also predicted the 1937 decline. IN FACT, A WELL-NIGH UNIVERSAL DISBELIEF THAT ANY IMPORTANT TREND IS POSSIBLE IS A PRE-REQUISITE OF THE CONDITION IMMEDIATELY PRECEDING IT, SINCE OTHERWISE PRICES WOULD ALREADY BE MOV-ING RAPIDLY IN THAT DIRECTION AS ACTION WAS TAKEN IN ANTICIPATION OF THE EVENT.

The same elements of dynamic symmetry which Beers believes apply to the patterns of stock price movements are likewise the basis of Elliott's 'Wave Principle' (see Section IV),[1] although Elliott says he made this discovery after empirically working out the Principle. Only the framework of the latter was outlined earlier, because a complete treatment would require more space than it was possible to allot, but some explanation of dynamic symmetry can be

---

[1] This refers to Section IV of the 1941 edition.

given. Dynamic symmetry is a long-recognized law of nat-
ural design seen, for example, in the proportions of the
human figure, growing plants, and some other manifesta-
tions of nature. It is ordinarily used by artists, designers,
and architects and, as a matter of fact, goes back to the
ancient Greeks and Egyptians. The law may be expressed
mathematically in what is known as a 'logarithmic spiral'
by the summation series of numbers 1, 2, 3, 5, 8, 13, 21,
34, 55, 89, 144, etc. (each term being the sum of the two
preceding terms). Note how Elliott's recurrent rhythms
of five waves and three waves build up the same way. So
far, so good. It is at this point that a mental leap must be
taken to accept the thesis of Elliott and Beers that the law
applies not only to the physical construction or growth of
living things in the universe, but also to the actions of mass
man, the stock market being merely an expression or re-
flection of those actions.

Thus, the law is regarded as applying to the price ranges
and time cycles of the market. To illustrate time, Beers
cites the important turning points since the June, 1932,
major bottom as follows, which may be better seen with
reference to the Frontispiece:

No. of months from bottom	Date	Dow-Jones Ind. Average Approx. High or Low for Month
3	Sept. 1932	81
5	Nov. 1932	69
8	Feb. 1933	50
13	July 1933	111
21	Mar. 1934	106
34	Apr. 1935	96
55	Jan. 1937	183

Corroborating the Beers forecast quoted earlier, Elliott's long-term 'wave analysis' in the spring of 1941 showed the market to be in the earlier phases of an important cyclical upward movement which might well eventually reach the 300 level. It is true that one could not see clearly just WHY *prices should rise to any such extent, but the 'why' is always much clearer in retrospect than it is in looking forward. Besides, if such situations were clearly defined, they would be evident to a great many, and that can never be the case on the eve of any important trend.*

Looking even farther ahead, it has been shown that the speculative opportunities for capital after the war are likely to be more rather than less. Allowing for the immediate dislocations, peace is fundamentally bullish. There will be much to reconstruct, and, although 'reconstruction' is likely to embrace a rather long period of years, it is worth remembering from a shorter term point of view that the end of World War I did not bring about any immediate collapse. In fact, no previous period in American financial history more pointedly accentuated the fallibility of human judgments and forecasts than was reflected in early 1919, when there were numerous forebodings of another depression lying ahead. The depression came, it is true, but considerably later than expected and after its probability had been largely forgotten, while to everyone's amazement 1919 recorded one of the most extraordinary bull markets in Stock Exchange history.

One reason, of course, was the inflation that sent stock prices, food prices, clothing, and rents, to fantastic levels. Then was created one of our first alphabetical designations — HCL (the high cost of living). And that is something we may hear of again, despite the hopes in Washington that inflation can be controlled.

Viewed in that light, a level of 300 for the Dow-Jones Industrial Average does not sound quite so fantastic. The 1940 level of corporate earnings would hardly even need to increase. Given a Confidence *in the future that would evaluate earnings in terms of prices at 15 to 1 (and we have had such ratios) instead of 5 to 1, stock prices would triple. Or given a* Fear *of the future, i.e., fear of inflation, causing a desire to own things instead of dollars, the same thing would happen. Investors have had inflation dinned into their ears ever since the dollar was first devalued in 1933. There was no inflation — at least in the sense expected — and they became increasingly skeptical. But — as in the old fable of the boy and the wolf — it was a foregone conclusion that when and if inflation actually 'caught', everyone would be inclined to disbelieve the actuality. In the early part of 1941, there were more signs of true inflation than at any time in over twenty years, but there was certainly no rush to exchange dollars for goods or stocks as on the false alarms of 1933 and 1937.*

Whatever the reasons may appear to be in the future, the author believes it is far more logical to assume that there will be opportunity for profit in the coming years than to take a defeatist attitude on the whole subject. Indeed, all history indicates that the aftermath of the war will include a great reconstruction boom in Europe, a revival of international trade, and an inflationary movement nearly everywhere. This does not imply that stock prices will just be rising year after year. It only means that they will change, rising substantially at times and falling at others, but not just pursuing a monotonous trend toward lower levels in a gradual process of attrition because of Hitler and the New Deal — those two Betes Noire *of the average investor in 1940.*

As long as there is movement, the opportunities for stock market profits will exist, and the methods discussed in this book are designed to take advantage of those opportunities. That is all one can hope to do, because the market cannot be made to behave as one might like to have it. The background may differ, or the character of the movement may not always be the same, but if any approach is soundly based upon some factor inherent in the nature of market price changes, it will continue to work just as well as it has in the past — come what may."

REFERENCES

to

Some Methods Discussed

Fundamental Measures (Section I)

Townsend-Skinner's Financial Accounting
Townsend-Skinner & Co., 52 Broadway, New York 4,
N. Y.

Trend Methods (Section II)

Orthodox Dow Theory
Dow Theory Comment, Rhea, Greiner & Co., Colorado
Springs, Colorado
Barbour's Dow Theory Service, 12 East Grand Ave.,
Chicago 90, Illinois

Character-of-the-Market Methods (Section III)

Buying Power vs. Selling Pressure
Lowry's Investment Reports, 250 Park Ave., New York
17, N. Y.
Mills' Buying and Selling
Mansfield Mills Co., 2 East Ave., Larchmont, N. Y.
Supply and Demand Measures
Lamotte & Whitman, Post-Office Box 123, Boston 1,
Mass.
Moving Volume Curve
Investographs, 31 Gibbs St., Rochester 4, N. Y.
Hood's Group Action
Oakman Hood, 8 Fuller Road, Wellesley Hills 82, Mass.

Formula Plans (Section IV)

BURLINGAME PLAN
Burlingame Corp., 53 State St., Boston 9, Mass.
HOWE METHOD
Howe & Rusling, Inc., 183 East Main St., Rochester, N. Y.
NEW ENGLAND PLAN
Samuel S. Cadwell Co., 420 Lexington Ave., New York 17, N. Y.

Cycle Forecasting (Section V)

SMITH'S DECENNIAL PATTERN
Brookmire Economic Service, 551 Fifth Ave., New York 17, N. Y.
SIDEREAL RADIATION AND THE STOCK MARKET
Lake States Securities Corp., 634 South Spring St., Los Angeles 14, California
ELLIOTT'S WAVE PRINCIPLE
John C. Sinclair, Francis I. duPont Co., 630 Fifth Ave., New York 20, N. Y.

Measures of Psychology (Section VI)

ODD LOT INDEXES
Drew Investment Associates, 53 State St., Boston 9, Mass.

Mediums for Timing Methods (Section VII)

GROUP SELECTION
Ray*Signals, 15 William St., New York 5, N. Y.
R. W. Mansfield Co., 117 Liberty St., New York 6, N. Y.
(Also see Hood's Group Action under Section III)